Lecture Notes in Artificial Intelligence 795

Subseries of Lecture Notes in Computer Science
Edited by J. G. Carbonell and J. Siekmann

Lecture Notes in Computer Science

Edited by G. Goos and J. Hartmanis

Warren A. Hunt, Jr.

FM8501: A Verified Microprocessor

Springer-Verlag

Berlin Heidelberg New York
London Paris Tokyo
Hong Kong Barcelona
Budapest

Series Editors

Jaime G. Carbonell
School of Computer Science, Carnegie Mellon University
Schenley Park, Pittsburgh, PA 15213-3890, USA

Jörg Siekmann
University of Saarland
German Research Center for Artificial Intelligence (DFKI)
Stuhlsatzenhausweg 3, D-66123 Saarbrücken, Germany

Author

Warren A. Hunt, Jr.
Computational Logic, Inc.
1717 West 6th Street, Suite 290
Austin, TX 78703-4776, USA

CR Subject Classification (1991): B.6, I.2.2-3, F.4.1, B.2.4, B.4.4, B.7.2

ISBN 3-540-57960-5 Springer-Verlag Berlin Heidelberg New York
ISBN 0-387-57960-5 Springer-Verlag New York Berlin Heidelberg

CIP data applied for

Typesetting: Camera ready by author
SPIN: 10132079   45/3140-543210 - Printed on acid-free paper

Preface

The hardware specification and verification ideas presented in this monograph germinated while I was taking a graduate class from Boyer and Moore in 1982. It was during their class that I was first introduced to logic. By the end of this class, I had written an instruction-interpreter specification for a Z80 microprocessor [51]. At this point, I had not seen any other work for mathematically specifying digital hardware except Boolean logic and ISP descriptions. At this point also, I was a digital design engineer for Cyb Systems, Inc., where I was designing Multibus[26] compatible cards for a Unix minicomputer. These designs were based upon the Motorola 68000 microprocessor [35]. During 1983 and 1984 I worked full time as a board designer, but I continued to be interested in formalizing a microprocessor. This interest was motivated both from an intellectual curiosity and from my personal frustration at attempting to engineer correctly designed boards. Each time I designed a board, I had to agglomerate specifications provided by device manufacturers in an attempt to produce some board with greater functionality. This was performed in a "rigorous" manner, but without any mathematical connecting tissue.

In 1985 I returned to the University of Texas to complete my degree. Originally, I had hoped to mathematically specify an existing microprocessor for my dissertation work, but I felt that the documentation available to me did not adequately specify all their operational aspects. I also realized that to specify and verify an existing microprocessor would require me to have access to a commercial design – this would require a non-disclosure agreement which would prevent me from publishing the results of my effort, thus no degree could result. In the beginning of 1985, I began the FM8501 effort which resulted in this monograph and this monograph was submitted as a dissertation at the end of 1985 in partial fulfillment of the PhD degree requirements at the University of Texas at Austin under the advisorship of Bob Boyer and J Moore.

The FM8501 microprocessor was invented as a generic microprocessor somewhat similar to a PDP-11 [13] — "FM" stood for functional machine and "8501" stood for the first machine of 1985. This was an optimistic naming convention; the FM8502, a 32-bit variant of the FM8501, wasn't completed until 1987. The principal idea of the FM8501 effort was to see if it was possible to express the user-level specification and the design implementation using a formal logic,

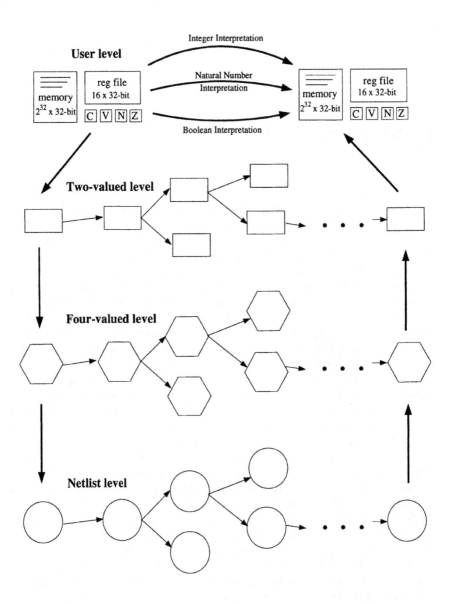

Figure 0.1: Specification Levels

the Boyer-Moore logic; this approach permitted us to complete a mechanically checked proof that the FM8501 implementation fully implemented its specification.

The implementation model for the FM8501 was inadequate for industrial hardware design. Circuits were expressed by overloading functions in the Boyer-Moore logic. This modeling technique allowed the specification of the necessary combinational connecting gates and registers, but did not allow wires to be named explicitly. Further, this approach did not provide a direct migration path to CAD languages, from which a physical device could be built. Since the FM8501 effort Bishop Brock and I have formalized a simple hierarchical, occurrence-oriented hardware description language (HDL) [25, 9]. The formalization of this HDL made the hardware circuits explicit – a formal circuit semantics and syntax exists for the HDL – and provides a simple means of converting designs into commercial CAD languages. Our HDL semantics include four logical values: true, false, undefined, and floating, thus providing a richer modeling capability than used with the FM8501.

Our current approach can be contrasted with the FM8501 effort by comparing our recent FM9001 microprocessor verification. Figure 0.1 shows the four specification levels we used for the FM9001; only the top two levels exist in the FM8501 effort. The two-valued level was the implementation level for the FM8501. The FM8501 had separate data input and data output busses because we were not able to model bidirectional wires. For the FM9001, the two-valued level is a Boolean model of the implementation with the tri-state memory interface bus abstracted away. The four-valued level is functionally equivalent to the netlist level. The netlist level describes the actual gates, wires, I/O pads, and test logic that are actually needed to construct the FM9001 microprocessor. The FM9001 design verification takes into consideration the I/O pads and test logic as well as the functional gates and registers. We had LSI Logic, Inc., fabricate the FM9001 design using one of their gate-array families. We have not discovered any errors in the fabricated devices after several months of testing.

The FM8501 effort was an important step in our evolution to the design verification methodology we now employ.

Warren A. Hunt, Jr.
Austin, Texas

January, 1992

Acknowledgements

My colleague Bill Young reformatted this document from Scribe^{TM} to LaTeX. He also remade all of the drawings. This conversion was a larger job than either of us expected. I am quite thankful for his effort, because without it this book would not have been possible.

This work originally appeared as the author's dissertation, Department of Computer Science, the University of Texas at Austin. The work was partially sponsored by the National Science Foundation (Grants DCR-8202943 and DCR-8122039), the Department of the Navy, Space and Naval Warfare Systems Command (Contract N00039-85-K-0085), and British Petroleum North America, Inc. It appeared as Technical Report 47, Institute for Computing Science, the University of Texas at Austin, February, 1986.

W. A. H.

Contents

Chapter 1

Introduction

Formal description of computing devices allows for accurate characterization of the computational foundation used by all computer programs. Computer system specification and construction is a time-intensive task. Specifications are usually vague and *correct* construction of a vaguely specified device is impossible. The ability to describe computing devices formally yields many benefits: known semantics, symbolic execution and transformation, proofs of correctness, and unambiguous specification. Presented herein is an attempt to describe digital hardware circuits within a formal system. In support of the methods presented, the verification of a microprocessor is presented – this microprocessor embodies many aspects of digital hardware design.

1.1 Nature of this Research

Computer evolution seems to follow a known path. New computers or computing systems are introduced, followed by prototypes, test sites, and production models. As users of computers, we have come to be skeptical about new products, due to their usual lack of documentation and operational correctness. *Bugs* found in early releases turn into *features* in later models or are removed at great cost. In the case of computer system families, market pressure seems to ensure that a *bigger* and *better* machine is built, usually changing the meaning or effect of some basic operations.

The ability to describe a computing device unambiguously has advantages not typically enjoyed by the commercial computing establishment. The reasons that formal methods have not been employed is both logical and idiotic: market pressure drives manufactures to build new products as quickly as possible; this pressure reduces the emphasis on product correctness. Accuracy, always a stated goal, takes a back seat to completion; however, the lack of accuracy leads to a tarnished product image and frustrated customers. The complexity of computers and computer devices is rising and informal natural language descriptions of operational characteristics fall far short of precisely specifying computing device operation.

The formal specification and verification of computer hardware is necessary to cope with the size and complexity of today's machines. Through the use of automated reasoning about formal systems, it is possible to accurately specify and completely verify computer system operation. This research shows a method for specifying and verifying digital computer hardware within a formal system. With automated theorem-proving systems it is possible to verify many aspects of digital computer operation. Most previous digital computer verification efforts were made by hand.

The hardware verification methods developed for this work were constructed in conjunction with available automated theorem-proving systems, and not by some hardware description language. Mathematical operations are defined inside a formal theory, then these operations are shown equivalent to some graph of (hardware) gates. The mathematical operations are characterized by commonly used functions, such as addition, subtraction, and shifting. The implementation (gate graph) is characterized by nests of Boolean functions applied to components of bit-vectors. Automated theorem-proving helps us to bridge the semantic gap between functions and gates.

1.2   The Meaning of Verification

The word *verification*, when written in this paper, is used to compare two objects inside a formal theory. To *verify* something, two different representations of some operation are shown to be equivalent under some set of assumptions; all functions and assumptions being represented in a formal logic. Verification to "first principles" seems unlikely, unless the first principles that are of interest can be represented inside the theory in which the verification is to take place.

Since the theory used to represent digital hardware is not quantum mechanics or some finer model, there is a gap between my lowest level objects and the physical world of hardware. Assumptions about hardware devices are described later in this paper.

1.3   Research Goal

The primary goal of the research performed in support of this document is to be able to accurately describe digital circuits commonly found in digital computers. To achieve this goal, I designed and verified a microprocessor, named "FM8501", which has a user-mode instruction set inspired by the PDP-11 [12]. A block diagram for this microprocessor is shown in Figure 1.1.

The selection of a microprocessor comes from a personal frustration of using many of the common commercially available products; the documentation does not accurately describe the operation of these devices and it is long winded and

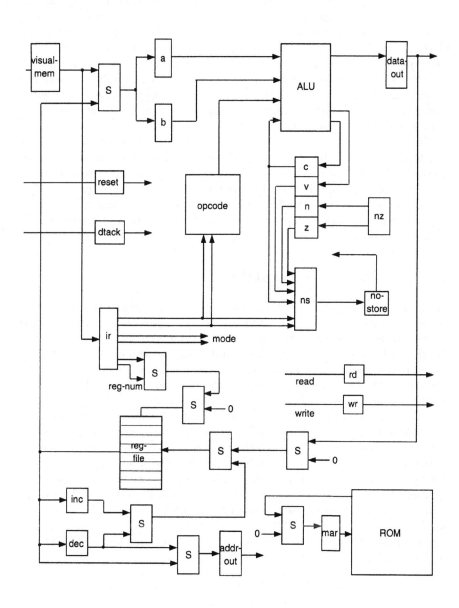

Figure 1.1: FM8501: Block Diagram of a Formally Specified Microprocessor

imprecise. Looking at the *Fourth Edition, M68000 16/32-bit Microprocessor Programmer's Reference Manual* [35], I find several hundred pages of diagrams and text. The number of assumptions I must make when reading this book is staggering. To compound problems, I must carry these assumptions with me if I am to successfully program this device. For example, what does adding to the PC mean? Well, it means adding a value to the program counter. But, what does that mean? Does it mean that the program counter cannot be odd; on the M68000 it is illegal to fetch an instruction from a numerically odd memory location and if attempted causes an exception. What happens when the program counter contains the largest positive number that can be represented and then is incremented? The questions go on and on and on...

The main contribution of this research is to show that a microprocessor or like device can be better described with several pages of formulas instead of hundreds of pages of text. The compact formal description is better suited to the task of description: it takes less time to read, it is unambiguous, and it provides an accurate basis for building systems that use it. And once a device is specified within a formal system, it is possible to verify its correctness with respect to the same.

1.4   Dissertation Outline

The material presented in this dissertation has the shape of an hourglass. There are many different types of computers and computing machinery; I will narrow my field of investigation to that of digital hardware circuits. At the neck of the glass, which is where the physical world meets the formal representation of hardware devices, I defend my hardware model and show its relation with the physical world. After entering a formal world, the glass falls away from me as I expand my hardware model into a complete functionally defined computer.

Following this introduction chapter, is a chapter discussing general hardware models and the hardware model that I use. The chapter on notation describes the connection between logic gates and the formal notation used for the remainder of this paper. Various data types and operations with these data types are described next. This dissertation then proceeds in a bottom up manner. The approach taken to prove the correctness of hardware is presented. Using this approach, a number of simple functions are grouped into an ALU. Later, this ALU is integrated in the FM8501 microprocessor. Conclusions and insights are last, followed by an appendix containing all formulas used in defining and verifying FM8501.

Chapter 2

A Hardware Model

Logic is not very good at representing device physics; however, if logic can be used, it is a beautiful foundation for describing the operation of devices. To be able to represent digital hardware devices with logic, a simplified view of hardware must be constructed. To construct this view, I will trim away many aspect of digital hardware, leaving only a gate-level view. After simplifying digital hardware to gates, a connection between formal logic and hardware gates will be established. Logic gates are the foundation of my digital hardware model.

To model time-sequenced computing devices a register-transfer style language is used. This is a common approach for representing digital hardware circuits. Register-transfer languages describe digital hardware as combinational logic separated by clocked registers.

Characterization of my model for computer hardware will be further refined in a later section in this chapter by comparing it to other hardware description models. Also a review of other hardware verification methods and research is presented, and comparisons to my model are made where appropriate.

2.1 Narrowing the Scope of Investigation

This research is concerned with bistate logic and logic devices typically used when building digital computers; these devices include *and, or, not, nand, nor, equv,* and *xor* gates, latches, register files, RAM, and ROM. Aspects of computer design that cannot be represented as Boolean logic are not considered.

This research is not concerned with device physics or topics related to the physical construction of basic gates. The semantics of gates are taken for granted (i.e., the Boolean-and function b-and[1], is a two argument function that returns a single value which is either *true* or *false*.) This work is not technology dependent; the results are valid for any logic family.

---

[1] This function along with the other logical connectives are defined later.

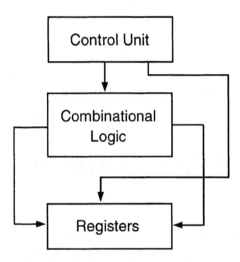

Figure 2.1: Typical Register-transfer Model

This presentation does not concern itself with packaging of circuits or the construction of boards or chips. Problems such as heat transfer, thermal expansion of chips and boards, circuit board technology, cooling, vibration, shock, and operating environments, are not investigated. The ability to discern whether a specific hardware device is manufactured correctly is not addressed (i.e., device defects, testing, wiring errors, etc.).

This study does not consider circuits such as analogue-to-digital converters, digital-to-analogue converters, FM or AM modulation, power devices or voltage regulators, transistor circuits, amplifiers, or any other analogue device. These types of circuits are not readily converted to Boolean valued logic.

2.2   The Register-transfer Model

This section describes a register-transfer model of digital computer hardware in general terms. The register-transfer model is shown in Figure 2.1. This diagram could represent a CPU or a whole computing system. Within synchronous computers, the state (registers and memory) are updated as a function of the combinational logic and the previous state. The control section directs the data flow through the combinational logic and controls the latching of the registers. There are no loops within the combinational logic – loops are present, but they are broken by clocked registers.

Kuck [31] describes combinational logic and sequential logic, which are essential components of the register-transfer model, for synchronous computing devices.

> A *combinational logic circuit* consists of a network of elementary logic function devices without any logical feedback loop.

> In a real computer, there are a number of registers and combinational logic circuits. Abstractly, it is convenient to lump all of the combinational logic in a system into one box and all of the registers into another box, as shown in Figure 2.1.[2] Thus the combinational logic makes simple transformations of the data in the registers. The clock pulses allow information to enter the registers and flow through the next stage of combinational logic, and the clock period is determined by the longest time delay around the loop – from the registers back to the registers. Because the data is repeatedly transformed on successive time steps, such a scheme is called a *sequential logic circuit*.

> Taken together, combinational logic and sequential logic form the basis of all real computer logic design.

A complete computer system can be modeled with the addition of a control unit. The control unit provides information, consistent with its programming, that directs the sequencing of data through the combinational logic, and in to and out of registers. Control units may have a fixed internal *program* that they execute or may interpret a *microprogram* [48, 49]. Referring back to Figure 2.1, Kuck integrates a control unit with sequential logic to describe the register-transfer abstraction.

> ... also shows control lines from the control unit to the combinational logic of the processor. These lines carry decoded instruction signals to control points in the combinational logic. For example, when the clock pulse triggers a register to accept a word of data and thus presents it as an input to the following combinational logic, we may wish to gate that word to one of several destinations, depending on the particular operation being performed. Control points in the combinational logic are used to control the path taken by such words. Other control points may be used to select a destination register for the outputs of the combinational logic. It is also obvious that we sometimes wish to select inputs from memory and sometimes wish to switch output to memory rather than processor registers. The above level of abstraction (combinational logic and registers) is often called a *register transfer* level of computer description.

---

[2] The control box and control lines are not shown in Kuck's diagram.

2.3   The FM8501 Model

The model used for FM8501 is based on a register-transfer paradigm. However, we use formally defined functions to describe both the combinational logic and the sequencing.

2.3.1   Hardware Functions

Combinational logic is described by recursively defined functions that generally map bit-vector inputs to a bit-vector output. We most often define such "hardware functions" to work on arbitrarily sized data. For example, instead of defining the combinational logic for a 16-bit wide adder, we define a recursive function for adding n-bit wide vectors. However, in their eventual use, hardware functions are applied to symbolic expressions denoting bit-vectors of fixed size. Such applications can be expanded out (by symbolic evaluation and the application of rewrite rules) to an *equivalent* expression involving only the seven Boolean gate functions: not, and, or, nand, nor, xor, and equv, and "glue" for creating bit-vectors. We regard such expressions as combinational logic.

The size of the combinational logic created is determined by the length of bit-vectors supplied as symbolic arguments. For example, a simple n-bit wide adder function expands into 63 gates when applied to 4-bit wide vectors. By identifying common subexpressions these 63 gates collapse into a gate graph with 23 gates in it. On the other hand, when applied to 64-bit wide vectors the adder expands into over 9×10^{19} gates, which collapses into 443 gates by identifying common subexpressions.

We prove our combinational logic correct by proving theorems about *general* applications of the hardware functions. For example, we prove the n-bit wide adder correct *for all n*. Such proofs are usually by induction and involve relatively little case analysis – usually just that caused by the Boolean logic laid down for one step in the recursion. We then obtain the correctness theorems for our gate graphs by *instantiation* of these general theorems.

2.3.2   Sequencing

To model sequencing we define self-recursive functions which take a "clock" argument plus other arguments representing state holding devices such as registers, ROMs, RAMs, memory, etc. Such "hardware interpreter" functions have a stylized definitional form: they call themselves recursively once each clock tick. The arguments to the recursive call specify how the state is modified each cycle as a function of the previous state. When the clock is exhausted, the final state is returned.

We can model the computation described by such a function with sequential logic provided hardware functions are used to determine the new state components and we fix the sizes of the registers, ROMs, etc.

We verify such hardware interpreters by proving them equivalent (in some sense) to more elegant functions. In these more elegant functions, the state is generally less elaborate. In addition, "time" runs at a different rate. For example, the FM8501 is described as a hardware interpreter with 19 state holding arguments. One step in the recursion of this function represents a microcycle. The specification of the FM8501 is a function with only six state holding arguments: the register file, the memory, and four condition code flags. Registers used by the FM8501 to hold intermediate microstate information and to communicate with the memory process are abstracted away in the specification. One step in the recursion of the specification function represents the execution of one macroinstruction. The number of microinstructions required to execute one macroinstruction of course varies with the instruction and the response of memory.

2.4 Related Hardware Verification Efforts

Of historical interest is the application of symbolic manipulation systems to digital hardware development and/or digital hardware verification.[3] This section describes recent digital hardware verification efforts. Several systems without associated symbolic manipulation systems are also mentioned due to their similarity of descriptive approach.

An early attempt at hardware verification through symbolic manipulation was made by Todd Wagner [46, 47]. Wagner's system is based on a transition algebra and this system can characterize some timing information. His system has a first order logic proof checker; however, the proofs given in his dissertation [46] are somewhat trivial.

J. Paul Roth, of the IBM Corporation, has been investigating hardware verification and testing for years. He is the inventor of the D-algorithm and PL/R. In his book [40], Roth discusses the last fifteen years of his work. He has a verification system for sequential logic. Much of his work concerns good, no-good functional testing of circuits right off the assembly line.

Using a resolution based theorem-prover, Louis Hanes proved the correctness of several small circuits [22]. A *C*-like language [30] was used to represent hardware and functional descriptions. For verification purposes, specifications were converted into clauses for use in a resolution-based theorem-prover. A 4-bit adder and a RAM memory were the most complex examples tackled.

Mike Gordon has used the LCF system [18] to prove a simple microcoded CPU correct [19]. The proof assumes the existence of adder, multiplexors, and other low-level objects. This system employed the mechanical assistance of the LCF system, and proofs are performed by the user by specifying rules to invoke. Induction is not supported by this system, and Gordon is not using this system anymore.

---

[3]Computerized drawing systems used in computer design are interesting, but not germane to this study.

Gordon is now working with a hardware specification language which uses higher-order logic (eg. quantified expressions) [20]. Higher-order logic allows the specification of induction through the use of quantifiers. This system is based on the LCF system, and logic terms are a datatype in ML [17]. Theorems are an abstract type in ML and derived inference rules can be programmed in ML. The HOL Proof Generating System [21] makes use of induction, and the verification of a chip used in the Cambridge Fast Ring has been performed.

Gordon's HOL work is in the same spirit as this work; however, only natural number and Boolean interpretations of bit-vectors have been defined, and the ability to relate asynchronous hardware inputs to high-level behaviorial descriptions is not demonstrated. This work stands apart from HOL by its development of natural numbers and integers from Peano's axioms; all the mathematics used for natural number and integer arithmetic proofs in FM8501 were performed within the Boyer-Moore system (theory). It appears that the HOL system is capable of doing similar work, but as yet, nothing as large as FM8501 has been attempted.

Harry Barrow of the Fairchild Laboratory for Artificial Intelligence Research has constructed a system called VERIFY [3, 4]. This system grew out of Gordon's original hardware verification work [19], and allows hardware systems to be created out of hierarchical elements called *modules*. Modules are considered to be finite state machines with inputs and and outputs, and some amount of internal state. Outputs are determined as functions of the inputs and internal state. Internal state is changed at *implicit clock ticks* and is described by equations just like the output equations. Confronted with a proof request, VERIFY attempts to automatically prove the request by recursive decomposition. This system has established the correctness of large circuits, one being the CPU verified by Gordon. This system is not capable of doing many of the proofs performed for FM8501; many of the proofs done here are inductive in nature and Barrow's system cannot perform inductions.

Steve German of GTE Laboratories is using the Boyer-Moore theorem-prover in conjunction with a hardware description language called Zeus [15]. This language attempts to express simultaneously the structure and function of hardware devices. After a hand translation of Zeus into the Boyer-Moore logic, the correctness of a comparator and a sequencer were established [16]. Although this system uses the same proof engine as used here, its basis lies in Zeus. The semantics for Zeus are incompletely specified thus making unambigious translation into the Boyer-Moore logic impossible. The dimension of the work verified within the Zeus/Boyer-Moore framework is much smaller than that presented here.

Steven D. Johnson is attempting to unify hardware and software specification using applicative programming languages [28, 29]; however, he has no automated reasoning system.

> An engineer starts with an abstractly descriptive *specification* and derives a concretely descriptive *realization*. These notations should be suited not only to what they describe but also to each other. Functional recursion equations serve here as specifications.

Johnson transforms initial specifications into iterative form, then into equivalent synchronous system descriptions. This work is formulated in an applicative language called DAISY. It appears that a theorem-prover could be added to the system.

Mary Sheeran has proposed *μFP - An Algebraic VLSI Design Language* [42]. This language is based on Backus' language FP [1, 2]. This is a functional approach to describing hardware, but her descriptions embody some geometric interpretations as well. There is no associated mechanical reasoning system, but like Johnson's DAISY, one could be added.

Other systems can be found in recent literature: DDL [14] and Interval Temporal Logic [33], just to name two.[4] Also, articles on microprogram verification have been presented [10]. One important proof procedure has been underutilized: induction. In addition, for any of these systems to be useful for large devices, automated theorem provers will be required.

---

[4]Many systems have been presented. Most are concerned with hardware representation and have no associated symbolic manipulation system.

Chapter 3

Notation and Bit Vectors

Hardware description languages are like conventional programming languages: they are plentiful, have varied syntax, and emphasize various data types and operations [4, 5, 18, 22, 29, 37, 42]. This chapter describes yet another hardware description language. In defense of this new description language is the associated reasoning system.

The accurate description of hardware devices would not be possible without a formally defined discourse. The discourse used is the Boyer-Moore logic and is introduced in this chapter.

The fundamental representation unit in digital computers is the bit. Bits are usually clustered into words (bit-vectors), which have some fixed width (number of bits in a word). A computing device memory is arranged as an array of words. A model for bits and bit-vectors is developed here.

3.1 Another Language–Why?

The language selection was driven by the availability of an automated, inductive theorem-prover. A method of representing hardware circuit descriptions within the Boyer-Moore logic was developed to allow the use of their automated theorem-prover when verifying the correctness of circuits [6, 7]. Most hardware description languages try to describe the wiring of a circuit – formalization and verification of circuits become secondary issues.

The use of the Boyer-Moore system has encourged the use of recursive functions as the primary description vechile for hardware functions. This recursive style has led to hardware functions that are not fixed in their operational size; hardware functions are defined without regard to the word size or number of registers which they manipulate.

The importance of having a theorem-prover capable of proving complex formulas with complex inductive proofs will be apparent later on. Induction has been underutilized as a proof procedure with regard to hardware verification. Recursion and induction allow the definition of and proofs about formal hardware functions that take arbitrary sized arguments. Also, induction allows correctness proofs of (micro) program loops. As will be shown later, the proof of FM8501 has hundreds of inductive proofs.

After the descriptions for hardware functions have been developed, one can readily see a one-to-one mapping between formal hardware descriptions and digital hardware circuits.

3.2   The Boyer-Moore Logic

A brief description of the Boyer-Moore logic is provided below in order to make the formalization comprehensible.[1] The book *A Computational Logic* by Boyer and Moore [6] provides a detailed description of the Boyer-Moore theorem prover and its logic.[2]

The Boyer-Moore logic is a quantifier-free first order logic with equality. The language is a form of pure-Lisp and consists of variables and function names combined in a prefix notation. Functions of no arguments serve as constants. Terms in the Boyer-Moore logic are either variables or of the form (fn t_1 ... tt t_n), where fn is an n-ary function name, and $t_1, \ldots, t_n$ are n terms. The term (fn $t_1, \ldots, t_n$) is usually represented in First-order logic syntax as fn($t_1, \ldots, t_n$).

There are two logical constants: (true) and (false) (abbreviated as t and f, respectively). The only primitive logical connective is the 3-place function if. The term (if x y z) (read informally as *If* x *then* t y *else* z) is axiomatized to return z if x is equal to f, and y otherwise. The other logical connectives: or, not, and, implies, etc., are defined in terms of if.

Equality is represented by the dyadic function equal. (equal x y) is axiomatized to return t if x and y are identical, and f otherwise. The theory includes the axiom of reflexivity of equality and an equality axiom for functions that permits the replacement of "equals for equals". Note that functions which return only t or f play the role of predicates.

The *Shell Principle* allows the user to add axioms describing inductively constructed objects. Natural numbers are axiomatized by adding a shell with a 1-place recognizer function numberp; a 1-place constructor function add1; a 1-place destructor function sub1; and a bottom object (zero). The result is an axiomatization similar to Peano's axioms for natural numbers. Abbreviations are used to represent numbers, e.g., (zero) is abbreviated by 0, and (add1 (add1 (add1 0))) is abbreviated by 3. The term (zerop x) returns f if x is a non-zero natural number, and t otherwise. Shell constructor functions applied to constants yield constants.

---

[1] This section was taken with permission from a technical report written by N. Shankar [41].

[2] A modification to the Boyer-Moore logic was made in connection with proving meta-theorems [7].

Lists are axiomatized by adding a shell with a 1-place recognizer listp; a 2-place constructor cons; and two 1-place destructor functions car and cdr. The empty list is usually represented by the special constant nil. Abbreviations are used to represent lists of constants, e.g., the list (cons (cons 1 (cons 2 nil))(cons 3 (cons 4 (cons 5 nil)))) is abbreviated by '((1 2) 3 4 5). (cons x y) returns the list whose first element is x and the remaining elements form the list y, e.g. (cons '(1 2) '(3 4 5)) returns '((1 2) 3 4 5). Conversely, (car x) returns the first element of a list, e.g., (car '((1 2) 3 4 5)) is '(1 2), and (cdr x) returns the remainder of the list, e.g., (cdr '((1 2) 3 4 5)) is '(3 4 5). Sequences of cars and cdrs are abbreviated, e.g., (caddr x) abbreviates (car (cdr (cdr x))). The term (listp (cons 1 nil)) returns t whereas (listp nil) is f. The basic theory includes shells for literal atoms (character strings), natural numbers, negative integers, and lists.

The definitions of new functions are admitted as axioms only if they satisfy the *Principle of Definition*. Under this principle, a definition is accepted only if it is recursively or non-recursively defined in terms of previously defined functions and there is some well-founded ordering, i.e., a partial ordering in which there are no infinite decreasing chains, on some measure of the arguments which decreases with every recursive call. The 2-place function lessp, which is the standard ordering predicate on natural numbers, is the most commonly used well-founded ordering. Every evaluation of functions admitted under this principle is guaranteed to terminate. In other words, every function admitted is total recursive. This ensures that no inconsistency is introduced by adding the definition as a new axiom.

The rules of inference in the Boyer-Moore logic consist of:

1. *Propositional Calculus:* All tautologies are theorems.

2. *A Principle of Noetherian Induction:* This permits the formulation of an induction that is justified by the well-founded orderings used to admit definitions.

3. *Instantiation:* Any instance of a theorem is a theorem.

The Boyer-Moore theorem prover is a mechanization of the above logic. The commands to the theorem prover include those for adding shells, defining new functions, and proving theorems. A new function *fn-name* with *n* arguments *arg1, ..., argn* and definition *body* is defined using the **defn** command as shown below:

(defn   *fn-name*   (*arg1 . . . argn*)   *body*)

To start the theorem prover off on the proof of a lemma *lemma-name* of type *lemma-type* which is stated as *statement*, the **prove-lemma** command is used as follows:

> (prove-lemma   *lemma-name*   (*lemma-type*)   *statement*)

prove-lemma takes an optional fourth argument by means of which an induction or the use of a lemma can be suggested to the theorem prover. The theorem prover is automatic in the sense that once prove-lemma has been invoked on a conjecture, the user may no longer interfere with the proof. The user can, however, "train" the theorem prover by means of a carefully selected sequence of definitions and lemmas. It can therefore be "trained" to check a particular proof and this is the sense in which the theorem prover is used as a high-level proof-checker.

This concludes the overview of the Boyer-Moore logic. Other details will be provided when needed to interpret the input to the theorem prover.

3.3 Bit Vectors

A formal representation of bit-vectors is central to the task of verifying hardware devices that operate on bit-vectors. Bit-vectors are literally vectors of bits. A bit (cell) can take on two values: *true* or *false* ("1" or "0"). RAM is just an array of bit-vectors. To be able to use bit-vectors as single arguments, there must be a way to glue bits together into a single object.

The *Shell Principle* is used to create a new data-type within the Boyer-Moore logic which represents bit-vectors.[3] The Boyer-Moore theorem-prover command used to create this new data-type is:

```
(add-shell bitv btm bitvp
          ((bit (one-of truep falsep) false)
           (vec (one-of bitvp) btm)))
```

Bit-vectors have a 2-place constructor function bitv, a bottom object (constant function) btm, a one place recognizer function bitvp, and two 1-place destructors functions bit and vec. The destructor function bit returns a single bit; this destructor function is restricted so that it can only return t or f; the bit destructor returns f when accessing something other than a bit-vector. The destructor function vec returns the remaining bit-vector with one bit stripped off; the vec destructor only returns a bit-vector that is recognized by the recognizer function bitvp; this destructor returns (btm) when accessing something other than a bit-vector.

---

[3]The word *logic* will usually refer to the Boyer-Moore logic. The Boyer-Moore theorem-prover is often just referred to as the *theorem-prover*.

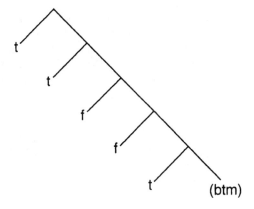

Figure 3.1: Pictorial representation of "10011"

Bit-vectors are used throughout the remainder of this paper. They are the data objects that many hardware functions operate on. The binary number "10011" can be written as

```
(bitv t (bitv t (bitv f (bitv f (bitv t (btm)))))).
```

A diagram depicting the structure of the bit-vector represented by the binary number "10011" is shown in Figure 3.1. The constructor function bitv glues together the bits. Hardware functions that transform bit-vectors generally work by breaking the glue, operating on a bit, and then constructing a new bit-vector as a result.

Finding the length of a bit-vector is a question that will be often posed. The need to know arises from the very nature of digital hardware–data are represented with finite length bit-vectors. Using the *Principle of Definition* a function can be defined that determines the size (length) of a bit-vector.

```
(defn size (a)
  (if (bitvp a)
      (if (equal a (btm))
          0
          (add1 (size (vec a))))
      0))
```

The function `size` is a 1-place function that counts the number of `bitv` constructors encountered. (`size a`) is determined as follows: if `a` is either not recognized by the bit-vector recognizer function `bitvp` or is (`btm`), its size is 0; otherwise, its size is one more than the size of (`vec a`).

The format picked for bit-vector representation is commonly called the *little endian* approach. The selection of a *big endian* or *little endian* format was not of particular importance. There has been much heated discussion over which *end* is up [32]. The misunderstandings caused by the *endian* problem points to the lack of clear representations for computer data storage and computer operations.

Chapter 4

Numeric Definitions and Operations

Digital computers operate on bits and bit-vectors. For instance, computers do not add natural numbers, or two's complement numbers, but transform bit-vectors into a bit-vector that we interpret as the sum of the interpretations of the input bit-vectors. For meaningful work to be performed by computers, we must get the computer to perform desired operations even though all information must be represented with bit-vectors. Therefore, the bit and bit-vector transformations performed by a computer have to have a formal basis in the operations we desire.

Natural number and integer arithmetic are operations that should be performed by computers with known accuracy.[1] Unfortunately, when reading descriptions of computer operation the following is likely to be found:

> Add the source operand to the destination operand, and store the result in the destination location. The size of the operation may be specified to be ... [35]

A solid foundation for the desired computer operations must be set down. The digital computer implementor needs to be aware of these foundations, and needs to be able to show a mapping between desired operations and hardware that implements these operations. Much work has been done in this area, but it usually fails to demonstrate convincingly the connection between desired operations and implementations [45]. This chapter characterizes two numeric data types. These characterizations include desired mathematical operations and their representation with bit-vectors.

---

[1] All operations performed by computers should be able to be characterized completely; thus, avoiding any confusion about a computer's operation.

4.1   Natural Number Representation

Natural number definition and their representation with bit-vectors is formally presented here. Additionally, several mathematical operations for natural numbers are defined. The bit-vector representations presented are not constrained to any specific word size, but are designed to work with any length vectors.

4.1.1   Natural Numbers

The theorem-prover *Shell Principle* is used to define natural numbers.[2]

```
(add-shell add1 zero numberp ((sub1 (one-of numberp) zero)))
```

This axiomatization of natural numbers is similar to Peano's axioms [36] for natural numbers. Natural number addition and subtraction are defined as follows, where 0 is an abbreviation for (zero).

```
(defn fix (x)
  (if (numberp x) x 0))

(defn plus (x y)
  (if (zerop x)
      (fix y)
      (add1 (plus (sub1 x) y))))

(defn difference (i j)
  (if (zerop i)
      0
      (if (zerop j)
          i
          (difference (sub1 i) (sub1 j)))))
```

Observe the simplicity of plus. To add x to y you add1 to y x times. That is, in Peano's system, addition is just counting. The usual properties of addition follow inductively: plus is associative, commutative, etc. It should be noted for

---

[2]This is not the actual theorem-prover command, as this data-type is part of the *booting* process of the theorem-prover. This data-type, the data-types for (true), (false), and (minus x), the definition for fixing any data object into a number, the definition for seeing if one natural number is less than another, and the definitions for natural number addition, subtraction, multiplication, division, and remainder, are part of the theorem-prover's standard initial knowledge base. All other definitions presented in this paper are entered into the theorem-prover through its user interface.

those unfamiliar with natural number subtraction that (equal (difference 5 3) 2) and (equal (difference 3 5) 0).

By themselves these functions say nothing about digital hardware addition and subtraction – by showing a mapping between natural numbers and bit-vectors a digital hardware adder can be constructed and proved correct.[3] The definitions are offered as "obviously correct" definitions of functions we wish to compute.

Natural number multiplication, division, and remainder, are also defined in a recursive style. As these functions will be soon used, they are presented here. The definition for the predicate function lessp is also defined.

```
(defn lessp (x y)
  (if (or (equal y 0) (not (numberp y)))
      f
      (if (or (equal x 0) (not (numberp x)))
          t
          (lessp (sub1 x) (sub1 y)))))

(defn times (i j)
  (if (zerop i)
      0
      (plus j (times (sub1 i) j))))

(defn quotient (i j)
  (if (zerop j)
      0
      (if (lessp i j)
          0
          (add1 (quotient (difference i j) j)))))

(defn remainder (i j)
  (if (zerop j)
      (fix i)
      (if (lessp i j)
          (fix i)
          (remainder (difference i j) j))))
```

4.1.2 Bit-vectors for Natural Numbers

Mappings between bit-vectors and natural numbers are straight-forward to define [43] and are shown below.

---

[3]This mapping and proof are forthcoming in this document.

```
(defn nat-to-bv (n size)
  (if (zerop size)
      (btm)
      (bitv (if (zerop (remainder n 2)) f t)
            (nat-to-bv (quotient n 2)
                       (sub1 size)))))

(defn bv-to-nat (x)
  (if (bitvp x)
      (if (equal x (btm))
          0
          (plus (if (bit x) 1 0)
                (times 2 (bv-to-nat (vec x)))))
      0))
```

The function nat-to-bv takes two arguments: n and size. n is the natural
number to be converted into a bit-vector, and size specifies the length of the
bit-vector. If a number is larger than can be represented in size bits, there
will be some information lost – this will be characterized in a moment. The
function bv-to-nat converts a bit-vector into a natural number. The length of
the bit-vector is immaterial.

The following two lemmas describe the relationship of composing the above
functions. In the Boyer-Moore theorem-proving system, a prove-lemma is a
request for the system to prove a statement within the logic. If the lemma
can be proved, knowledge concerning the lemma is added to the theorem-prover
database. This knowledge can be used later, when the theorem-prover is invoked
with another request.

```
(defn exp (i j)
  (if (zerop j)
      1
      (times i (exp i (sub1 j)))))

(prove-lemma nat-to-bv-to-nat (rewrite)
  (equal (bv-to-nat (nat-to-bv n size))
         (remainder n (exp 2 size))))


(defn fix-bv (x)
  (if (bitvp x) x (btm)))
```

```
(prove-lemma bv-to-nat-to-bv (rewrite)
  (implies (equal size (size a))
           (equal (nat-to-bv (bv-to-nat a) size)
                  (fix-bv a)))))
```

The first **prove-lemma** request presented says the following: the name of the **prove-lemma** request is **nat-to-bv-to-nat**, its type is **rewrite**, and the theorem-prover request is to prove that **(bv-to-nat (nat-to-bv n size))** is equal to **(remainder n (exp 2 size))))**. This proof request shows that **nat-to-bv** may truncate n if it is larger than 2^{size}.[4] The second **prove-lemma** request says that if bit-vector **a** is converted into a natural number and then back into a bit-vector, no information (bits) is lost.

4.2 Integer Number Representation

Integers are represented within the Boyer-Moore logic as a signed natural numbers. Due to the use of a sign signifier, the previously defined mathematical natural number operations do not work for integers. An integer addition function is defined here, which also may be used for natural numbers. Integer subtraction is accomplished by negating the integer to be subtracted and handing this value to the integer adder. For representing integers within a fixed-sized bit-vector a two's complement scheme is used. [45]

4.2.1 Integer Numbers

As an extension to the natural number datatype, negative numbers are axiomatized within the logic as follows.

```
(add-shell minus nil negativep
  ((negative-guts (one-of numberp) zero)))
```

The theorem-prover's acceptance of the above command allows the pasting of a sign signifier onto a natural number. A number by itself is nonnegative; a number with a **minus** in front of it is considered negative. One should note that **(minus 0)** is possible; the type restriction **(one-of numberp)** accepts all natural numbers including zero.[5] A 1-place recognizer function **tcp** allows anything to be tested to see if it is a *good* integer; all positive and negative numbers are recognized except minus zero.

---

[4]Once proved this fact is built into the system's data base as a **rewrite** rule. While such strategic decisions as how to use a rule were crucial to the mechanical checking of our results, the reader need not be concerned with what "rewrite" precisely means here since it does not affect the meaning or logical validity of the formula proved.

[5]**(minus 0)** is here abbreviated by **-0**.

```
(defn tcp (x)
  (or (numberp x)
      (and (negativep x)
           (not (zerop (negative-guts x)))))))
```

As integers are not a single datatype, the definitions for integer addition and subtraction have to consider the different guises in which integers appear.

```
(defn add (x y)
  (if (negativep x)
      (if (negativep y)
          (minus (plus (negative-guts x) (negative-guts y)))
          (if (lessp y (negative-guts x))
              (minus (difference (negative-guts x) y))
              (difference y (negative-guts x))))
      (if (negativep y)
          (if (lessp x (negative-guts y))
              (minus (difference (negative-guts y) x))
              (difference x (negative-guts y)))
          (plus x y))))

(defn tc-minus (x)
  (if (negativep x)
      (negative-guts x)
      (if (zerop x) 0 (minus x))))
```

To subtract the (natural or integer) number y from the (natural or integer) number x one writes (add x (tc-minus y)). Therefore, to subtract 5 from 3 the formulation (add 3 (tc-minus 5)) is appropriate. Note that the function add returns -0 only if both arguments to add are -0.

4.2.2   Bit-vectors for Integer Numbers

Mapping between bit-vectors and integers is more complex than the mapping between bit-vectors and natural numbers. The bit-vector representation for integers must include the sign of the number. The bit-vector representation used here for integers is the two's complement system [45]. Shown below are functions for converting integers into two's complement bit-vectors and back again.

```
(defn compl (x)
  (if (bitvp x)
      (if (equal x (btm))
          (btm)
          (bitv (not (bit x)) (compl (vec x))))
      (btm)))

(defn incr (c x)
  (if (bitvp x)
      (if (equal x (btm))
          (btm)
          (bitv (xor c (bit x))
                (incr (and c (bit x)) (vec x))))
      (btm)))

(defn bitn (x n)
  (if (zerop n)
      f
      (if (equal n 1)
          (bit x)
          (bitn (vec x) (sub1 n)))))

(defn tc-to-bv (x size)
  (if (negativep x)
      (incr t
            (compl (nat-to-bv (negative-guts x) size)))
      (nat-to-bv x size)))

(defn bv-to-tc (x)
  (if (bitn x (size x))
      (minus (bv-to-nat (incr t (compl x))))
      (bv-to-nat x)))
```

The functions compl and incr complement a bit-vector and increment a bit-vector respectively. The function bitn retrieves n-th bit from the bit-vector x; bit numbering starts with one. The function tc-to-bv converts the integer x into a two's complement bit-vector of length size. The function bv-to-tc converts a (two's complement) bit-vector into an integer.

The ability to convert a bit-vector into an integer and back into a bit-vector of the same length is shown below. This composition shows that each bit-vector has a unique integer representation, and that an identical bit-vector can be reconstructed through the composition.[6]

---

[6]In its original form, this prove-lemma had a fourth argument. The fourth argument to a prove-lemma request allows a user to more carefully direct the theorem-prover's approach to proofs. As these hints are not material to the discussion in this dissertation they have been deleted, but can all be found in the complete listing contained in the Appendix.

```
(prove-lemma bv-to-tc-to-bv (rewrite)
  (implies (equal size (size a))
           (equal (tc-to-bv (bv-to-tc a) size)
                  (fix-bv a))))
```

It is possible to convert natural numbers into integers and back again; these operations can be imagined by composing two of the above functions.

The axiomatization of natural numbers and integers is independent of any computer machinery. Additionally, the definitions for addition, subtraction, multiplication, division, and remainder, are defined only with respect to the integer and natural number axiomatization. Bit-vectors are used exclusively by computers. The definitions for converting bit-vectors to numbers and back again link numbers as we know them to computer consumable bit-vectors. Concerning integers and natural numbers, the bit-vector transformations performed by digital hardware must have a meaning with respect to the mathematical definitions presented above to have a useful numeric interpretation.

Chapter 5

The Verification Approach

This chapter is a short, but necessary, digression in the presentation of the FM8501 microprocessor. The description of FM8501 is a number of recursive function definitions within the Boyer-Moore logic. These definitions are middlemen in a manner of thinking: they are compared to operational specifications and they are expanded into Boolean digital hardware. In Figure 5.1, the description of FM8501 is thought to be in the center box. To the left, these definitions are compared to operational specifications, and to the right, these definitions are expanded into digital hardware devices.

The conversion of the recursive definitions defining FM8501 is performed automatically once the various register sizes are specified. The verification that FM8501 meets its operational specifications is the subject of the remainder of this dissertation. The equivalence of an operational specification to digital hardware is only as good as the operational specification. It is the user's responsibility to write meaningful specifications.

We now illustrate our approach. This example does not illustrate our handling of registers, microcode, or time. However, the basic idea below is generalized to handle these concepts later.

Suppose we wish to specify and design verify a 4-bit adder. Let a and b be two n-bit wide bit vectors, representing the natural numbers i and j we wish to add. Suppose the output of the adder is a bit-vector $n+1$ bits wide representing some natural number k. The specification of our circuit is $k = (\text{plus } i\ j)$ Note that to write this specification formally we need the bv-to-nat function which maps from bit-vectors to natural numbers.

To describe our circuit design we write a function, here named bv-adder, which takes a and b and a carry flag c as input and yields a bit vector one bit longer than a. A simple ripple carry adder, for arbitrarily wide bit-vectors, is defined as follows:

```
(defn bv-adder (c a b)
  (if (bitvp a)
      (if (equal a (btm))
          (bitv c (btm))
          (bitv (b-xor c (b-xor (bit a) (bit b)))
                (bv-adder (b-or (b-and (bit a) (bit b))
                                (b-or (b-and (bit a) c)
                                      (b-and (bit b) c)))
                          (vec a)
                          (vec b))))
      (bitv c (btm))))
```

Since this is the first hardware function we have exhibited, we will briefly explain how it works. Implicit in the definition is the assumption that a and b are the same size; what bv-adder does if they are not is unimportant. If they are not bit-vectors or are empty we return the 1-bit wide vector containing the carry input c. Otherwise, we create a new bit-vector with bitv. The least significant bit is generated by exclusive or'ing together the input carry and the least significant bits of a and b. The rest of the vector is obtained by recursively adding the other bits in a and b with an input carry computed combinationally as the majority function of the bits just exclusive or'ed.

Assuming (and (sizep a 4) (sizep b 4) (boolp c)) we can prove that the natural number represented by (bv-adder f a b) is the mathematical sum of those represented by a and b. That is:

```
(bv-to-nat (bv-adder f a b))
             =
(plus (bv-to-nat a) (bv-to-nat b))
```

In fact, we prove a generalized version of this theorem, in which the role of the carry flag c is explained and a and b are assumed only to be of equal size (but not necessarily size 4). The proof of the generalized theorem is by induction on a and b and is quite straightforward. The proof of the above instance is then trivial.

Assumptions:

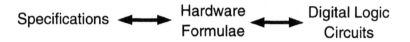

Figure 5.1: Diagram of proof relationships

Under the assumption above, we can also prove that (bv-adder f a b) is equal to:

```
(bitv (b-xor c (b-xor a-1 b-1))
     (bitv (b-xor *1 (b-xor a-2 b-2))
          (bitv (b-xor *2 (b-xor a-3 b-3))
               (bitv (b-xor *3 (b-xor a-4 b-4))
                    (bitv (b-or (b-and a-4 b-4)
                              (b-or (b-and a-4 *3)
                                   (b-and b-4 *3)))
                         (btm))))))
```

where the following abbreviations are used for commonly used subterms:

```
a- x:       (bitn a  x)
b- y:       (bitn b  y)
c:          f
*1:         (b-or (b-and a-1 b-1)
                 (b-or (b-and a-1 c) (b-and b-1 c)))
*2:         (b-or (b-and a-2 b-2)
                 (b-or (b-and a-2 *1) (b-and b-2 *1)))
*3:         (b-or (b-and a-3 b-3)
                 (b-or (b-and a-3 *2) (b-and b-3 *2)))
```

This expression can be more conventionally represented as shown in the bottom of Figure 5.2.

Observe that we could just as easily obtain a 16-bit or a 32-bit wide adder from bv-adder. The above example situation is pictorially illustrated in Figure 5.2.

Assumptions: (and (sizep a 4) (sizep b 4) (boolp c))

Theorem: (bv-to-nat (bv-adder f a b))

                    =

                (plus (bv-to-nat a) (bv-to-nat b))

Given that: a = (bitv a0 (bitv a1 (bitv a2 (bitv a3 (btm))))))
             b = (bitv b0 (bitv b1 (bitv b2 (bitv b3 (btm))))))
then   (bv-adder f a b) represents the schematic below.

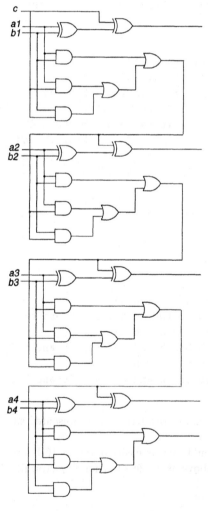

Figure 5.2: Illustration of the Verification Approach

Chapter 6

FM8501: A Conventional Description

The purpose of this chapter is to introduce the FM8501 within a conventional framework.[1] An *intuitive* feeling for the microprocessor will help you relate the coming formulae with other commerical devices.

FM8501 is a 16-bit microprocessor with word addressing only. It is a single state machine, not having supervisior modes nor interupt levels. It contains the normal complement of arithmatic operations found on commerical microprocessors [12, 35], and a general-purpose, conditional-move instruction. FM8501 is not unique in size or capabilities. Its uniqueness stems from it having been mechanically verified against a complete formal, functional description.

This microprocessor has not been implemented in silicon or with TTL logic; many conventional implementation issues are not described. For example, the pin-out for this processor is unknown. Signals are characterized as being on or off, not by logic "1" or "0." The amount and type of power required for operation has not been specified, etc. Additionally, nothing is said as to a possible clock rate for FM8501.

6.1 Introduction and Features

FM8501 is a complete, stand-alone microprocessor with a symmetrically organized instruction set. Its features include:

- 16-bit general purpose processor

- word addressing yielding a 64K word (128K byte) memory size

---

[1]The sub-section titles here mirror the ones used in the M68000 16/32-bit Microprocessor [35].

- eight general purpose registers (one also being the program counter)

- 16-bit instructions

- register-register, register-memory, or memory-memory operation is allowed with all instructions

- two-address instruction format

- register, register indirect, register indirect with post-increment, or register indirect with pre-decrement addressing mode are individually supported for both operands for all instructions

- general-purpose conditional move instruction

- Boolean, natural number, and integer operational specification

- separate ALU for effective address generation

- memory mapped I/O

- compact functional description

6.2   Block Diagram

The block diagram for FM8501 is shown in Figure 6.1. This diagram shows the various registers and the data flow between them. Data enters the microprocessor at the top left-hand corner of the figure and leaves at the top right-hand corner. Input data may flow into the register file or into latches for processing by the ALU. Output from the ALU can be stored into the register file after being latched in the data output register. The instruction register is located in the middle of the figure and along with the microrom controls the execution of instructions. On the lower left-hand corner are an incrementer and decrementer for generating the next program counter and for doing the pre-decrement and post-increment operations.

To avoid further complicating Figure 6.1, we have not shown all the data paths. For example, we do not show how the control bits in the microcode ROM determine the read output line.

6.3   Programmer's Model

The FM8501 microprocessor has eight 16-bit general-purpose registers, one of them being the program counter. A diagram of the register set is shown in Figure 6.2. The use of register R0 is overloaded as it is also the program counter. All registers may be used as index registers or as software stack pointers. The four status bits C, V, N, and Z, stand for carry, overflow, negative, and zero, respectively.

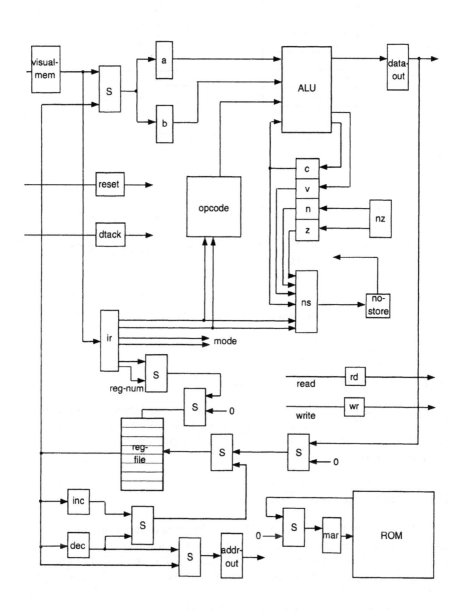

Figure 6.1: An Internal Block Diagram of FM8501

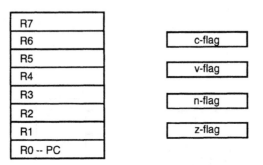

Figure 6.2: Programming Model

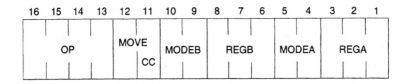

Figure 6.3: Instruction Word

6.4 Data Representation

FM8501 has only one operand size: a 16-bit word. Each register and memory location contain 16-bit values. Memory is organized on a word-addressable basis, and there are 2^{16} uniquely addressable memory locations. All instructions operate on words.

6.5 Instruction Format

All FM8501 instructions are one word in size. Every instruction specifies a source and a destination location, each of which is either in a register or in memory. Instructions for the FM8501 specify two kinds of information: the operation to be performed and the location of the operands on which the operation is performed.

Figure 6.3 shows the various fields in an instruction. The field named MOVE specifies whether the operation to be performed is to be a move instruction or a data manipulation instruction. When a move instruction is specified, the OP field specifies the type of move to be performed; otherwise, the OP field specifies the operation to be performed. The CC bit specifies whether to set all or none of the condition-code bits. REGA and REGB specify the registers to be used and MODEA and MODEB specify the type of addressing to be used.

Every instruction has a source and a destination. If two sources are required, the destination operand serves as the other source before being modified. Every instruction is either one of the four following forms:

operand-b ← operator *operand-a*
operand-b ← *operand-b* operator *operand-a*
operand-b ← *operand-a*
operand-b ←(condition) *operand-a*

The first two are operator forms; an operator such as negation or addition, is applied to source operand(s). The last two forms are move instructions; the first is an unconditional move and the second is a conditional move instruction.

The move instruction is unique in the repect that its operation can be conditional with regard to the setting of the condition-code bits. Move instructions can be specified to be unconditional or they can be specified to be conditional upon the setting of any condition-code bit.

6.6 Addressing

Operand addressing is specified by the register and mode fields in an instruction. Four different addressing modes are supported by FM8501: register, register indirect, register indirect with pre-decrement, register indirect with post-increment. A register operand is the contents of a register. For the indirect modes, the contents of a register specify the address of the desired operand in memory. In the register indirect with pre-decrement mode, the contents of the register specified is decremented before being used as a memory address; the decremented value of the register is stored back into the register before memory is accessed. In the register indirect with post-increment mode, the contents of the register specified is incremented after the instruction operation has been completed. For instructions that specify both operands as the same register, the pre-decrements and post-increments occur first to *operand-a* and then to *operand-b*.

6.7 Instruction Set

The instruction set is composed of two groups of instructions: move and function. The move group is composed of a number of conditional move instructions. The function group is composed of instructions that transform data with some function. The instruction set of FM8501 has been summarized in Table 6.2.

MODE	Register	Operand	Description
00	An	An	Register direct
01	An	(An)	Register indirect
10	An	-(An)	Register indirect pre-decrement
11	An	(An)+	Register indirect post-increment
00	Bn	Bn	Register direct
01	Bn	(Bn)	Register indirect
10	Bn	-(Bn)	Register indirect pre-decrement
11	Bn	(Bn)+	Register indirect post-increment

where n is 000, 001, 010, 011, 100, 101, 110, or 111.

Table 6.1: Instruction Register Mode Summary

The letters "b" and "a" used in the "Operation" column signify *operand-a* and *operand-b*.

6.8   Signal Description

The signals of the FM8501 microprocessor are shown in Figure 6.4. There are several major groups: address, data output, data input, control output, control input, and clock and power. All output signals are bi-state, and are internally synchronized. All input signals are assumed to be bi-state, and input values are sampled at the falling edge of the input clock signal.

6.8.1   Address Bus

These bi-state outputs provide the address for a bus transfer. All bus transfers, both read and write, set the address bus. The address bus is capable of addressing 2^{16} 16-bit words of data.

6.8.2   Data Out Bus

During write operations these bi-state lines are set to the value to be written. The location for this data is specified by the address bus.

6.8.3   Data Input

During read operations these lines are sampled for bi-state input values that are to be read into the microprocessor. The location assumed to be responding to a read request is specified by the contents of the address bus.

OPCODE	MOVE	Operation	Description
0000	0	$b \leftarrow a$	Move
0001	0	$b \leftarrow a + 1$	Increment
0010	0	$b \leftarrow b + a + c$	Add with carry
0011	0	$b \leftarrow b + a$	Add
0100	0	$b \leftarrow 0 - a$	Negation
0101	0	$b \leftarrow a - 1$	Decrement
0110	0	$b \leftarrow b - a - c$	Subtract with borrow
0111	0	$b \leftarrow b - a$	Subtract
1000	0	$b \leftarrow a \gg 1$	Rotate right, shifted through carry
1001	0	$b \leftarrow a \gg 1$	Arithmetic shift right, top bit duplicated
1010	0	$b \leftarrow a \gg 1$	Logical shift right, top bit zero
1011	0	$b \leftarrow b \otimes a$	Exclusive or
1100	0	$b \leftarrow b \vee a$	Or
1101	0	$b \leftarrow b \wedge a$	And
1110	0	$b \leftarrow \neg a$	Not
1111	0	$b \leftarrow a$	Move
0000	1	$b \leftarrow (\neg c)a$	Move if no carry
0001	1	$b \leftarrow (c)a$	Move if carry
0010	1	$b \leftarrow (\neg v)a$	Move if no overflow
0011	1	$b \leftarrow (v)a$	Move if overflow
0100	1	$b \leftarrow (\neg z)a$	Move if not zero
0101	1	$b \leftarrow (z)a$	Move if zero
0110	1	$b \leftarrow (\neg n)a$	Move if not negative
0111	1	$b \leftarrow (n)a$	Move if negative
1000	1	$b \leftarrow a$	Move
1001	1	$b \leftarrow a$	Move
1010	1	$b \leftarrow a$	Move
1011	1	$b \leftarrow a$	Move
1100	1	$b \leftarrow a$	Move
1101	1	$b \leftarrow a$	Move
1110	1	$b \leftarrow a$	Move
1111	1	$b \leftarrow a$	Move

Table 6.2: Instruction Set Summary

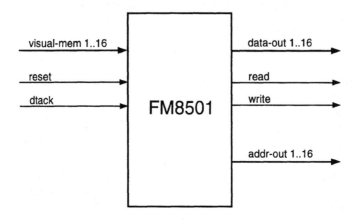

Figure 6.4: FM8501 Functional Signal Groups

6.8.4 Reset Input

This input line is always sampled, and if set, will reset FM8501 one clock cycle later. For resetting to completely occur, this line should be set for at least two clock ticks.

6.8.5 Data Acknowledge Input

This input line, often called "Dtack," is an asynchronous bi-state input that is sampled every clock edge during read and write operations. This input tells the microprocessor that the unit responding to a read or write operation has completed its operation.

6.8.6 Read and Write Outputs

These bi-state output lines specify that either a read or write bus cycle is in progress. These lines are never both active at once.

6.8.7 Clock and Power

As this device is not implemented, the amount and type of power required is unspecified. This is also true of the clock.

6.9 Bus Operation

There are two types of bus cycles: read and write. These two different cycles differ in the sense that only the data flow changes directions. Both bus cycles have the following common points: each cycle is initiated by the read (write) signal, upon initiation of read (write) signal the address bus has the address to be read (written), the microprocessor holds the read (write) line and the address bus steady during the bus cycle, the reset input signal is assumed to be off during the whole cycle, and the processor waits for the data acknowledge input signal to become valid before completing.

The read cycle asserts the read output line; the write output line remains unasserted during a read cycle. The processor waits for its data acknowledge input signal to become valid before reading its data input port. The processor assumes that its data input port does not change after the assertion of its data acknowledge input signal and remains constant so long as the read output signal is asserted. The processor also assumes that the data acknowledge input signal does not change during the read bus cycle after becomming active.

The write cycle asserts the write output; the read output line remains unasserted during a write cycle. The processor waits for its data acknowledge input signal to become valid before terminating a write bus cycle. The processor assumes that the data acknowledge input signal does not change during the write bus cycle after becomming active.

Chapter 7

Commonly Used Functions

To describe and specify the FM8501 formally we must define many mathematical functions for manipulating Booleans, bit-vectors, numbers, integers, etc. In this and successive chapters we display the definitions and properties of these functions. A number of functions that are common to the formal descriptions to follow are presented here. Some of these functions have been seen before, but are included for completeness. Only short descriptions of these functions are presented.

7.1   Bit and Bit-vector Manipulation

The logical functions are:

```
(defn b-or (x y) (or x y))

(defn b-nor (x y) (if x f (if y f t)))

(defn b-not (x) (if x f t))

(defn b-and (x y) (and x y))

(defn b-nand (x y) (if x (if y f t) t))

(defn b-equv (x y) (if x (if y t f) (if y f t)))

(defn b-xor (x y) (if x (if y f t) (if y t f)))

(defn fix-bool (x) (if x t f))
```

The function `fix-bool` takes any input and returns t if x is not equal to f; otherwise, this function returns f.

The functions for constructing bit-vectors and measuring their sizes are presented below.

```
(add-shell bitv btm bitvp
            ((bit (one-of truep falsep) false)
             (vec (one-of bitvp) btm)))
```

```
(defn size (a)
     (if (bitvp a)
         (if (equal a (btm))
             0
             (add1 (size (vec a))))
         0))
```

```
(defn trunc (a n)
     (if (zerop n)
         (btm)
         (bitv (bit a)
               (trunc (vec a) (sub1 n)))))
```

```
(defn bitn (x n)
     (if (zerop n)
         f
         (if (equal n 1)
             (bit x)
             (bitn (vec x) (sub1 n)))))
```

The function `size` measures the number of `bitv` constructor functions. `trunc` makes a into a bit-vector of size n. Function `bitn` returns bit n from bit-vector x.

The bit-vector logical functions are presented next. Functions `bv-not`, `bv-or`, `bv-and`, and `bv-xor`, are bit-vector functions not, or, and, and exclusive or, respectively. `v-append` glues two bit-vectors together. `v-lsr` is a logical right shift function for bit-vectors. `v-asr` is an arithmatic right shifter, and `v-ror` is a rotate right function. The "bv" versions are identical.

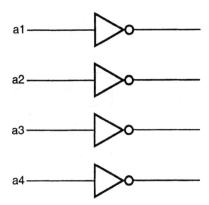

Figure 7.1: Schematic of Four-bit Vector Not

```
(defn bv-not (a)
     (if (bitvp a)
         (if (equal a (btm))
             (btm)
             (bitv (b-not (bit a))
                   (bv-not (vec a))))
         (btm)))
```

To illustrate the sense in which these functions describe digital hardware, observe under the hypothesis (sizep a 4), that

```
(bv-not a)
   =
(bitv (b-not a-1)
      (bitv (b-not a-2)
            (bitv (b-not a-3)
                  (bitv (b-not a-4)
                        (btm)))))
```

where $a_i =$(bitn a i). A conventional representation of the four-bit vector not function (bv-not a), where (sizep a 4), is shown in Figure 7.1.

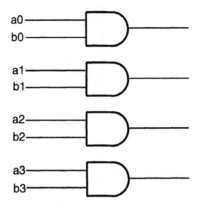

Figure 7.2: Schematic of Four-bit Vector And

```
(defn bv-or (a b)
     (if (bitvp a)
         (if (equal a (btm))
             (btm)
             (bitv (b-or (bit a) (bit b))
                   (bv-or (vec a) (vec b))))
         (btm)))
```

```
(defn bv-and (a b)
     (if (bitvp a)
         (if (equal a (btm))
             (btm)
             (bitv (b-and (bit a) (bit b))
                   (bv-and (vec a) (vec b))))
         (btm)))
```

A conventional representation of the four-bit vector and function (bv-and a b) where (and (sizep a 4) (sizep b 4)), a_i = (bitn a i), and b_j = (bitn b j), is shown in Figure 7.2.

```
(defn bv-xor (a b)
     (if (bitvp a)
         (if (equal a (btm))
```

```
              (btm)
              (bitv (b-xor (bit a) (bit b))
                    (bv-xor (vec a) (vec b))))
          (btm)))


(defn v-lsr (a)
     (if (bitvp a)
         (if (equal a (btm))
             (btm)
             (v-append (vec a) (bitv f (btm))))
         (btm)))


(defn v-append (a b)
     (if (bitvp a)
         (if (equal a (btm))
             b
             (bitv (bit a) (v-append (vec a) b)))
         b))


(defn v-ror (a c)
     (if (bitvp a)
         (if (equal a (btm))
             (btm)
             (v-append (vec a) (bitv c (btm))))
         (btm)))


(defn v-asr (a)
     (if (bitvp a)
         (if (equal a (btm))
             (btm)
             (v-append (vec a)
                       (bitv (bitn a (size a)) (btm))))
         (btm)))


(defn bv-asr (a) (v-asr a))

(defn bv-ror (a c) (v-ror a c))

(defn bv-lsr (a) (v-lsr a))
```

The functions b-bv-zerop and b-bv-nzerop test a bit-vector for all fs or not all fs. The b-bv-equal function tests two bit-vectors for equality. Their definitions are given below.

```
(defn b-bv-nzerop (a)
    (if (bitvp a)
        (if (equal a (btm))
            f
            (b-or (bit a) (b-bv-nzerop (vec a))))
        f))

(defn b-bv-zerop (a)
    (b-not (b-bv-nzerop a)))

(defn bv-equal (a b)
    (if (bitvp a)
        (if (equal a (btm))
            t
            (b-and (b-equv (bit a) (bit b))
                   (bv-equal (vec a) (vec b))))
        f))
```

The hardware *if* functions are presented next: the "Boolean if," b-if; the "bit-vector if," bv-if; and the "bv-cv if," bv-cv-if. bv-cv is a constructor function used to glue a bit-vector together with two other bits: carry and overflow. This constructor is used by the ALU to return three values.

```
(defn b-if (c a b)
    (b-nand (b-nand c a)
            (b-nand (b-not c) b)))

(defn bv-if (c a b)
    (if (bitvp a)
        (if (equal a (btm))
            (btm)
            (bitv (b-if c (bit a) (bit b))
                  (bv-if c (vec a) (vec b))))
        (btm)))

(add-shell bv-cv nil bv-cvp
            ((bv (one-of bitvp) btm)
             (c (one-of truep falsep) false)
             (v (one-of truep falsep) false)))
```

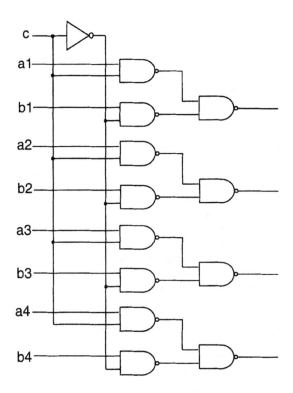

Figure 7.3: Schematic of Four-bit Vector If

```
(defn bv-cv-if (c a b)
     (bv-cv (bv-if c (bv a) (bv b))
            (b-if c (c a) (c b))
            (b-if c (v a) (v b))))
```

Observe that for 4-bit wide vectors (bv-if c a b) can be depicted as shown in Figure 7.3. To demonstrate the theorem-prover actually proving a hardware function equivalent to a specification, the theorem-prover output for the correctness of the bv-if function is included below.[1] The specification of the bv-if is that it returns a if c is true and b if c is flase, assuming that c is Boolean, and

---

[1] The reader may note that the formulas in the theorem-prover output are in upper-case. When Zetalisp on the Symbolics 3600 reads our formulas and user commands, it translates them to upper-case. Thus, when we type a definition for bv-if, the theorem-prover sees and defines the function BV-IF.

a and b are bit-vectors of equal size.

```
(PROVE-LEMMA BV-IF-SPECIFICATION NIL
  (IMPLIES (AND (BOOLP C)
               (BITVP A)
               (BITVP B)
               (EQUAL (SIZE A) (SIZE B)))
          (EQUAL (BV-IF C A B) (IF C A B))))
```

This simplifies, clearly, to the following two new conjectures:

```
Case 2. (IMPLIES (AND (BOOLP C)
                     (BITVP A)
                     (BITVP B)
                     (EQUAL (SIZE A) (SIZE B))
                     (NOT C))
                (EQUAL (BV-IF C A B) B)).
```

This again simplifies, unfolding BOOLP, to:

```
        (IMPLIES (AND (BITVP A)
                     (BITVP B)
                     (EQUAL (SIZE A) (SIZE B)))
                (EQUAL (BV-IF F A B) B)).
```

Name the above subgoal *1.

```
Case 1. (IMPLIES (AND (BOOLP C)
                     (BITVP A)
                     (BITVP B)
                     (EQUAL (SIZE A) (SIZE B))
                     C)
                (EQUAL (BV-IF C A B) A)),
```

which we would usually push and work on later by induction. But if we must use induction to prove the input conjecture, we prefer to induct on the original formulation of the problem. Thus we will disregard all that we have previously done, give the name *1 to the original input, and work on it.

So now let us consider:

```
(IMPLIES (AND (BOOLP C)
```

```
            (BITVP A)
            (BITVP B)
            (EQUAL (SIZE A) (SIZE B)))
      (EQUAL (BV-IF C A B) (IF C A B))),
```
which we named *1 above. We will appeal to induction. There are three
plausible inductions. However, they merge into one likely candidate
induction. We will induct according to the following scheme:

```
  (AND (IMPLIES (AND (BITVP A)
                     (EQUAL A (BTM)))
               (p C A B))
       (IMPLIES (AND (BITVP A)
                     (NOT (EQUAL A (BTM)))
                     (p C (VEC A) (VEC B)))
               (p C A B))
       (IMPLIES (NOT (BITVP A)) (p C A B))).
```
Linear arithmetic and the lemma VEC-LESSP can be used to show that the
measure (COUNT A) decreases according to the well-founded relation LESSP
in each induction step of the scheme. Note, however, the inductive
instance chosen for B. The above induction scheme produces three new
conjectures:

Case 3. (IMPLIES (AND (EQUAL A (BTM))
```
                      (BOOLP C)
                      (BITVP A)
                      (BITVP B)
                      (EQUAL (SIZE A) (SIZE B)))
                 (EQUAL (BV-IF C A B) (IF C A B))),
```

which simplifies, expanding the functions BITVP, SIZE, EQUAL, and
BV-IF, to:

```
      (IMPLIES (AND (BOOLP C)
                    (BITVP B)
                    (EQUAL 0 (ADD1 (SIZE (VEC B))))
                    (NOT C))
               (EQUAL (BTM) B)).
```

But this again simplifies, using linear arithmetic, to:

```
      T.
```

Case 2. (IMPLIES (AND (NOT (EQUAL A (BTM)))
```
                      (NOT (EQUAL (SIZE (VEC A)) (SIZE (VEC B))))
                      (BOOLP C)
                      (BITVP A)
                      (BITVP B)
                      (EQUAL (SIZE A) (SIZE B)))
```

```
                  (EQUAL (BV-IF C A B) (IF C A B))),
```

which simplifies, rewriting with BIT-IS-BOOLEAN, B-IF-WORKS, and
SIZE-HYPS-CONTRADICTORY, and expanding SIZE, BV-IF, VEC, BOOLP, BIT,
and EQUAL, to:

```
      T.
```

```
Case 1. (IMPLIES (AND (NOT (EQUAL A (BTM)))
                      (EQUAL (BV-IF C (VEC A) (VEC B))
                             (IF C (VEC A) (VEC B)))
                      (BOOLP C)
                      (BITVP A)
                      (BITVP B)
                      (EQUAL (SIZE A) (SIZE B)))
                 (EQUAL (BV-IF C A B) (IF C A B))).
```

This simplifies, rewriting with BIT-IS-BOOLEAN, B-IF-WORKS, and
BITV-BIT-VEC, and opening up the functions BOOLP, SIZE, BV-IF, VEC, and
BIT, to three new conjectures:

```
Case 1.3.
        (IMPLIES (AND (NOT (EQUAL A (BTM)))
                      (NOT C)
                      (EQUAL (BV-IF C (VEC A) (VEC B))
                             (VEC B))
                      (BITVP A)
                      (BITVP B)
                      (NOT (EQUAL B (BTM)))
                      (EQUAL (ADD1 (SIZE (VEC A)))
                             (ADD1 (SIZE (VEC B)))))
                 (EQUAL (BV-IF F A B) B)),
```

which again simplifies, appealing to the lemmas ADD1-EQUAL,
BITV-BIT-VEC, B-IF-WORKS, and BIT-IS-BOOLEAN, and opening up the
functions BOOLP and BV-IF, to:

```
      T.
```

```
Case 1.2.
        (IMPLIES (AND (NOT (EQUAL A (BTM)))
                      (NOT C)
                      (EQUAL (BV-IF C (VEC A) (VEC B))
                             (VEC B))
                      (BITVP A)
                      (BITVP B)
                      (EQUAL B (BTM))
                      (EQUAL (ADD1 (SIZE (VEC A))) 0))
```

```
(EQUAL (BV-IF F A (BTM))
       (BTM))),
```

which again simplifies, using linear arithmetic, to:

T.

Case 1.1.

```
(IMPLIES (AND (NOT (EQUAL A (BTM)))
              C
              (EQUAL (BV-IF C (VEC A) (VEC B))
                     (VEC A))
              (BOOLP C)
              (BITVP A)
              (BITVP B)
              (EQUAL B (BTM))
              (EQUAL (ADD1 (SIZE (VEC A))) 0))
         (EQUAL (BITV (BIT A)
                      (BV-IF C (VEC A) (BTM)))
                A)),
```

which again simplifies, using linear arithmetic, to:

T.

That finishes the proof of *1. Q.E.D.

[5.9 5.3]
BV-IF-SPECIFICATION

The pair of floating point numbers above are the times taken to construct and to print (respectively) the proof, measured in seconds on a Symbolics, Inc., 3600 Lisp Machine.

7.2 Adder and Subtracter Definitions

Presented here are functions for adding and subtracting bit-vectors. These functions are used both in the FM8501 and its specification. Indeed, the ALU for the FM8501 is used in the specification. The next chapter explains how we use these functions in the specification without begging the question of the correctness of the hardware.

The functions for adding and subtracting bit-vectors require only one base function `bv-adder`.[2] The other functions `bv-adder-carry-out`, `bv-adder--overflowp`, `bv-adder-output`, `bv-subtracter-overflowp`, `bv-subtracter--carry-out`, and `bv-subtracter-output`, are defined in terms of `bv-adder`. These functions are presented below.

```
(defn bv-adder (c a b)
    (if (bitvp a)
        (if (equal a (btm))
            (bitv c (btm))
            (bitv (b-xor c (b-xor (bit a) (bit b)))
                (bv-adder (b-or (b-and (bit a) (bit b))
                            (b-or (b-and (bit a) c)
                                (b-and (bit b) c)))
                        (vec a)
                        (vec b))))
        (bitv c (btm))))

(defn bv-adder-output (c a b)
    (trunc (bv-adder c a b) (size a)))

(defn bv-adder-carry-out (c a b)
    (bitn (bv-adder c a b)
        (add1 (size a))))

(defn bv-adder-overflowp (c a b)
    (b-and (b-equv (bitn a (size a))
                (bitn b (size b)))
        (b-xor (bitn a (size a))
                (bitn (bv-adder-output c a b)
                    (size a)))))

(defn bv-subtracter-carry-out (c a b)
    (b-not (bv-adder-carry-out (b-not c)
                            (bv-not a)
                            b)))
```

---

[2]Note that any other type of bit-vector adder could have been used in place of `bv-adder`. Only two lemmas need be proved about `bv-adder`; afterwards, the definition of `bv-adder` is not consulted. We have also proved the correctness of a propagate-generate adder and a conditional-sum adder. These parallel adders calculate their result with fewer gate delays but at a greater cost in gates than a ripple carry adder.

```
(defn bv-subtracter-overflowp (c a b)
     (bv-adder-overflowp (b-not c)
                         (bv-not a)
                         b))

(defn bv-subtracter-output (c a b)
     (bv-adder-output (b-not c)
                      (bv-not a)
                      b))
```

The function bv-adder-carry-out returns the carry out from an addition of two bit-vectors. bv-adder-overflowp determines if an overflow condition occurred when considering the two's complement addition of integers. bv-adder-output returns the bit-vector representing the addition of two bit-vectors.[3] The subtracter functions are similar to the addition functions, but for subtraction.

7.3   Incrementer and Decrementer

Two functions have been defined which perform a natural number increment or decrement on bit-vectors. These functions "wrap around", that is, if the largest natural number representable by a bit-vector is incremented, the natural number interpretation of the result is zero.

```
(defn v-nat-inc
     (a)
     (nat-to-bv (add1 (bv-to-nat a))
                (size a)))

(defn v-nat-dec
     (a)
     (if (zerop (bv-to-nat a))
         (nat-to-bv (sub1 (exp 2 (size a)))
                    (size a))
         (nat-to-bv (sub1 (bv-to-nat a))
                    (size a))))
```

The definition of v-nat-dec is more complex than the v-nat-inc definition because (equal (sub1 0) 0).

---

[3]The theorems that these functions *really* perform useful mathematical operations are given in the ALU section which follows.

Chapter 8

The ALU

The ALU performs all transformations on data within FM8501.[1] This ALU performs 15 different logical and arithmetic operations, most of which have operational meaning with respect to several mathematically defined data-types (Boolean vectors, natural numbers, and integers).

The ALU function is used both in the FM8501 and its specification. Since the ALU contributes more than half of the combinational logic of the FM8501, one must consider the possibility that its use as its own specification devaluates the overall specification and verification effort. Why do we use the ALU in the specification and in what sense have we verified it?

To specify the FM8501 we will present (in the FM8501 specification chapter) a more elegant but equivalent function definition that abstracts away much of the internal structure and state of the FM8501 implementation. In designing this more abstract machine we had to decide what kind of objects were held in its registers and memory: bit-vectors, natural numbers, or integers.

Had we chosen natural numbers, the abstract ALU would have had a very elegant specification for the natural number arithmetic operations, but it would have offered an unsatisfyingly complex specification for the logical and integer operations. The crux of the problem is that in a typical von Neumann machine, such as FM8501, a data object can be interpreted in many different ways and no single interpretation gives satisfying specifications to all operations.

For simplicity, we chose bit-vectors as the abstract object representation format. The ALU itself operates directly on bit-vectors. The specification of the ALU is with respect to bit-vectors, e.g. we say, in effect, "the *add* instruction takes two bit-vectors and returns the bit-vector computed by the ALU".

To prevent this from being vacuous we prove three theorems about the ALU. One explains (some of) its operations when the input and output bit-vectors are interpreterd as bit-vectors, one explains (some of) its operations when the input

---

[1] The incrementing of the program counter, the pre-decrement and post-increment operations are performed by separate hardware.

and output bit-vectors are interpreted as natural numbers, and one explains (some of) its operations when the input and output bit-vectors are interpreted as integers. We regard these theorems as the specifications of the ALU.

This chapter presents the definition of the ALU and three verified specificatons of it.

8.1   ALU Hardware Function

The ALU is a function of four arguments and returns three results. The input arguments are two bit-vectors, a and b; a carry bit, c; and a four-bit opcode, op-code. The ALU returns three values for all opcodes: a bit-vector, a carry bit, and an overflow bit glued together with a bv-cv. The definition of the ALU follows:

```
(defn bv-alu-cv (a b c op-code)
  (bv-cv-if (bitn op-code 4)
    (bv-cv-if (bitn op-code 3)
      (bv-cv-if (bitn op-code 2)
        (bv-cv-if (bitn op-code 1)
                (bv-cv a                    ; Op-code 15 - move
                       f
                       f)
                (bv-cv (bv-not a)           ; Op-code 14 - not
                       f
                       f))
          (bv-cv-if (bitn op-code 1)
                (bv-cv (bv-and a b)         ; Op-code 13 - and
                       f
                       f)
                (bv-cv (bv-or a b)          ; Op-code 12 - or
                       f
                       f)))

      (bv-cv-if (bitn op-code 2)
        (bv-cv-if (bitn op-code 1)
                (bv-cv (bv-xor a b)         ; Op-code 11 - xor
                       f
                       f)
                (bv-cv (bv-lsr a)           ; Op-code 10 - lsr
                       (bitn a 1)
                       f))
        (bv-cv-if (bitn op-code 1)
                (bv-cv (bv-asr a)           ; Op-code 9 - asr
```

```
                         (bitn a 1)
                         f)
               (bv-cv (bv-ror a c)          ; Op-code 8 - ror
                      (if (zerop (size a))
                          c
                          (bitn a 1))
                      f))))
(bv-cv-if (bitn op-code 3)
  (bv-cv-if (bitn op-code 2)
    (bv-cv-if (bitn op-code 1)
                                      ; Op-code 7 - sub
              (bv-cv (bv-subtracter-output f a b)
                     (bv-subtracter-carry-out f a b)
                     (bv-subtracter-overflowp f a b))
                                      ; Op-code 6 - subb
              (bv-cv (bv-subtracter-output c a b)
                     (bv-subtracter-carry-out c a b)
                     (bv-subtracter-overflowp c a b)))
    (bv-cv-if (bitn op-code 1)          ; Op-code 5 - dec
              (bv-cv (bv-subtracter-output
                     t (nat-to-bv 0 (size a)) a)
                     (bv-subtracter-carry-out
                     t (nat-to-bv 0 (size a)) a)
                     (bv-subtracter-overflowp
                     t
                     (nat-to-bv 0 (size a)) a))
                                      ; Op-code 4 - neg
              (bv-cv (bv-subtracter-output
                     f a (nat-to-bv 0 (size a)))
                     (bv-subtracter-carry-out
                     f a (nat-to-bv 0 (size a)))
                     (bv-subtracter-overflowp
                     f a
                     (nat-to-bv 0 (size a))))))
  (bv-cv-if (bitn op-code 2)
    (bv-cv-if (bitn op-code 1)
                                      ; Op-code 3 - add
              (bv-cv (bv-adder-output f a b)
                     (bv-adder-carry-out f a b)
                     (bv-adder-overflowp f a b))
                                      ; Op-code 2 - addc
              (bv-cv (bv-adder-output c a b)
                     (bv-adder-carry-out c a b)
```

```
                              (bv-adder-overflowp c a b)))
        (bv-cv-if (bitn op-code 1)              ; Op-code 1 - inc
                  (bv-cv (bv-adder-output
                             t a (nat-to-bv 0 (size a)))
                         (bv-adder-carry-out
                             t a (nat-to-bv 0 (size a)))
                         (bv-adder-overflowp
                             t a (nat-to-bv 0 (size a))))
                  (bv-cv a              ; Op-code 0 - noop, move
                         f
                         f))))))
```

8.2 ALU Specification

The specification and proof of correctness statement for the ALU are wrapped up
in three lemmas. The three lemmas specify what operations the ALU performs
with respect to the Boolean bit-vector, natural number, and integer interpretation of its input and output bit-vectors. This section discusses each of these in
turn. Not all opcodes have interpretations with respect to all three data-types.
For instance, the ALU bit-vector "exclusive or" function has only a Boolean bit-
vector specification; exclusive or has no *nice* properties with respect to natural
numbers or integers operations.

The Boolean bit-vector specification is presented below. This specification
is a theorem about `bv-alu-cv`. This proof has several hypotheses: `(boolp c)`
specifying that c is either t or f, `(bitvp a)` specifying that a is a bit-vector,
`(bitvp b)` specifying that b is a bit-vector, and `(equal (size a) (size b))`
specifying that the lengths of bit-vectors a and b are equal. The conclusion of
the theorem is a conjuction of 11 formulae, each of which specifies for a different
opcode the three values returned by `bv-alu-cv`. For example the sixth conjunct:

```
(equal (bv-alu-cv a b c (nat-to-bv 10 4))        ; Lsr
       (bv-cv (v-lsr a)
              (bitn a 1)
              f))
```

specifies the behavior of `bv-alu-cv` for opcode 10, the logical shift right operation: the bit-vector returned is `(v-lsr a)`, the carry flag returned is `(bitn a
1)`, and the overflow flag returned is f. Note that this theorem about `bv-alu-cv`
does not constrain the sizes of a and b (except that they be equal). That is,
having proved this theorem we can obtain a correct ALU for any word size by
appropriately expanding `bv-alu-cv`.

```
(prove-lemma bv-alu-cv-correct-boolean nil
  (implies (and (bitvp a)
                (bitvp b)
                (equal (size a) (size b))
                (boolp c))

           (and (equal (bv-alu-cv a b c (nat-to-bv 15 4)) ; Move
                       (bv-cv a f f))

                (equal (bv-alu-cv a b c (nat-to-bv 14 4)) ; Not
                       (bv-cv (v-not a) f f))

                (equal (bv-alu-cv a b c (nat-to-bv 13 4)) ; And
                       (bv-cv (v-and a b) f f))

                (equal (bv-alu-cv a b c (nat-to-bv 12 4)) ; Or
                       (bv-cv (v-or a b) f f))

                (equal (bv-alu-cv a b c (nat-to-bv 11 4)) ; Xor
                       (bv-cv (v-xor a b) f f))

                (equal (bv-alu-cv a b c (nat-to-bv 10 4)) ; Lsr
                       (bv-cv (v-lsr a)
                              (bitn a 1)
                              f))

                (equal (bv-alu-cv a b c (nat-to-bv 9 4))  ; Asr
                       (bv-cv (v-asr a)
                              (bitn a 1)
                              f))

                (equal (bv-alu-cv a b c (nat-to-bv 8 4))  ; Ror
                       (bv-cv (v-ror a c)
                              (if (zerop (size a))
                                  c
                                  (bitn a 1))
                              f))

                (implies (equal a b)                      ; Lsl
                         (and (equal (bv (bv-alu-cv
                                          a b c (nat-to-bv 3 4)))
                                     (v-lsl a))
```

```
                      (equal (c (bv-alu-cv
                                 a b c (nat-to-bv 3 4)))
                             (bitn a (size a)))))

       (implies (equal a b)                              ; Asl
                (and (equal (bv (bv-alu-cv
                                  a b c (nat-to-bv 3 4)))
                            (v-asl a))
                     (equal (c (bv-alu-cv
                                 a b c (nat-to-bv 3 4)))
                            (bitn a (size a)))))

       (implies (equal a b)                              ; Rol
                (and (equal (bv (bv-alu-cv
                                  a b c (nat-to-bv 2 4)))
                            (v-rol a c))
                     (equal (c (bv-alu-cv
                                 a b c (nat-to-bv 2 4)))
                            (if (zerop (size a))
                                c
                                (bitn a (size a)))))))))))
```

The ALU has no facilities for performing left-shifts. This seeming lack of functionality can be circumvented by using the adder within the ALU. If a and b are both equal to the bit-vector to be left-shifted, then the adder can be used as a left shifter as shown above by opcodes 2 and 3.

The natural number specification for the ALU is presented below. Again, not all opcodes are specified, as some have no interesting natural number interpretation. Like the Boolean specification, the conclusion is a conjunction, but this time we are interested in the natural number interpretation of the inputs and outputs. For example, here opcode 10–logical right shift–is shown to divide natural numbers by two and set the carry flag to t if a is odd and to f if a is even.

Conjunct 9 and 10 of the theorem below specify the bit-vector and carry flag produced by the add opcode 3. Namely, the bit-vector represents the *sum* of the numbers represented by a and b, unless that number is too large, in which case it is the *sum* mod 2^n where n is the word size. The carry flag is set to t or f according to whether the sum is too large. The overflow flag is not interpreted here.

```
(prove-lemma bv-alu-cv-correct-natural-number nil
  (implies
    (and (bitvp a)
         (bitvp b)
         (equal (size a) (size b))
         (boolp c))
                                                    ; Lsr
    (and (equal (bv-alu-cv a b c (nat-to-bv 10 4))
                (bv-cv (nat-to-bv (quotient (bv-to-nat a) 2)
                                  (size a))
                       (not (zerop (remainder
                                      (bv-to-nat a) 2)))
                       f))
                                                    ; Sub - bv
         (equal (bv (bv-alu-cv a b c (nat-to-bv 7 4)))
                (if (not (lessp (bv-to-nat b)
                                (bv-to-nat a)))
                    (nat-to-bv (difference (bv-to-nat b)
                                           (bv-to-nat a))
                               (size a))
                    (nat-to-bv (difference (exp 2 (size a))
                                           (difference (bv-to-nat a)
                                                       (bv-to-nat b)))
                               (size a))))

                                                    ; Sub-carry
         (equal (c (bv-alu-cv a b c (nat-to-bv 7 4)))
                (lessp (bv-to-nat b) (bv-to-nat a)))
                                                    ; Subb - bv
         (equal (bv (bv-alu-cv a b c (nat-to-bv 6 4)))
                (if (not (lessp (bv-to-nat b)
                                (plus (bv-to-nat a)
                                      (carry c))))
                    (nat-to-bv (difference
                                 (bv-to-nat b)
                                 (plus (bv-to-nat a)
                                       (carry c)))
                               (size a))
                    (nat-to-bv (difference
                                 (exp 2 (size a))
                                 (difference (plus
                                               (bv-to-nat a)
                                               (carry c))
```

```
                              (bv-to-nat b)))
                  (size a))))
                                        ; Subb-carry
(equal (c (bv-alu-cv a b c (nat-to-bv 6 4)))
       (lessp (bv-to-nat b)
              (plus (bv-to-nat a) (carry c))))

                                        ; Dec - bv
(equal (bv (bv-alu-cv a b c (nat-to-bv 5 4)))
       (if (zerop (bv-to-nat a))
           (nat-to-bv (sub1 (exp 2 (size a)))
                      (size a))
         (nat-to-bv (sub1 (bv-to-nat a))
                    (size a))))
                                        ; Dec - carry
(equal (c (bv-alu-cv a b c (nat-to-bv 5 4)))
       (zerop (bv-to-nat a)))
                                        ; Add - bv
(equal (bv (bv-alu-cv a b c (nat-to-bv 3 4)))
       (if (lessp (plus (bv-to-nat a)
                        (bv-to-nat b))
                  (exp 2 (size a)))
           (nat-to-bv (plus (bv-to-nat a)
                            (bv-to-nat b))
                      (size a))
         (nat-to-bv
          (remainder (plus (bv-to-nat a)
                           (bv-to-nat b))
                     (exp 2 (size a)))
          (size a))))
                                        ; Add-carry
(equal (c (bv-alu-cv a b c (nat-to-bv 3 4)))
       (not (lessp (plus (bv-to-nat a)
                         (bv-to-nat b))
                   (exp 2 (size a)))))

                                        ; Addc - bv
(equal (bv (bv-alu-cv a b c (nat-to-bv 2 4)))
       (if (lessp (plus (bv-to-nat a)
                        (bv-to-nat b)
                        (carry c))
                  (exp 2 (size a)))
           (nat-to-bv (plus (bv-to-nat a)
                            (bv-to-nat b)
                            (carry c))
```

```
                                      (size a))
                    (nat-to-bv
                      (remainder (plus (bv-to-nat a)
                                       (bv-to-nat b)
                                       (carry c))
                                 (exp 2 (size a)))
                      (size a))))
                                                    ; Addc-carry
            (equal (c (bv-alu-cv a b c (nat-to-bv 2 4)))
                   (not (lessp (plus (bv-to-nat a)
                                     (bv-to-nat b)
                                     (carry c))
                               (exp 2 (size a)))))
                                                    ; Inc - bv
            (equal (bv (bv-alu-cv a b c (nat-to-bv 1 4)))
                   (if (lessp (add1 (bv-to-nat a))
                              (exp 2 (size a)))
                       (nat-to-bv (add1 (bv-to-nat a))
                                  (size a))
                       (nat-to-bv 0 (size a))))
                                                    ; Inc-carry
            (equal (c (bv-alu-cv a b c (nat-to-bv 1 4)))
                   (not (lessp (add1 (bv-to-nat a))
                               (exp 2 (size a)))))))))
```

The integer specification and proof is similar to the natural number specification, but we interpret the overflow flag instead of the carry flag.

```
(prove-lemma alu-correct-twos-complement nil
  (implies
    (and (bitvp a)
         (not (equal a (btm)))
         (bitvp b)
         (not (equal b (btm)))
         (equal (size a) (size b))
         (boolp c))
                                                    ; Asr - bv
    (and (equal (bv (bv-alu-cv a b c (nat-to-bv 9 4)))
                (tc-to-bv (mod2 (bv-to-tc a))
                          (size a)))
                                                    ; Asr-overflow
         (equal (v (bv-alu-cv a b c (nat-to-bv 9 4)))
                f)
```

```
                                                      ; Sub - bv
(equal (bv (bv-alu-cv a b c (nat-to-bv 7 4)))
       (tc-to-bv
        (if (tc-in-rangep
               (add (bv-to-tc b)
                    (tc-minus (bv-to-tc a)))
               (size a))
            (add (bv-to-tc b)
                 (tc-minus (bv-to-tc a)))
          (if (negativep
                (add (bv-to-tc b)
                     (tc-minus (bv-to-tc a))))
              (add (bv-to-tc b)
                   (add (exp 2 (size a))
                        (tc-minus
                          (bv-to-tc a))))
            (add (bv-to-tc b)
                 (add (minus (exp 2 (size a)))
                      (tc-minus
                        (bv-to-tc a))))))
        (size a)))
                                              ; Sub - overflow
(equal (v (bv-alu-cv a b c (nat-to-bv 7 4)))
       (not (tc-in-rangep (add (bv-to-tc b)
                               (tc-minus
                                 (bv-to-tc a)))
                          (size a))))


                                              ; Subb - bv
(equal (bv (bv-alu-cv a b c (nat-to-bv 6 4)))
       (tc-to-bv
        (if (tc-in-rangep
               (add (bv-to-tc b)
                    (tc-minus (add (bv-to-tc a)
                                   (carry c))))
               (size a))
            (add (bv-to-tc b)
                 (tc-minus (add (bv-to-tc a)
                                (carry c))))
          (if (negativep
                (add (bv-to-tc b)
                     (tc-minus
                       (add (bv-to-tc a)
                            (carry c)))))
```

```
              (add (bv-to-tc b)
                  (add (exp 2 (size a))
                      (tc-minus
                        (add (bv-to-tc a)
                            (carry c)))))
          (add (bv-to-tc b)
              (add (minus (exp 2 (size a)))
                  (tc-minus
                    (add (bv-to-tc a)
                        (carry c))))))
    (size a)))
                                                ; Subb-overflow
(equal (v (bv-alu-cv a b c (nat-to-bv 6 4)))
      (not (tc-in-rangep
            (add (bv-to-tc b)
                (tc-minus (add (bv-to-tc a)
                              (carry c))))
            (size a))))

                                            ; Dec - bv
(equal (bv (bv-alu-cv a b c (nat-to-bv 5 4)))
      (tc-to-bv
        (if (tc-in-rangep (add (bv-to-tc a) -1)
                          (size a))
            (add (bv-to-tc a) -1)
          (if (negativep (add (bv-to-tc a) -1))
              (add (bv-to-tc a)
                  (add -1
                      (exp 2 (size a))))
            (add (bv-to-tc a)
                (add -1
                    (minus
                      (exp 2 (size a))))))))
        (size a)))
                                              ; Dec - overflow
(equal (v (bv-alu-cv a b c (nat-to-bv 5 4)))
      (not (tc-in-rangep (add (bv-to-tc a) -1)
                          (size a))))


                                              ; Neg - bv
(equal (bv (bv-alu-cv a b c (nat-to-bv 4 4)))
      (tc-to-bv
        (if (tc-in-rangep (tc-minus
                            (bv-to-tc a))
                          (size a))
```

```
               (tc-minus (bv-to-tc a))
             (if (negativep (tc-minus
                               (bv-to-tc a)))
                 (add (exp 2 (size a))
                       (tc-minus (bv-to-tc a)))
                 (add (minus (exp 2 (size a)))
                       (tc-minus (bv-to-tc a)))))
           (size a)))
                                               ; Neg-overflow
(equal (v (bv-alu-cv a b c (nat-to-bv 4 4)))
       (not (tc-in-rangep (tc-minus (bv-to-tc a))
                           (size a))))


                                       ; Add -  bv
(equal (bv (bv-alu-cv a b c (nat-to-bv 3 4)))
       (tc-to-bv
        (if (tc-in-rangep (add (bv-to-tc a)
                                (bv-to-tc b))
                           (size a))
            (add (bv-to-tc a) (bv-to-tc b))
          (if (negativep (add (bv-to-tc a)
                               (bv-to-tc b)))
              (add (bv-to-tc a)
                    (add (bv-to-tc b)
                          (exp 2 (size a))))
            (add (bv-to-tc a)
                  (add (bv-to-tc b)
                        (minus
                          (exp 2 (size a)))))))
           (size a)))
                                           ; Add - overflow
(equal (v (bv-alu-cv a b c (nat-to-bv 3 4)))
       (not (tc-in-rangep (add (bv-to-tc a)
                                (bv-to-tc b))
                           (size a))))

                                      ; Addc - bv
(equal (bv (bv-alu-cv a b c (nat-to-bv 2 4)))
       (tc-to-bv
        (if (tc-in-rangep (add (bv-to-tc a)
                                (add (bv-to-tc b)
                                      (carry c)))
                           (size a))
            (add (bv-to-tc a) (add (bv-to-tc b)
                                    (carry c)))
```

```
                (if (negativep (add (bv-to-tc a)
                                    (add (bv-to-tc b)
                                         (carry c))))
                    (add (bv-to-tc a)
                         (add (bv-to-tc b)
                              (add (carry c)
                                   (exp 2 (size a)))))
                    (add (bv-to-tc a)
                         (add
                          (bv-to-tc b)
                          (add (carry c)
                               (minus
                                (exp 2
                                     (size a)))))))
            (size a)))
                                               ; Addc - overflow
(equal (v (bv-alu-cv a b c (nat-to-bv 2 4)))
       (not (tc-in-rangep (add (bv-to-tc a)
                               (add (bv-to-tc b)
                                    (carry c)))
                          (size a))))

                                               ; Inc - bv
(equal (bv (bv-alu-cv a b c (nat-to-bv 1 4)))
       (tc-to-bv
        (if (tc-in-rangep (add (bv-to-tc a) 1)
                          (size a))
            (add (bv-to-tc a) 1)
          (if (negativep (add (bv-to-tc a) 1))
              (add (bv-to-tc a)
                   (add 1 (exp 2 (size a))))
            (add (bv-to-tc a)
                 (add 1
                      (minus
                       (exp 2 (size a)))))))
        (size a)))
                                               ; Inc - overflow
(equal (v (bv-alu-cv a b c (nat-to-bv 1 4)))
       (not (tc-in-rangep (add (bv-to-tc a) 1)
                          (size a))))))
```

Note that for the integer interpretation to hold, the two bit-vectors a and b must have a size greater than zero.

Chapter 9

Instruction Fields

Accessors have been defined for accessing FM8501 instruction words. A pictorial
diagram of an instruction word is shown in Figure 6.3. These functions are used
in both the FM8501 definition and its specification. That is, in the abstract
machine we fetch the various fields of an instruction with the same functions as
we do in the FM8501 itself.

One might wonder why we chose to make instructions at the abstract level
be bit-vectors instead of richer structures with symbolic names for opcodes and
registers. Why is the specification of FM8501 at the machine code level instead of
the assembly code level? The reason is that FM8501 is a von Neumann machine
and instructions are fetched from a read/write memory – instructions are also
data objects.

```
(defn bv-op-code (i-reg)
      (bitv (bitn i-reg 13)
            (bitv (bitn i-reg 14)
                  (bitv (bitn i-reg 15)
                        (bitv (bitn i-reg 16) (btm)))))))

(defn b-move-op (i-reg)
      (bitn i-reg 12))

(defn b-cc-set (i-reg)
      (bitn i-reg 11))

(defn bv-alu-op-code (i-reg)
      (bv-if (b-move-op i-reg)
             (nat-to-bv 0 4)
             (bv-op-code i-reg)))
```

The function bv-op-code returns the top four bits of a 16-bit bit-vector. These
four bits specify the instruction to be executed by the FM8501 microprocessor.
The function b-move-op returns a bit which specifies either a move operation
or a conventional operation. b-cc-set is interpreted as a command to set all or
none of the FM8501 flags. The function bv-alu-op-code will be seen in both the
hardware description and the specification of FM8501. This function supplies
the four-bit value to be given to the ALU. This function passes the results from
bv-op-code to the ALU if the instruction does not specify a move operation;
otherwise, a zero is supplied to the ALU.

The specification of the addressing modes as coded within instructions is
shown below. There are four different modes for both operand-a and operand-
b. These modes are register direct, register indirect, register indirect pre-
decrement, and register indirect post-increment. Functions b-direct-reg-a and
b-direct-reg-b return t when a register direct addressing mode is specified,
functions b-indirect-reg-a and b-indirect-reg-b return t when a register
indirect addressing mode is specified, functions b-indirect-reg-a-inc and b--
indirect-reg-b-inc return t when a register indirect with post-increment is
coded, and function b-indirect-reg-a-dec and b-indirect-reg-b-dec return
t if a register indirect with pre-decrement is specified.

```
(defn b-direct-reg-b (i-reg)
      (b-nor (bitn i-reg 9)
             (bitn i-reg 10)))

(defn b-indirect-reg-b (i-reg)
   (b-and (bitn i-reg 9)
          (b-not (bitn i-reg 10))))

(defn b-indirect-reg-b-inc (i-reg)
      (b-and (bitn i-reg 9)
             (bitn i-reg 10)))

(defn b-indirect-reg-b-dec (i-reg)
      (b-and (b-not (bitn i-reg 9))
             (bitn i-reg 10)))

(defn b-direct-reg-a (i-reg)
      (b-nor (bitn i-reg 4) (bitn i-reg 5)))

(defn b-indirect-reg-a (i-reg)
   (b-and (bitn i-reg 4)
          (b-not (bitn i-reg 5))))
```

```
(defn b-indirect-reg-a-dec (i-reg)
      (b-and (b-not (bitn i-reg 4))
             (bitn i-reg 5)))

(defn b-indirect-reg-a-inc (i-reg)
      (b-and (bitn i-reg 4) (bitn i-reg 5)))
```

The following functions specify the register number to be used for the above addressing modes. Each of these functions returns a three-bit value specifying one of eight registers to be used.

```
(defn bv-oprd-b (i-reg)
      (bitv (bitn i-reg 6)
            (bitv (bitn i-reg 7)
                  (bitv (bitn i-reg 8) (btm)))))

(defn bv-oprd-a (i-reg)
      (bitv (bitn i-reg 1)
            (bitv (bitn i-reg 2)
                  (bitv (bitn i-reg 3) (btm)))))
```

Chapter 10

Update and Accessor Functions

RAMs and ROMs are modeled by lists of bit-vectors. When implementing
FM8501, RAMs and ROMs of the necessary sizes are considered to be available devices. The functions defined here are used to simulate the accessing and
updating of registers, RAMs, and ROMs. These functions are used both in the
FM8501 definition and its specification.

We start by defining functions for accessing and updating the nth element of
list lst:

```
(defn nth (n lst)
     (if (zerop n)
         (car lst)
         (nth (sub1 n) (cdr lst))))

(defn update-nth (c n lst value)
     (if (and (truep c) (listp lst))
         (if (zerop n)
             (cons value (cdr lst))
             (cons (car lst)
                   (update-nth c
                               (sub1 n)
                               (cdr lst)
                               value)))
         lst))
```

Note that update-nth replaces the nth element of lst with value conditional
upon the flag c.

We next define the function used to access elements of a RAM or ROM. Note that here we use a bit vector, v-n, rather than a natural number to specify the element to be accessed:

```
(defn v-nth (v-n lst)
      (nth (bv-to-nat v-n) lst))
```

The expression (v-nth *addr rm*) models the accessing of the element at location *addr* in RAM or ROM *rm*.

The function update-v is used to model a write-enabled register:

```
(defn update-v (c cell value)
      (if (truep c) value cell))
```

The function update-v-nth is used to model a write-enabled RAM. Note that the address v-n is a bit-vector rather than a natural number.

```
(defn update-v-nth (c v-n lst value)
      (update-nth c
                  (bv-to-nat v-n)
                  lst value))
```

The expression (update-v-nth *c addr rm val*) models a write of *val* to location *addr* in RAM *rm* conditional upon *c*.

Chapter 11

The FM8501 Hardware Interpreter

Self-recursive functions are used to model sequential logic–these self-recursive functions are called interpreters. The formal parameters of interpreters model registers and RAMs. On each recursive call of an interpreter, the formal parameters are updated by functions that can be thought of a combinational logic.

The hardware definition of the FM8501 microprocessor is cast within an interpreter. This interpreter works at the fundamental clock frequency of the microprocessor, and defines the internal working of the FM8501. The FM8501 interpreter, called `big-machine`, represents three different aspects of the microprocessor: the timed nature of this device, the state-holding devices, and the combinational logic that transforms the state each time unit. Additionally, `big-machine` contains a memory process, which is not part of the `big-machine` hardware. The functions composing the memory process characterize the expected operation of a memory connected to FM8501.

The function `big-machine` is a self-recursive function of 20 arguments. Most of the arguments represent RAMs or registers, while the remainder model external state and time. This function recurses through time; this is characterized by a cdring of the variable `oracle` with each recursive call. The function `big-machine` is presented below.

```
(defn big-machine
      (mar read write dtack reset no-store data-out
           reg-file addr-out c-flag v-flag z-flag n-flag
           a-reg b-reg i-reg visual-mem real-mem
           memory-watch-dog-history oracle)
      (if (nlistp oracle)
          (list mar read write dtack reset no-store
```

```
                    data-out reg-file addr-out c-flag v-flag
                    z-flag n-flag a-reg b-reg i-reg visual-mem
                    real-mem memory-watch-dog-history)
        (big-machine (mar mar i-reg dtack reset no-store)
                     (read mar i-reg)
                     (write mar i-reg no-store)
                     (dtack (car oracle))
                     (reset (car oracle))
                     (no-store no-store c-flag v-flag
                               z-flag n-flag i-reg mar)
                     (data-out data-out a-reg b-reg
                               c-flag i-reg mar)
                     (reg-file reg-file data-out i-reg
                               mar no-store reset)
                     (addr-out addr-out reg-file i-reg
                               mar reset)
                     (c-flag c-flag a-reg b-reg i-reg mar)
                     (v-flag v-flag a-reg b-reg c-flag
                             i-reg mar)
                     (z-flag z-flag a-reg b-reg c-flag
                             i-reg mar)
                     (n-flag n-flag a-reg b-reg c-flag
                             i-reg mar)
                     (a-reg a-reg visual-mem reg-file
                            i-reg mar reset)
                     (b-reg b-reg visual-mem reg-file
                            i-reg mar reset)
                     (i-reg i-reg visual-mem mar)
                     (visual-mem real-mem read write
                                 addr-out
                                 memory-watch-dog-history
                                 (dtack (car oracle))
                                 (reset (car oracle)))
                     (real-mem real-mem read write
                               addr-out data-out
                               memory-watch-dog-history
                               (dtack (car oracle))
                               (reset (car oracle)))
                     (watch-dog read write
                                (dtack (car oracle))
                                data-out addr-out)
        (cdr oracle))))
```

Each time **big-machine** recurses, it checks to see if there are remaining clock ticks by (nlistp oracle). If so, big-machine calls itself with its formal parameters modified by functions which have the same name as the formal parameter being modified; otherwise, this function halts and returns the final state as a list of the current values of its arguments.

As an introduction to the operation of big-machine, a short description of the formal parameters is given. big-machine is a function of 20 arguments. The meaning of the various arguments are:

- mar: microstore memory address register,

- read: bit-register for read output signal,

- write: bit-register for write output signal,

- dtack: bit-register for data acknowledgement input signal,

- reset: bit-register for processor reset input signal,

- no-store: bit-register which tells the processor to store or not to store on a conditional move instruction,

- data-out: data output register,

- reg-file: 8 word internal register file,

- addr-out: address output register,

- c-flag: bit-register for carry flag,

- v-flag: bit-register for overflow flag,

- z-flag: bit-register for zero flag,

- n-flag: bit-register for negative flag,

- a-reg: register containing input a to the ALU,

- b-reg: register containing input b to the ALU,

- i-reg: instruction register,

- visual-mem: register buffering input data to the processor,

- real-mem: the memory that the processor accesses, this memory is separate from the processor,

- memory-watch-dog-history: history used in the characterization of the memory process,

- oracle: a list of two element lists, each member of the two element list are asynchronous inputs to the processor.

11.1   The Control Unit

The control unit controls the internal working of the FM8501 microprocessor. The functions that calculate the next value of the formal parameters of big-machine depend on the control unit.[1]

The control unit is comprised of a ROM and a microaddress register. The ROM contains a stored program–the microcode–which is used to control the data-flow within the FM8501 microprocessor. The microaddress register (mar) is a four-bit wide register which can contain one of 16 microaddresses. The mar is used to select one of the 16 microinstructions.

The microcode for FM8501 is a list of bit-vectors, each of which is a microinstruction. Each microinstruction is 20 bits wide and contains 17 fields. The first 16 fields are 1 bit in length and control the data-flow through the microprocessor. The last 4 bits comprise the last field and this field specifies the address of the next microinstruction.

The function make-micro-word, shown below, takes a list of 16 control bits and one natural number (indicating the next microaddress) and generates the corresponding microinstruction by concatenating the control bits to the 4-bit natural number bit-vector representation of the next microaddress. This function merely makes it easier to write down microinstructions. The constant function micro-store defines the microcode.[2]

```
(defn nxsz nil 4)

(defn make-micro-word (l)
     (if (nlistp l)
         (btm)
         (if (nlistp (cdr l))
             (nat-to-bv (car l) (nxsz))
             (bitv (if (equal (car l) 't) t f)
                   (make-micro-word (cdr l))))))

(defn make-micro-rom (l)
     (if (nlistp l)
         nil
         (cons (make-micro-word (car l))
               (make-micro-rom (cdr l)))))
```

---

[1]Note that the memory process does not depend on the control unit, or for that matter, does not depend on the FM8501 hardware at all. The part of big-machine which defines the memory process will be identified later.

[2]The semicolon character (";") specifies that the remainder of a line is to be ignored; it is the beginning comment character.

```
(defn micro-store nil
;                                     1 1 1 1 1 1 1 1    Micro-
;                     1 2 3 4 5 6 7 8 9 0 1 2 3 4 5 6 7  address
 (make-micro-rom '((f f f f f f f f f t f f f f f f 1)    ; 0
                   (f t f t f t f f f t f t f f f f 2)    ; 1
                   (f f f t f f f f t f f f f f f f 3)    ; 2
                   (f f f f f f f f f f t f f f f t f 4)  ; 3
                   (f f f f t f f t f t f t f f f f 5)    ; 4
                   (f f f f t f f f t f f f f f f f 6)    ; 5
                   (f f f f t f f f f t t f f f f f 7)    ; 6
                   (f f f f f f f t f t f t f f f f 8)    ; 7
                   (f f f f f f f f t f f f f f f f 9)    ; 8
                   (f f f f f f f f f t f f t f f f 10)   ; 9
                   (f f f f f f f f f t f f f t f f 11)   ; 10
                   (t f t f f f f f f f f f f f f t 12)   ; 11
                   (f f f f t f t f f t f f f f f f 13)   ; 12
                   (f f f f f f t f f t f f f f f f 1)    ; 13
                   (f f f f f f f f f t f f f f f f 0)    ; 14
                   (f f f f f f f f f t f f f f f f 0)))) ; 15

(defn micro-rom (addr)
      (v-nth addr (micro-store)))
```

A short description of the effect of each microinstruction is presented below. Note that the natural number entry in each microinstruction specifies the next microinstruction. Some microstates wait for external events, such as a memory read, and may wait an arbitrary amount of time before proceeding.

The accessors for the 16 control fields and the next microaddress field are defined below.

```
(defn b-dout-incdec (x) (bitn x 1))

(defn b-force-inc (x) (bitn x 2))

(defn b-en-no-store (x) (bitn x 3))

(defn b-ir-mem-ref (x) (bitn x 4))

(defn b-oprda-oprdb (x) (bitn x 5))

(defn b-pc-regnum (x) (bitn x 6))

(defn b-postinc (x) (bitn x 7))
```

Microinstruction	Description
0	Reset state
1	PC → addr-out, PC + 1 → PC, start read
2	Read wait
3	Memory[addr-out] → i-reg
4	Conditionally pre-decrement Operand-A, store pre-decrement result to Operand-A and addr-out
5	Read wait, if Mode-A is an indirect mode
6	Either Memory[addr-out] or Operand-A → a-reg
7	Conditionally pre-decrement Operand-B, store pre-decrement result to Operand-B and addr-out
8	Read wait, if Mode-B is an indirect mode
9	Either Memory[addr-out] or Operand-B → b-reg
10	ALU[a-reg,b-reg,c-flag] → data-out, conditionally set the flag-registers, set no-store
11	Start write, wait if Mode-B is an indirect mode conditionally store data-out to reg-file or Memory
12	Conditionally post-increment Operand-A
13	Conditionally post-increment Operand-B
14	Unused
15	Unused

Table 11.1: Microinstruction Descriptions

```
(defn b-predec (x) (bitn x 8))

(defn b-rd (x) (bitn x 9))

(defn b-seq (x) (bitn x 10))

(defn b-we-a-reg (x) (bitn x 11))

(defn b-we-addr-out (x) (bitn x 12))

(defn b-we-b-reg (x) (bitn x 13))

(defn b-we-alu-result (x) (bitn x 14))

(defn b-we-ir (x) (bitn x 15))

(defn b-wr (x) (bitn x 16))

(defn bv-next (x)
     (bitv (bitn x 17)
           (bitv (bitn x 18)
                 (bitv (bitn x 19)
                       (bitv (bitn x 20) (btm))))))
```

For example, to obtain the first microinstruction from the microrom one writes
(micro-rom (bv-to-nat 0 (nxsz))). And to obtain the first bit of the first
microinstruction one may write (b-dout-incdec (micro-rom (bv-to-nat 0
(nxsz)))).

As an aid of the use of the various bits in the microinstruction, the functions
that use each microinstruction field accessor are listed by each field which they
access and are shown in the following table. For example, the b-ir-mem-ref bit
is used in the determination of the new values for the read and mar registers.

11.2 Miscellanous Functions

Several miscellanous functions which do not fall in any one particular catagory
are presented here. The first of these functions determines whether the current
operand mode causes a memory reference.

Field	Functions Which Access Field
b-dout-incdec	reg-file
b-force-inc	reg-file
b-en-no-store	mar
b-ir-mem-ref	read, mar
b-oprda-oprdb	addr-out, reg-file, b-oprd-mem-ref, bv-reg-select
b-pc-regnum	reg-file, bv-reg-select
b-postinc	reg-file
b-predec	addr-out, reg-file
b-rd	read
b-seq	mar
b-we-a-reg	a-reg
b-we-addr-out	addr-out
b-we-b-reg	b-reg
b-we-alu-result	n-flag, z-flag, v-flag, c-flag, data-out, no-store
b-we-ir	i-reg
b-wr	reg-file, write
bv-next	mar

Table 11.2: Cross Reference for Microinstruction Accessors

```
(defn b-oprd-mem-ref (mar i-reg)
     (b-if (b-oprda-oprdb (micro-rom mar))
          (b-not (b-direct-reg-a i-reg))
          (b-not (b-direct-reg-b i-reg))))
```

The register file `reg-file` is a RAM with eight registers. To address a particular register a 3-bit address is supplied to the RAM device. The function `bv-reg-select` supplies the address to the register file.

```
(defn bv-reg-select (i-reg mar reset)
     (bv-if (b-or reset
                  (b-pc-regnum (micro-rom mar)))
          (nat-to-bv 0 3)
          (bv-if (b-oprda-oprdb (micro-rom mar))
               (bv-oprd-a i-reg)
               (bv-oprd-b i-reg))))
```

FM8501 has a conditional move instruction. In support of this is a function `b-store-alu-result` that determines if the result of the ALU operation is to be stored (either to the register file or to the memory). All instructions, except the move instructions, unconditionally store their result. There are eight conditional move instructions: move if no carry, move if carry, move if no overflow, move if overflow, move if not zero, move if zero, move if not negative, and move if negative. This function returns t unless the current instruction is a conditional move for which the test fails.

```
(defn b-store-alu-result (c-flag v-flag z-flag n-flag i-reg)
  (b-or (b-or (b-not (b-move-op i-reg))
              (bitn (bv-op-code i-reg) 4))
        (b-or (b-or (b-or (b-and (b-not c-flag)
                                 (bv-equal (bv-op-code i-reg)
                                           (nat-to-bv 0 4)))
                          (b-and c-flag
                                 (bv-equal (bv-op-code i-reg)
                                           (nat-to-bv 1 4))))
                    (b-or (b-and (b-not v-flag)
                                 (bv-equal (bv-op-code i-reg)
                                           (nat-to-bv 2 4)))
                          (b-and v-flag
                                 (bv-equal (bv-op-code i-reg)
                                           (nat-to-bv 3 4)))))
              (b-or (b-or (b-and (b-not z-flag)
                                 (bv-equal (bv-op-code i-reg)
                                           (nat-to-bv 4 4)))
                          (b-and z-flag
                                 (bv-equal (bv-op-code i-reg)
                                           (nat-to-bv 5 4))))
                    (b-or (b-and (b-not n-flag)
                                 (bv-equal (bv-op-code i-reg)
                                           (nat-to-bv 6 4)))
                          (b-and n-flag
                                 (bv-equal (bv-op-code i-reg)
                                           (nat-to-bv 7 4)))))))))
```

11.3 The FM8501 Combinational Logic

We are now ready to define the combination logic functions which calculate the new formal parameters for recursive calls of big-machine. The function big-machine has 20 formal parameters: 14 represent combinational hardware (and are a part of FM8501), 2 supply asynchrounous inputs to the micropro-cessor (but are external to the processor), 3 model the memory process (and are external to the processor) and 1 models time. This section describes the 14 combinational logic functions that are within FM8501. The others are discussed in the next section.

At this point it is necessary to specify the size of the machine's data paths. Some of the functions that follow depend on the machine word size. FM8501 is a 16-bit microprocessor and this is specified as follows:

```
(defn machine-size nil 16)
```

The function mar calculates the next value of the microstore address register mar. This function conditionally updates the value of the microstore address register with one of three values: mar itself, zero when reseting, or (bv-next (micro-rom mar)) which is the next microaddress specified by the microrom.

```
(defn mar (mar i-reg dtack reset no-store)
 (update-v
  (b-or
      (b-or reset
             (b-or dtack (b-seq (micro-rom mar))))
      (b-or (b-and (b-en-no-store (micro-rom mar))
                    no-store)
             (b-and (b-not (b-oprd-mem-ref mar i-reg))
                    (b-not (b-ir-mem-ref (micro-rom mar))))))
   mar
   (bv-if reset
          (nat-to-bv 0 (nxsz))
          (bv-next (micro-rom mar)))))
```

Observe the use of the micro-rom control bits b-seq, b-en-no-store, and b-ir-mem-ref, as well as the previously defined function b-oprd-mem-ref which itself uses the b-oprda-oprdb control bit, to determine whether mar is changed.

Function read and write set the output latches read and write with either t or f. The signals are used by external devices, such as memory, to determine if the processor is requesting an external read or write.

```
(defn read (mar i-reg)
       (b-and (b-or (b-oprd-mem-ref mar i-reg)
                    (b-ir-mem-ref (micro-rom mar)))
              (b-rd (micro-rom mar))))
```

```
(defn write (mar i-reg no-store)
    (b-and (b-wr (micro-rom mar))
           (b-and (b-oprd-mem-ref mar i-reg)
                  (b-not no-store))))
```

The function no-store specifies whether the microprocessor is to store the result of the current instruction. This function relies upon the function b--store-alu-result to determine the new value and the b-we-alu-result control bit to determine if an update is to occur.

```
(defn no-store (no-store c-flag v-flag z-flag n-flag i-reg mar)
    (update-v (b-we-alu-result (micro-rom mar))
              no-store
              (b-not (b-store-alu-result c-flag v-flag
                                         z-flag n-flag
                                         i-reg))))
```

The bit-vector output of the ALU is latched into the data-out register by the function data-out. The register update is controlled by the microrom.

```
(defn data-out (data-out a-reg b-reg c-flag i-reg mar)
    (update-v (b-we-alu-result (micro-rom mar))
              data-out
              (bv (bv-alu-cv a-reg b-reg c-flag
                             (bv-alu-op-code i-reg)))))
```

The register file reg-file may be updated four times given six opportunities during each FM8501 instruction execution. The function reg-file conditionally updates the register file at each of the six opportunities: program counter (PC) increment, operand-a pre-decrement, operand-b pre-decrement, store ALU result, operand-a post-increment, operand-b post-increment. The function reg-file includes the hardware for the PC increment, and the pre-decrement and post-increment operations. The reg-file function is shown below.

```
(defn reg-file (reg-file data-out i-reg mar no-store reset)
 (update-v-nth
  (b-or
   (b-or reset
         (b-force-inc (micro-rom mar)))
```

```
    (b-or
        (b-or (b-pc-regnum (micro-rom mar))
              (b-and (b-wr (micro-rom mar))
                     (b-and (b-not no-store)
                            (b-direct-reg-b i-reg))))
          (b-or (b-and (b-predec (micro-rom mar))
                       (b-if (b-oprda-oprdb (micro-rom mar))
                             (b-indirect-reg-a-dec i-reg)
                             (b-indirect-reg-b-dec i-reg)))
                (b-and (b-postinc (micro-rom mar))
                       (b-if (b-oprda-oprdb (micro-rom mar))
                             (b-indirect-reg-a-inc i-reg)
                             (b-indirect-reg-b-inc i-reg)))))))
    (bv-reg-select i-reg mar reset)
    reg-file
    (bv-if
     (b-or (b-dout-incdec (micro-rom mar))
           reset)
     (bv-if reset
            (nat-to-bv 0 (machine-size))
            data-out)
     (bv-if
      (b-or (b-force-inc (micro-rom mar))
            (b-if (b-oprda-oprdb (micro-rom mar))
                  (b-indirect-reg-a-inc i-reg)
                  (b-indirect-reg-b-inc i-reg)))
      (bv-adder-output t
                       (nat-to-bv 0 (machine-size))
                       (v-nth (bv-reg-select i-reg mar reset)
                              reg-file))
      (bv-subtracter-output t
                       (nat-to-bv 0 (machine-size))
                       (v-nth (bv-reg-select i-reg mar reset)
                              reg-file))))))
```

The `addr-out` function conditionally updates the `addr-out` register. This output register is used by external devices as the address of reads or writes.

```
(defn addr-out (addr-out reg-file i-reg mar reset)
 (update-v
  (b-we-addr-out (micro-rom mar))
  addr-out
  (bv-if
```

```
(b-and (b-predec (micro-rom mar))
       (b-if (b-oprda-oprdb (micro-rom mar))
             (b-indirect-reg-a-dec i-reg)
             (b-indirect-reg-b-dec i-reg)))
(bv-subtracter-output t
                      (nat-to-bv 0 (machine-size))
                      (v-nth (bv-reg-select i-reg mar reset)
                             reg-file))
(v-nth (bv-reg-select i-reg mar reset)
       reg-file)))))
```

There are four flag registers in FM8501. These flags are the carry, overflow,
zero and negative flags. These flags are stored in 1-bit registers. The carry
flag c-flag and the v-flag take their input directly from the ALU carry and
overflow outputs. The zero flag z-flag is conditionally set to t if the bit-vector
result from the ALU is all fs. The negative flag n-flag is identical to the most-
significant bit of the bit-vector result from the ALU. Displayed below are the
four combinational logic functions for updating the flag registers.

```
(defn c-flag (c-flag a-reg b-reg i-reg mar)
      (update-v (b-and (b-we-alu-result (micro-rom mar))
                       (b-cc-set i-reg))
                c-flag
                (c (bv-alu-cv a-reg b-reg c-flag
                              (bv-alu-op-code i-reg)))))

(defn v-flag (v-flag a-reg b-reg c-flag i-reg mar)
      (update-v (b-and (b-we-alu-result (micro-rom mar))
                       (b-cc-set i-reg))
                v-flag
                (v (bv-alu-cv a-reg b-reg c-flag
                              (bv-alu-op-code i-reg)))))


(defn z-flag (z-flag a-reg b-reg c-flag i-reg mar)
 (update-v
      (b-and (b-we-alu-result (micro-rom mar))
             (b-cc-set i-reg))
      z-flag
      (b-bv-zerop (bv (bv-alu-cv a-reg b-reg c-flag
                                 (bv-alu-op-code i-reg)))))))
```

```
(defn n-flag (n-flag a-reg b-reg c-flag i-reg mar)
   (update-v (b-and (b-we-alu-result (micro-rom mar))
                    (b-cc-set i-reg))
             n-flag
             (bitn (bv (bv-alu-cv a-reg b-reg c-flag
                                  (bv-alu-op-code i-reg)))
                   (machine-size))))
```

Two registers, a-reg and b-reg are used to hold the a and b values for the ALU.
These functions accept input from the register file or from the external memory
input buffer visual-mem and conditionally place this input in a-reg and b-reg.

```
(defn a-reg (a-reg visual-mem reg-file i-reg mar reset)
   (update-v (b-we-a-reg (micro-rom mar))
             a-reg
             (bv-if (b-direct-reg-a i-reg)
                    (v-nth (bv-reg-select i-reg mar reset)
                           reg-file)
                    visual-mem)))

(defn b-reg (b-reg visual-mem reg-file i-reg mar reset)
   (update-v (b-we-b-reg (micro-rom mar))
             b-reg
             (bv-if (b-direct-reg-b i-reg)
                    (v-nth (bv-reg-select i-reg mar reset)
                           reg-file)
                    visual-mem)))
```

The last FM8501 combinational logic function is i-reg. This function returns instructions as requested, and looks to the external memory input buffer
visual-mem for input.

```
(defn i-reg (i-reg visual-mem mar)
   (update-v (b-we-ir (micro-rom mar))
             i-reg visual-mem))
```

As the implementable hardware functions which comprise FM8501 have now
been completed, it is possible to generate the Boolean logic to implement the
above functions. This expansion is done in much the same way as other ex-
pansions and is shown in a later chapter. Note that the expansion assumes the

existence of registers `dtack`, `reset`, and `visual-mem`. These registers are necessary, but their input is generated external to FM8501. We discuss the `dtack`, `reset`, and the `visual-mem` functions in the next section.

11.4 External Functions

Several formal parameters of `big-machine` are used to model events outside of FM8501. This section discusses the other six `big-machine` parameter modifying functions. These six functions can be divided into three catagories: the oracle, the asynchronous external inputs, and the memory process.

The formal `big-machine` parameter `oracle` represents time. So long as this parameter contains a list, `big-machine` steps forward in time. When non-empty, the oracle specifies asynchronous input values. For each unit of time, the first element (the `car`) of the oracle contains the current asynchronous input values for `dtack` and `reset`. These values are organized into a list, where members of this list are accessed by external functions. The external functions accessing oracle elements may also supply them to the hardware through a synchronizing register.

The functions `dtack` and `reset` read two current asynchronous oracle values and pass them to the registers `dtack` and `reset`. This operation is external to FM8501, and is not part of the FM8501 hardware.

```
(defn dtack (current-oracle-entry)
      (fix-bool (car current-oracle-entry)))

(defn reset (current-oracle-entry)
      (fix-bool (cadr current-oracle-entry)))
```

If the `oracle` is recognized by the recognizer `listp` the `big-machine` formal parameter `oracle` is cdred, thus uncovering a new set of asynchronous oracle values.

The memory process is characterized by three `big-machine` formal parameters and their associated functions: `visual-mem`, `real-mem`, and `watch-dog`. `visual-mem` is the hole through which the microprocessor sees the external world. All bit-vector inputs from external devices pass through the `visual-mem` register. The `big-machine` formal parameter `real-mem` contains the contents of the external memory as seen by `big-machine`. The parameter `memory-watch-dog--history` contains history for the functions which model the memory process.

The function `visual-mem` acts as a memory which responds to read requests. This function updates the contents of the parameter `visual-mem` each clock, with either some arbitrary value (known as `default-visual-mem-value`) or the contents of an element of `real-mem` as specified by the `addr-out` register.

Before the function visual-mem returns the contents of a memory location,
it attempts to insure that the memory request is valid. The rules for when
visual-mem returns a memory value are as follows: the read output (parameter)
must have contained t for two consecutive clock ticks, the write output must
have contained f for two consecutive clock ticks, the addr-out output must have
been stable for two consecutive clock ticks, the asynchronous input placed in the
dtack register must have been t for two consecutive clock ticks, and the reset
register must be f. The function visual-mem is presented momentarily.

To be able to compute all of the access checks above, it is necessary to supply one clock tick's worth of history for the parameters read, write, dtack, and
addr-out. The parameter memory-watch-dog-history is used to store these
values for one clock tick. Additionally, the parameter data-out has one clock
tick's worth of history stored. To perform this history storage, the *Shell Principle* is used to define a 5-place constructor function along with five destructor
functions. This constructor is invoked with each recursive call of big-machine,
thereby saving the contents of five objects. The definition of the watch-dog shell
and the expression we use to save some parameter values for one clock tick are
shown below.

```
(add-shell watch-dog nil watch-dogp
           ((read-1 (none-of) false)
            (write-1 (none-of) false)
            (dtack-1-oracle (none-of) false)
            (data-out-1 (one-of bitvp) btm)
            (addr-out-1 (one-of bitvp) btm)))

(watch-dog read write
           (dtack (car oracle))
           data-out addr-out)
```

The function visual-mem consults the memory-watch-dog-history to ensure that all of its conditions for supplying a memory value are met. The function visual-mem returns an unspecified value if any of its conditions are not met.
The definition of the arbitrary memory value and the function visual-mem are
given below.

```
(dcl default-visual-mem-value nil)

(defn visual-mem
  (real-mem read write addr-out memory-watch-dog-history
            dtack-oracle reset-oracle)
  (trunc
```

```
    (if (and (and read
                  (read-1 memory-watch-dog-history))
             (and (not write)
                  (not (write-1 memory-watch-dog-history)))
             (equal addr-out
                    (addr-out-1 memory-watch-dog-history))
             (and dtack-oracle
                  (dtack-1-oracle memory-watch-dog-history))
             (not reset-oracle))
        (v-nth addr-out real-mem)
        (default-visual-mem-value))
    (machine-size)))
```

Note that the function `visual-mem` attempts to capture the expected operating characteristics of memory connected to FM8501. If memory connected to FM8501 meets these requirements, then the operation of the microprocessor is as specified (in the next chapter).

The function `real-mem` operates in much the same way as the `visual-mem` function; however, this function updates an element of the `big-machine` parameter `real-mem`. The definition for the `real-mem` function is given below.

```
(defn real-mem
 (real-mem read write addr-out data-out
           memory-watch-dog-history dtack-oracle
           reset-oracle)
 (update-v-nth
  (and (and write
            (write-1 memory-watch-dog-history))
       (and (not read)
            (not (read-1 memory-watch-dog-history)))
       (equal addr-out
              (addr-out-1 memory-watch-dog-history))
       (and dtack-oracle
            (not (dtack-1-oracle memory-watch-dog-history)))
       (not reset-oracle))
  addr-out real-mem data-out))
```

This concludes the specification of the hardware required to construct a FM8501 microprocessor. To come is the specification of FM8501 and the verification that the FM8501 hardware functions perform correctly.

Chapter 12

FM8501: A Formal Specification

This chapter specifies the FM8501 microprocessor from the outside looking in. This specification can be thought of as a programmer's description; a programmer would study the coming specification to learn how to program FM8501. The specification function for FM8501 is at the instruction level, that is, each time the specification function "ticks" an instruction is interpreted.

12.1 RAM, Flags, and the Register File

The programmer visible state for FM8501 is composed of four 1-bit flag registers, one eight element 16-bit random access register file, and one 2^{16} element RAM. The programmer visible registers are: the carry flag, c-flag; the overflow flag, v-flag; the zero flag, z-flag; the negative flag, n-flag; the register file, reg-file; and the external RAM memory, real-mem.

Instructions are fetched from the RAM real-mem and executed. The contents of the memory RAM, the register file, or the flag registers may be changed during the execution of any instruction. The programmer should think of FM8501 as an instruction interpreter, which always executes the instruction pointed to by the first element of the register file (this first element of the register file is commonly called a program counter).

12.2 The Instruction Interpreter

The specification for FM8501 is an instruction interpreter; this specification interpreter is named soft. The function soft is a self-recursive function with seven formal parameters. Six of the formal parameters represent the programmer visable state, while the seventh models time.

```
(defn soft (reg-file real-mem c-flag v-flag z-flag n-flag lst)
 (if (nlistp lst)
     (list reg-file real-mem c-flag v-flag z-flag n-flag)
   (soft
    (reg-file-after-oprd-b-post-increment reg-file real-mem
                                          c-flag v-flag
                                          z-flag n-flag)
    (real-mem-after-alu-write reg-file real-mem c-flag
                              v-flag z-flag n-flag)
    (update-v (b-cc-set (current-instruction reg-file real-mem))
              c-flag
              (c (bv-alu-cv-results reg-file real-mem
                                    c-flag)))
    (update-v (b-cc-set (current-instruction reg-file real-mem))
              v-flag
              (v (bv-alu-cv-results reg-file real-mem
                                    c-flag)))
    (update-v (b-cc-set (current-instruction reg-file real-mem))
              z-flag
              (zerop (bv-to-nat (bv (bv-alu-cv-results reg-file
                                                       real-mem
                                                       c-flag)))))
    (update-v (b-cc-set (current-instruction reg-file real-mem))
              n-flag
              (negativep (bv-to-tc (bv (bv-alu-cv-results
                                        reg-file
                                        real-mem
                                        c-flag)))))
    (cdr lst))))
```

Each time soft recurses, it checks to see if there are remaining instructions by
(nlistp lst). If so, soft calls itself, modifying its formal parameters in accor-
dance with the functions that interpret instructions. In the following sections
the functions which are composed to make soft are discussed.

12.3   Conditional Storage of the ALU Results

The FM8501 microprocessor has a conditional move instruction. This instruction
can be used for program code conditional branching, conditional subroutine
return, etc. To decide whether the results of the ALU operation are to be
stored, the function b-store-alu-results-with-ifs is defined.

```
(defn b-store-alu-result-with-ifs
     (c-flag v-flag z-flag n-flag i-reg)
     (or (not (b-move-op i-reg))
         (bitn (bv-op-code i-reg) 4)
         (equal (bv-op-code i-reg)
                (nat-to-bv (if c-flag 1 0) 4))
         (equal (bv-op-code i-reg)
                (nat-to-bv (if v-flag 3 2) 4))
         (equal (bv-op-code i-reg)
                (nat-to-bv (if z-flag 5 4) 4))
         (equal (bv-op-code i-reg)
                (nat-to-bv (if n-flag 7 6) 4))))
```

This function accesses the current instruction (which is passed to this function through the formal parameter i-reg) to check for a move instruction. If (not (b-move-op i-reg)) is t then the above function returns t; otherwise, the move operation code must be checked against the four flag bits. For instance, if the move operation code is 0001 and the value of c-flag is t then a move occurs; if the move operation is 0001 and c-flag is f then the function b-store-alu-results-with-ifs returns f. Note that this function is equivalent to the much different FM8501 function b-store-alu-results. The function presented above is used by other functions which are a part of soft.

12.4 Register File Update

There are six possible changes which can occur to the register file reg-file during the execution of a FM8501 instruction: program counter increment, operand-a pre-decrement, operand-b pre-decrement, ALU result storage, operand-a post-increment, and operand-b post-increment. The execution of any instruction causes the program counter to be incremented. The other five changes depend on the contents of the instruction, but a single operand cannot be both pre-decremented and post-incremented.

To more conveniently model the various register file updates, six register file update functions have been defined. To model the register file activity during the execution of an instruction, these six functions are composed, one atop another, six deep. Before presenting these functions, we present a function that returns the current instruction.

```
(defn current-instruction (reg-file real-mem)
     (v-nth (nth 0 reg-file) real-mem))
```

The function `reg-file-after-pc-increment` returns a register file with its program counter having been incremented.

```
(defn reg-file-after-pc-increment (reg-file)
     (update-nth t 0 reg-file
                    (v-nat-inc (nth 0 reg-file)))))
```

The next possible register file change is a possible pre-decrement of operand-a. The function `reg-file-after-oprd-a-pre-decrement` performs this conditional update on operand-a, after incrementing the program counter.

```
(defn reg-file-after-oprd-a-pre-decrement (reg-file real-mem)
 (update-v-nth
  (b-indirect-reg-a-dec (current-instruction reg-file
                                               real-mem))
  (bv-oprd-a (current-instruction reg-file real-mem))
  (reg-file-after-pc-increment reg-file)
  (v-nat-dec (v-nth (bv-oprd-a (current-instruction reg-file
                                                     real-mem))
             (reg-file-after-pc-increment reg-file)))))
```

Similarly, the conditional update on operand-b is performed:

```
(defn reg-file-after-oprd-b-pre-decrement (reg-file real-mem)
 (update-v-nth
  (b-indirect-reg-b-dec (current-instruction reg-file
                                               real-mem))
  (bv-oprd-b (current-instruction reg-file real-mem))
  (reg-file-after-oprd-a-pre-decrement reg-file real-mem)
  (v-nat-dec (v-nth (bv-oprd-b (current-instruction reg-file
                                                     real-mem))
              (reg-file-after-oprd-a-pre-decrement
                reg-file
                real-mem)))))
```

After the pre-decrement operations on the register file, the next conditional update operation is the storing of the ALU result into the register file. Before we can present this operation, the ALU result for the current instruction must be calculated. The ALU has three data inputs: the carry input, c; and two bit-vector inputs a and b. The a ALU input receives operand-a; this operand is read from the register file or the memory, but not until the program counter is incremented and the conditional operand-a pre-decrement operation performed. The function which calculates operand-a is shown below.

```
(defn a-value-for-alu-after-oprd-a-pre-decrement
  (reg-file real-mem)
  (if (b-direct-reg-a (current-instruction reg-file real-mem))
      (v-nth (bv-oprd-a (current-instruction reg-file real-mem))
             (reg-file-after-pc-increment reg-file))
      (if (b-indirect-reg-a-dec (current-instruction reg-file
                                                     real-mem))
          (v-nth
           (v-nat-dec
            (v-nth (bv-oprd-a (current-instruction reg-file
                                                   real-mem))
                   (reg-file-after-pc-increment reg-file)))
           real-mem)
          (v-nth (v-nth (bv-oprd-a (current-instruction reg-file
                                                        real-mem))
                        (reg-file-after-pc-increment reg-file))
                 real-mem))))
```

Operand-b for the ALU is also obtained from either the register file or the memory, but not until the program counter incremented, and the conditional pre-decrement for operand-a and operand-b has occurred.

```
(defn b-value-for-alu-after-oprd-b-pre-decrement
  (reg-file real-mem)
  (if (b-direct-reg-b (current-instruction reg-file real-mem))
      (v-nth (bv-oprd-b (current-instruction reg-file real-mem))
             (reg-file-after-oprd-a-pre-decrement reg-file
                                                  real-mem))
      (if (b-indirect-reg-b-dec (current-instruction reg-file
                                                     real-mem))
          (v-nth
           (v-nat-dec
            (v-nth (bv-oprd-b (current-instruction reg-file
                                                   real-mem))
                   (reg-file-after-oprd-a-pre-decrement
                    reg-file real-mem)))
           real-mem)
          (v-nth
```

```
        (v-nth (bv-oprd-b (current-instruction reg-file
                                               real-mem))
               (reg-file-after-oprd-a-pre-decrement reg-file
                                                     real-mem))
    real-mem)))))
```

After obtaining the ALU inputs, the results of the ALU are calculated based
upon the current instruction.

```
(defn bv-alu-cv-results (reg-file real-mem c-flag)
 (bv-alu-cv
     (a-value-for-alu-after-oprd-a-pre-decrement reg-file
                                                 real-mem)
     (b-value-for-alu-after-oprd-b-pre-decrement reg-file
                                                 real-mem)
     c-flag
     (bv-alu-op-code (current-instruction reg-file
                                          real-mem))))
```

And using the ALU result, the contents of the register file can determined (from
program counter increment to conditional ALU results storage).

```
(defn reg-file-after-alu-write
 (reg-file real-mem c-flag v-flag z-flag n-flag)
 (update-v-nth
  (and (b-store-alu-result-with-ifs
        c-flag v-flag z-flag n-flag
        (current-instruction reg-file real-mem))
       (b-direct-reg-b (current-instruction reg-file real-mem)))
  (bv-oprd-b (current-instruction reg-file real-mem))
  (reg-file-after-oprd-b-pre-decrement reg-file real-mem)
  (bv (bv-alu-cv-results reg-file real-mem c-flag))))
```

The last two possible updates which can occur to the register file are the two
operand post-increment operations. Again these functions are composed one
after another on top of the previous function's register file result.

```
(defn reg-file-after-oprd-a-post-increment
 (reg-file real-mem c-flag v-flag z-flag n-flag)
 (update-v-nth
  (b-indirect-reg-a-inc (current-instruction reg-file
```

```
                                             real-mem))
   (bv-oprd-a (current-instruction reg-file real-mem))
   (reg-file-after-alu-write reg-file real-mem c-flag v-flag
                             z-flag n-flag)
   (v-nat-inc
              (v-nth (bv-oprd-a (current-instruction reg-file
                                                     real-mem))
                     (reg-file-after-alu-write reg-file real-mem
                                               c-flag v-flag
                                               z-flag n-flag)))))


(defn reg-file-after-oprd-b-post-increment
  (reg-file real-mem c-flag v-flag z-flag n-flag)
  (update-v-nth
    (b-indirect-reg-b-inc (current-instruction reg-file
                                               real-mem))
    (bv-oprd-b (current-instruction reg-file real-mem))
    (reg-file-after-oprd-a-post-increment reg-file real-mem
                                          c-flag v-flag
                                          z-flag n-flag)
  (v-nat-inc
    (v-nth (bv-oprd-b (current-instruction reg-file
                                           real-mem))
           (reg-file-after-oprd-a-post-increment reg-file
                                                 real-mem
                                                 c-flag
                                                 v-flag
                                                 z-flag
                                                 n-flag)))))
```

The reader who is disappointed by the complex nature of the reg-file specification is reminded that this is due to the design of FM8501 rather than the use of formalism. If an instruction can cause four of six possible alterations to the reg-file and the reg-file is visible to the user, the specification must explain each possible modification.

The reader will also note that the specification is "just" the composition of the six possible updates caused by the microcode; that is, *if* the microcode does what we said it does. The disappointed reader is invited to verify that the sequential execution of the microcode composes the modifications to the register file as shown. This is the final part of the correctness proof, which is still to come.

If the execution of a single instruction were independent of how that instruction modifies the state of the machine, the specification would not be so complicated. However, machines with complex addressing modes (like the PDP-

11) necessarily expose some aspects of the order of register updates during the execution of a single instruction. Such is the nature of von Neumann machines.

12.5   Memory Update

The execution of a FM8501 instruction may cause the ALU result to be written to memory. To model this event, the following function is defined.

```
(defn real-mem-after-alu-write
 (reg-file real-mem c-flag v-flag z-flag n-flag)
 (update-v-nth
  (and
   (b-store-alu-result-with-ifs c-flag v-flag z-flag n-flag
                               (current-instruction reg-file
                                                    real-mem))
   (not (b-direct-reg-b (current-instruction reg-file
                                             real-mem))))
   (v-nth (bv-oprd-b (current-instruction reg-file real-mem))
          (reg-file-after-oprd-b-pre-decrement reg-file
                                               real-mem))
  real-mem
  (bv (bv-alu-cv-results reg-file real-mem c-flag))))
```

This function updates memory if operand-b is memory based and the function `b-store-alu-result-with-ifs` indicates a store.

12.6   Flag Interpretations

Due to the non-deterministic nature of the type of ALU operation being performed, the meaning of the flags must be defined for the three mathmatically defined datatypes: bit-vectors, natural numbers, and integers. The values for the carry flag `c-flag` and the overflow flag `v-flag` were already defined in the ALU chapter.

The definition of `soft` sets the `z-flag` to:

```
(zerop
  (bv-to-nat
    (bv (bv-alu-cv-results reg-file real-mem c-flag))))
```

Alternative interpretations of this flag are established by two theorems:

```
(prove-lemma bit-vector-interpretation-of-z-flag (rewrite)
  (equal (zerop
           (bv-to-nat
             (bv (bv-alu-cv-results reg-file real-mem c-flag))))
         (v-zerop
           (bv (bv-alu-cv-results reg-file real-mem c-flag)))))

(prove-lemma integer-interpretation-of-z-flag (rewrite)
  (equal (zerop
           (bv-to-nat
             (bv (bv-alu-cv-results reg-file real-mem c-flag))))
         (equal 0
                (bv-to-tc (bv (bv-alu-cv-results reg-file real-mem
                                                 c-flag))))))
```

One additional theorem is displayed giving the bit-vector interpretation of the n-flag.

```
(prove-lemma bit-vector-interpretation-of-n-flag (rewrite)
  (equal (negativep
           (bv-to-tc
             (bv (bv-alu-cv-results reg-file real-mem c-flag))))
         (bitn (bv (bv-alu-cv-results reg-file real-mem c-flag))
               (size (bv (bv-alu-cv-results reg-file real-mem
                                            c-flag))))))
```

No interpretation is supplied for the negative flag concerning its meaning with regard to natural numbers.

12.7 The Reset Specification

Upon being reset, the FM8501 microprocessor sets the program counter to zero. After the reset input line is turned off, program execution begins with the instruction at location zero in the memory. The specification of the reset process is shown below.

```
(defn soft-reset (reg-file real-mem c-flag v-flag z-flag n-flag
                           oracle)
  (if (nlistp oracle)
      (list reg-file real-mem c-flag v-flag z-flag n-flag)
      (soft (update-nth t 0 reg-file (nat-to-bv 0 (machine-size)))
            real-mem
            c-flag
            v-flag
            z-flag
            n-flag
            (cdr oracle))))
```

Note that the above function continues by calling the FM8501 specification `soft`.

This concludes the specification of the FM8501 microprocessor. In the next chapter, the theorems relating the FM8501 hardware to the specifications shown in this chapter are presented.

Chapter 13

Correctness of FM8501

The correctness of the FM8501 hardware with respect to its specification is demonstrated by several theorems. We wish to prove that any final state computed by **soft** can be computed by the FM8501, i.e., by **big-machine**, by running it long enough on the appropriate initial state. However, there are several complications. First, we must make certain assumptions about the types of the arguments to the two functions, e.g., that **reg-file** is an 8 word by 16 bit RAM. Second, we must be able to get into an appropriate initial state of **big-machine**. Third, we must address the fact that **big-machine** returns a more elaborate final state than **soft**, e.g., when **big-machine** halts its final state includes a value for the **read** line, which is irrelevant to our specification. Fourth, we must address the fact that **big-machine** has a "faster" clock than **soft**; many ticks of the **big-machine** clock are required to implement one tick of the **soft** clock.

13.1   The Proof Environment

Before attempting to establish the correctness of FM8501, the register, RAM, and ROM sizes are fixed. The following function is used to characterize the "environment" in which we conduct our equivalence proofs and in which we will eventually expand **big-machine** into the FM8501 hardware description.

```
(defn standard-hyps (mar read write dtack reset no-store
                          data-out reg-file addr-out
                          c-flag v-flag z-flag n-flag
                          a-reg b-reg i-reg visual-mem real-mem)
  (and (sizep mar (nxsz))
       (boolp read)
       (boolp write)
       (boolp dtack)
```

```
(boolp reset)
(boolp no-store)
(sizep data-out (machine-size))
(ramp reg-file (machine-size) 8)
(sizep addr-out (machine-size))
(boolp c-flag)
(boolp v-flag)
(boolp z-flag)
(boolp n-flag)
(sizep a-reg (machine-size))
(sizep b-reg (machine-size))
(sizep i-reg (machine-size))
(sizep visual-mem (machine-size))
(ramp real-mem (machine-size) (exp 2 16))))
```

13.2   Resetting FM8501

Our main correctness theorem requires that we get the FM8501 into a state in which the mar is 1, the read and write registers are f and the reset register is t. We call such a state an *initial state*. We can get the FM8501 into an initial state by appropriate use of the reset line.

We reach an initial state by first asserting the reset line for at least three clock ticks and entering what we call a *reset state* in which the mar is 0, the read and write registers are f and the reset register is t.

```
(prove-lemma reset-to-state-0 (rewrite)
  (implies (and (standard-hyps mar read write dtack reset no-store
                                data-out reg-file addr-out c-flag
                                v-flag z-flag n-flag a-reg b-reg
                                i-reg visual-mem real-mem)
                (equal m (big-machine mar read write dtack reset
                                       no-store data-out
                                       reg-file addr-out
                                       c-flag v-flag z-flag n-flag
                                       a-reg b-reg i-reg
                                       visual-mem real-mem
                                       memory-watch-dog-history
                                       (list (list dt1 t)
                                             (list dt2 t)
                                             (list dt3 t)))))
           (and (equal (car m) (nat-to-bv 0 (nxsz)))    ; mar = 0
                (equal (cadr m) f)                       ; read = f
```

```
(equal (caddr m) f)                      ; write = f
(equal (caddddr m) t)                    ; reset = t
(equal (nth 0 (caddddddddr m))
       (nat-to-bv 0 (machine-size)))))))
```

What does the formula above tell us? First, note that we assume the internal
registers are as specified by standard-hyps. Such an assumption will be made
in every formula proven about big-machine. The other hypothesis, equating m
to the application of big-machine, is in essence the establishment of an abbreviation convention: let m denote the final state obtained by running big-machine
three clock ticks with the reset line asserted, starting from any state whatsoever.
Observe that the values on the dtack line may be arbitrary. The conclusion of
the theorem states that in state m, mar is 0, read and write are f, reset is t,
and the program counter is 0. That is, m is a reset state in which the program
counter is 0.

Observe that we do not completely characterize m. For example, what is
the final value of the reg-file? To answer that question we would have to
consider all of the possible starting states of the microcode. Depending on what
microstate we were in when the first reset is asserted, writes to the reg-file
might occur later since it takes one cycle for the reset input line to be latched
into the register reset and another for that to cause the mar to be set to 0.
Similarly the condition flags might be overwritten during resetting.

However, real-mem is defined not to change during reset. The function for
managing external memory, real-mem, takes as one of its arguments the reset
line itself (not the internal latch reset) and guarantees that memory is not
written while reset is asserted. Thus, an initialization program that starts in
location 0 of real-mem survives resetting.[1]

Once we enter a reset state, the operation of the machine is completely
deterministic. Additional clock ticks while reset is asserted do not change the
state. When the reset input has become f for two clock ticks we enter an initial
state:

```
(prove-lemma state-0-to-0-wait-to-1 (rewrite)
  (implies (and (standard-hyps mar0 f f dtack t no-store data-out
                               reg-file addr-out c-flag v-flag
                               z-flag n-flag a-reg b-reg i-reg
                               visual-mem real-mem)
                (equal mar0 (nat-to-bv 0 (nxsz))))
           (equal (big-machine mar0 f f dtack t no-store data-out
                               reg-file addr-out c-flag v-flag
                               z-flag n-flag a-reg b-reg i-reg
```

---

[1] Commonly found in microprocessor designs is a memory ROM which contains instructions
that are executed upon reset.

```
                        visual-mem real-mem
                        watch-dog-history
                        (state-0-to-0-wait-to-1-oracle n))
        (list (nat-to-bv 1 (nxsz))
              f f f f no-store data-out
              (update-nth t 0 reg-file
                          (nat-to-bv 0 (machine-size)))
              addr-out c-flag v-flag z-flag n-flag
              a-reg b-reg i-reg
              (trunc (default-visual-mem-value) 16)
              real-mem
              (watch-dog f f f data-out addr-out)))))
```

As an inspection of the Appendix will show, (state-0-to-0-wait-to-1-oracle
n) is an oracle containing n+3 ticks with the dtack line off throughout, the reset
line asserted during the first n+1 ticks, and the reset line off for the last two
ticks.

The theorem above tells us that if we start the machine in an arbitrary reset
state (note: the starting mar is 0, read and write are f and reset is t) and run
for n+3 ticks with the reset line as described, we arrive at an initial state: mar is
1, read, write, dtack, and reset are f, the reg-file is unmodified except at 0
where it is 0, and all other internal registers are unmodified. That is, if in a reset
state, reset can be asserted for any positive number of clock ticks and then, two
ticks after reset has become f we are in an initial state. Observe that real-mem
is not modified by the transition into an initial state. Thus, an initialization
program at location 0 of real-mem will be activated upon proceeding from the
initial state.

Having established that we can get the FM8501 into an initial state, we now
turn to its "equivalence" to soft when started in an initial state. We later
combine these two results into our main theorem.

13.3   Abstracting Big-Machine's State

Recall that big-machine returns its final state encoded as a list of length 19:

```
(list mar read write dtack reset no-store
      data-out reg-file addr-out
      c-flag v-flag z-flag n-flag
      a-reg b-reg i-reg
      visual-mem real-mem watch-dog-history)
```

On the other hand, `soft` returns a simpler final state:

```
(list reg-file real-mem c-flag v-flag z-flag n-flag)
```

To state the "equivalence" between `big-machine` and `soft`, we select from the `big-machine` state only those components of interest. The following function converts a `big-machine` state m to a `soft` state:

```
(defn abstract (m)
  (list (caddddddr m)              ; reg-file of m
        (caddddddddddddddddddr m)  ; real-mem of m
        (cadddddddddr m)           ; c-flag of m
        (caddddddddddr m)          ; v-flag of m
        (cadddddddddddr m)         ; z-flag of m
        (caddddddddddddr m)))      ; n-flag of m
```

13.4 The Oracles

We intend to show how computations by `soft` — a machine someone might want to program — can be carried out by a suitable application of `big-machine` — a machine someone can build. The user of `soft` provides seven inputs. The first six define the starting state: `reg-file`, `real-mem`, and the flags `c-flag`, `v-flag`, `z-flag` and `n-flag`. The seventh input is a list, `lst`, whose length specifies the number of machine instructions to be executed. (The elements of the list are irrelevant to the computation performed by `soft`.) These seven user inputs completely determine the computation performed by `soft`.

To carry out the computation on `big-machine` we start in an initial state (by resetting) and load the six state components provided by the user. This defines all of `big-machine`'s state except for `no-store`, `data-out`, `addr-out`, `a-reg`, `b-reg`, `i-reg`, `visual-mem`, and `watch-dog`, all of which are irrelevant because they will be written before they are first read. However, how long are we to let `big-machine` run? How many microcycles does it take to execute the number of instructions specified by `lst`?

From one perspective it does not matter how many microcycles it takes. It is sufficient to know merely that there exists a number that will do the job. The Boyer-Moore logic does not have existential quantification. To establish that something exists one must exhibit a function for constructing it. The function `oracle`, defined in the Appendix, constructs a `big-machine` oracle sufficient for executing the specified number of instructions. `oracle` takes as input the same arguments that `soft` does. Informally, you tell `oracle` exactly which `soft` computation you have in mind and it tells you exactly how long you should let `big-machine` run. Readers who merely want assurance that there exists an adequate oracle for `big-machine` need know no more about this function.

In fact, the function requires a great deal of knowledge about `big-machine` to construct and its definition is quite informative to the person interested in counting microcycles. For example, the number of microcycles it takes to execute a given instruction depends not only upon what the instruction is (which is a function of all the writes which have occurred previously) but upon how the memory process responds to read and write requests.

The microcode may go to memory four times per instruction. Each time it waits for acknowledgement from the memory. The four events causing waits are: instruction read, operand-a read, operand-b read, and ALU result write. How long are each of these waits? In defining `oracle` we might have assumed that each wait lasted a constant amount of time. That would have established the existence of an oracle under the built-in assumption that memory responded in constant time. However, we decided against this unrealistic assumption and adopted the opposite approach: the amount of time taken by each wait is supplied by some arbitrary oracle. Thus, for each machine instruction to be executed by `soft` we needed at most four numbers specifying the delays encountered when (if) the instruction goes to memory. We wanted these numbers completely unconstrained by the statement of our main theorem. Since the elements of the `soft` "oracle," `lst`, are irrelevant — only the length of `lst` matters to `soft`; we decided to treat each element as a 4-tuple — padding out nonexistent components with 0's. The final correctness theorem puts no constraints on `lst`. Any two lists of the same length lead to the same final `soft` state and thus we prove the correctness of `big-machine` under completely arbitrary memory wait times.

To construct a suitable `big-machine` oracle, the function `oracle` essentially simulates the operation of `soft` on each instruction and appends together the oracles necessary to execute each. The function `state-1-to-1-oracle` is the key function: given a `soft` state, specified by `reg-file`, `real-mem` and the four flags, and four numbers, specifying the instruction wait time, operand a and b wait times, and the memory write wait time, `state-1-to-1-oracle` returns an oracle suitable for causing `big-machine` to execute the instruction indicated by the program counter in `reg-file`. That is, `state-1-to-1-oracle` returns a list of pairs, one pair for each microcycle required, each of which specifies the values of the dtack and reset input lines. Put another way, `state-1-to-1-oracle` encodes the timing diagrams for the FM8501. The details are provided by the definitions and theorems in the Appendix.

We remind the reader, before resuming our description of the correctness theorem, that the constructive details of `oracle` are irrelevant: with no knowledge whatsoever of the defined function `oracle` the reader can glean from the correctness theorem the existence of dtack and reset inputs enabling `big-machine` to carry out the computations of `soft`.

13.5 Correctness of FM8501 Instruction Execution

Here is the theorem establishing the relationship between `big-machine` (in an initial state) and `soft`:

```
(prove-lemma big-machine-is-soft-machine (rewrite)
  (implies (and (equal mar1 (nat-to-bv 1 (nxsz)))
                (standard-hyps mar1 f f f f
                               no-store data-out
                               reg-file addr-out
                               c-flag v-flag z-flag n-flag
                               a-reg b-reg i-reg
                               visual-mem real-mem))
           (equal (abstract
                    (big-machine mar1 f f f f
                                 no-store data-out
                                 reg-file addr-out
                                 c-flag v-flag z-flag n-flag
                                 a-reg b-reg i-reg
                                 visual-mem real-mem
                                 watch-dog
                                 (oracle reg-file real-mem c-flag
                                         v-flag z-flag n-flag
                                         lst)))
                  (soft reg-file real-mem
                        c-flag v-flag z-flag n-flag lst))))
```

The hypothesis equating `mar1` to `(nat-to-bv 1 (nxsz))` merely establishes an abbreviation convention. The theorem can be read as follows. Suppose we have an arbitrary `soft` state characterized by `reg-file`, `real-mem` and the four condition flags (all satisfying our standard hypotheses). Consider the final state, which we shall call s, obtained by running `soft` n instructions, where n is the length of an arbitrary list `lst`. Then there exists an oracle, namely the one constructed by `oracle`, such that s is equal to the abstraction of the state obtained by running `big-machine` starting in any intial state with the given `reg-file`, `real-mem` and condition flags.

13.6 Correctness of FM8501

We are finally ready to combine the reset and instruction execution theorems. The final theorem tells us that if we start in a reset state, there exists a suitable oracle (namely `oracle-reset`) for making `big-machine` compute `soft-reset`:

```
(prove-lemma soft-reset-works (rewrite)
  (implies (and (equal mar0 (nat-to-bv 0 (nxsz)))
                (standard-hyps mar0 f f dtack t
                               no-store data-out
                               reg-file addr-out
                               c-flag v-flag z-flag n-flag
                               a-reg b-reg i-reg
                               visual-mem real-mem))
           (equal (abstract
                      (big-machine mar0 f f dtack t
                               no-store data-out
                               reg-file addr-out
                               c-flag v-flag z-flag n-flag
                               a-reg b-reg i-reg
                               visual-mem real-mem
                               memory-watch-dog-history
                               (oracle-reset reg-file real-mem
                                       c-flag v-flag
                                       z-flag n-flag
                                       lst)))
                  (soft-reset reg-file real-mem
                               c-flag v-flag z-flag n-flag
                               lst))))
```

Recall that function `soft-reset` is just like the function `soft` with the program counter set to 0. `oracle-reset` is just the concatenation of the previously discussed `state-0-to-0-wait-to-1-oracle` and `oracle`. We have already established that we enter a reset state by asserting reset for at least three clock ticks.

Chapter 14

Expansion of FM8501

We now describe how to generate hardware for the FM8501 from the definition
of big-machine. First, recall its definition:

```
(defn big-machine
      (mar read write dtack reset no-store data-out
           reg-file addr-out c-flag v-flag z-flag n-flag
           a-reg b-reg i-reg visual-mem real-mem
           memory-watch-dog-history oracle)
      (if (nlistp oracle)
          (list mar read write dtack reset no-store
                data-out reg-file addr-out c-flag v-flag
                z-flag n-flag a-reg b-reg i-reg visual-mem
                real-mem memory-watch-dog-history)
          (big-machine (mar mar i-reg dtack reset no-store)
                       (read mar i-reg)
                       (write mar i-reg no-store)
                       (dtack (car oracle))
                       (reset (car oracle))
                       (no-store no-store c-flag v-flag
                                 z-flag n-flag i-reg mar)
                       (data-out data-out a-reg b-reg
                                 c-flag i-reg mar)
                       (reg-file reg-file data-out i-reg
                                 mar no-store reset)
                       (addr-out addr-out reg-file i-reg
                                 mar reset)
                       (c-flag c-flag a-reg b-reg i-reg mar)
                       (v-flag v-flag a-reg b-reg c-flag
                               i-reg mar)
```

```
(z-flag z-flag a-reg b-reg c-flag
        i-reg mar)
(n-flag n-flag a-reg b-reg c-flag
        i-reg mar)
(a-reg a-reg visual-mem reg-file
        i-reg mar reset)
(b-reg b-reg visual-mem reg-file
        i-reg mar reset)
(i-reg i-reg visual-mem mar)
(visual-mem real-mem read write
            addr-out
            memory-watch-dog-history
            (dtack (car oracle))
            (reset (car oracle)))
(real-mem real-mem read write
          addr-out data-out
          memory-watch-dog-history
          (dtack (car oracle))
          (reset (car oracle)))
(watch-dog read write
           (dtack (car oracle))
           data-out addr-out)
(cdr oracle))))
```

We classify the 20 arguments of big-machine as follows: mar, read, write, no-store, data-out, reg-file, addr-out, c-flag, v-flag, z-flag, n-flag, a-reg, b-reg, and i-reg are *internal registers*; dtack, reset, and visual-mem are *input latch registers*, and finally memory-watch-dog-history, real-mem, and oracle are *external devices*.

The internal register arguments of big-machine have a special property: upon recursion, the new value of each internal register is a function only of the current values of internal registers and input latch registers. If we can compute with combinational logic the new value of each internal register upon recursion, then we can build hardware that computes the final values of all the internal registers given a correct sequence of values for the input latches. The idea is simple: allocate a physical register to each internal register argument and each latch argument; wire the registers with combinational logic so that on each clock pulse the new value of each internal register is computed from the internal and latch registers and written back into the appropriate internal register; wire the latch registers so that on each clock pulse they are written by lines coming in from the outside. Then each clock pulse causes the hardware to step the state forward once in the recursion of big-machine.

All that remains is to exhibit the hardware necessary to compute each internal register. This cannot be done unless we fix the sizes of the registers. We, of course, use `standard-hyps` to do this. In the table that constitutes most of this chapter we exhibit a hardware expression for each of the internal register arguments. We name each hardware expression with the name of the corresponding formal parameter of `big-machine`, except printed in upper-case italics. Thus, the expression for `mar` is named *MAR*. For each internal register argument we can prove, under the standard hypotheses, that the named hardware expression is equivalent to the expression appearing in the corresponding argument position in the recursive call in the definition of `big-machine`.

For example, we can prove, trivially, that:

```
(implies (standard-hyps mar read write dtack reset
                        no-store data-out reg-file addr-out
                        c-flag v-flag z-flag n-flag
                        a-reg b-reg i-reg visual-mem real-mem)
         (equal (mar mar i-reg dtack reset no-store)
                MAR))
```

The proof is trivial because *MAR* is obtained by mechanically expanding the definition of `mar`. Since the standard hypotheses specify the sizes of all our registers, we can obtain similar "hardware expressions" for all our internal registers by expanding all recursively defined functions just as we did in the early examples of `bv-if` and `bv-adder`.

We now explain how to interpret *MAR* as a description of hardware. *MAR* has the form (`update-v` *bool* `mar` *bv*), where *bool* is combinational logic and *bv* is a 4-bit wide bit-vector expression each bit of which is specified by combinational logic. Thus, to wire up the `mar` internal register we lay down a 4-bit wide write-enabled register, connect the write enable line to the combinational logic for *bool* and the input line to the 4-bit wide combinational logic for *bv*.

Similarly, *REG-FILE* is of the form (`update-v-nth` *bool* *addr* `reg-file` *bv*), where *bool* is combinational logic, *addr* is a 3-bit wide combinational logic bit-vector, and *bv* is a 16-bit wide combinational logic bit-vector. This is consistent with the standard hypothesis that `reg-file` is an 8-word, 16-bit wide RAM. To wire `reg-file` we lay down an 8-word, 16-bit wide write-enabled RAM and connect the write enable line to the logic for *bool*, the address line to the logic for *addr* and the input lines to the logic for *bv*.

ROMs, RAMs and registers have outputs; these outputs are accessed directly by referencing the output bit of interest. In the case of a bit-register, the name of the bit-register is used. In the case the *n*th bit of a bit-vector found in RAMs or bit-vector registers, the form (`bitn` *reg-name* *n*) is used, where *reg-name* is a bit-vector register or *reg-name* is an expression of the form (`v-nth` *addr* *rm*) where *rm* is the name of a 2-dimensional RAM or ROM and *addr* is a bit-vector expression of the appropriate size. Expressions requiring the contents of registers or RAM are wired to the appropriate output of the register, RAM, or ROM.

Finally, it should be noted for every RAM or ROM element, there is exactly one location referenced (whether for read by v-nth or write by update-v-nth) in the expressions below. Thus, on no cycle do we try to access a RAM or ROM at two locations.

The table below gives the hardware expressions for each of the internal registers of the FM8501. We have introduced certain abbreviations, namely the use of "variable symbols" that begin with asterisks, to name the common subexpressions. The meanings of these symbols are given at the conclusion of the table. The machine has 1,789 logical gates in it. Were common subexpressions not removed, it would have over 11 million gates. Multiple uses of a common subexpression represent opportunities for fan-out.

The output below was produced mechanically by expanding the internal register expressions inside the definition of big-machine after noting which arguments are internal registers and which are latches. It takes 552 seconds on a Symbolics 3600 to expand big-machine (producing a term with over 11 million gates in it), 812 seconds to find and rename the common subexpressions, and 5 seconds to check that all the constraints imposed by the standard hypotheses are met (e.g., that reg-file is addressed with the same 3-bit wide vector expansion in every case).

The following registers are wired as input latches:

```
dtack  (1 bit)
reset  (1 bit)
visual-mem  (16 bits)
```

The following registers are to be wired as shown:

MAR (4 bits):
```
(update-v (b-or (b-or reset (b-or dtack (bitn *1 10)))
                (b-or (b-and (bitn *1 3) no-store)
                      (b-and (b-not *5) (b-not *6))))
          mar
          (bitv (b-not (b-nand *4 (bitn *1 17)))
                (bitv (b-not (b-nand *4 (bitn *1 18)))
                      (bitv (b-not (b-nand *4 (bitn *1 19)))
                            (bitv (b-not (b-nand *4 (bitn *1 20)))
                                  (btm)))))))
```

READ (1 bit):
```
(b-and (b-or *5 *6) (bitn *1 9))
```

WRITE (1 bit):
```
(b-and *231 (b-and *5 *232))
```

NO-STORE (1 bit):
```
(update-v *16
          no-store
          (b-not
           (b-or (b-or *17 i-reg-16)
                 (b-or (b-or (b-or (b-and *26 (b-and *8 *7))
                                   (b-and c-flag (b-and i-reg-13 *7)))
                             (b-or (b-and (b-not v-flag) (b-and *8 *10))
                                   (b-and v-flag (b-and i-reg-13 *10))))
                       (b-or (b-or (b-and (b-not z-flag) (b-and *8 *13))
                                   (b-and z-flag (b-and i-reg-13 *13)))
                             (b-or (b-and (b-not n-flag) (b-and *8 *15))
                                   (b-and n-flag
                                          (b-and i-reg-13 *15)))))))))
```

DATA-OUT (16 bits):
```
(update-v
```

```
*16 data-out
(bitv *326
 (bitv *327
  (bitv *328
   (bitv *329
    (bitv *330
     (bitv *331
      (bitv *332
       (bitv *333
        (bitv *334
         (bitv *335
          (bitv *336
                (bitv *337
                    (bitv *338
                        (bitv *339
                            (bitv *340
                                (bitv *341
                                    (btm)))))))))))))))))
```

REG-FILE (16 x 8 bit ram):

```
(update-v-nth
 (b-or (b-or reset *238)
       (b-or (b-or *235 (b-and *231 (b-and *232 *233)))
             (b-or *288 (b-and (bitn *1 7) *239))))
 *240 reg-file
 (bitv
  (b-nand (b-nand *237 (b-not (b-nand *4 data-out-1)))
          (b-nand *243 (b-nand (b-nand *241 *242)
                               (b-nand *246 *242))))
  (bitv
   (b-nand (b-nand *237 (b-not (b-nand *4 data-out-2)))
           (b-nand *243 (b-nand (b-nand *241 (b-xor *244 *247))
                                (b-nand *246 *289))))
   (bitv
    (b-nand (b-nand *237 (b-not (b-nand *4 data-out-3)))
            (b-nand *243 (b-nand (b-nand *241 (b-xor *248 *249))
                                 (b-nand *246 *291))))
    (bitv
     (b-nand (b-nand *237 (b-not (b-nand *4 data-out-4)))
             (b-nand *243 (b-nand (b-nand *241 (b-xor *252 *251))
                                  (b-nand *246 *292))))
     (bitv
      (b-nand (b-nand *237 (b-not (b-nand *4 data-out-5)))
              (b-nand *243
                      (b-nand (b-nand *241 (b-xor *255 *254))
                              (b-nand *246 *293))))
      (bitv
       (b-nand (b-nand *237 (b-not (b-nand *4 data-out-6)))
```

```
            (b-nand *243
                    (b-nand (b-nand *241 (b-xor *258 *257))
                            (b-nand *246 *294))))
(bitv
 (b-nand (b-nand *237 (b-not (b-nand *4 data-out-7)))
         (b-nand *243
                    (b-nand (b-nand *241 (b-xor *261 *260))
                            (b-nand *246 *295))))
 (bitv
  (b-nand (b-nand *237 (b-not (b-nand *4 data-out-8)))
          (b-nand *243
                     (b-nand (b-nand *241 (b-xor *264 *263))
                             (b-nand *246 *296))))
  (bitv
   (b-nand (b-nand *237 (b-not (b-nand *4 data-out-9)))
           (b-nand *243
                      (b-nand (b-nand *241 (b-xor *267 *266))
                              (b-nand *246 *297))))
   (bitv
    (b-nand (b-nand *237 (b-not (b-nand *4 data-out-10)))
            (b-nand *243
                       (b-nand (b-nand *241 (b-xor *270 *269))
                               (b-nand *246 *298))))
    (bitv
     (b-nand (b-nand *237 (b-not (b-nand *4 data-out-11)))
             (b-nand *243
                        (b-nand (b-nand *241 (b-xor *273 *272))
                                (b-nand *246 *299))))
     (bitv
      (b-nand (b-nand *237 (b-not (b-nand *4 data-out-12)))
              (b-nand *243
                         (b-nand (b-nand *241 (b-xor *276 *275))
                                 (b-nand *246 *300))))
      (bitv
       (b-nand (b-nand *237 (b-not (b-nand *4 data-out-13)))
               (b-nand *243
                          (b-nand (b-nand *241 (b-xor *279 *278))
                                  (b-nand *246 *301))))
       (bitv
        (b-nand (b-nand *237 (b-not (b-nand *4 data-out-14)))
                (b-nand *243
                           (b-nand (b-nand *241 (b-xor *282 *281))
                                   (b-nand *246 *302))))
        (bitv
         (b-nand (b-nand *237 (b-not (b-nand *4 data-out-15)))
                 (b-nand *243
                            (b-nand (b-nand *241 (b-xor *285 *284))
                                    (b-nand *246 *303))))
```

```
            (bitv
             (b-nand
              (b-nand *237 (b-not (b-nand *4 data-out-16)))
              (b-nand *243
                      (b-nand (b-nand *241
                                      (b-xor (b-and *284 *285) *287))
                              (b-nand *246 *304))))
              (btm)))))))))))))))))))
```

ADDR-OUT (16 bits):

```
(update-v
 (bitn *1 12)
 addr-out
 (bitv
  (b-nand (b-nand *288 *242) (b-nand *290 *244)) .
  (bitv
   (b-nand (b-nand *288 *289) (b-nand *290 *247))
   (bitv
    (b-nand (b-nand *288 *291) (b-nand *290 *249))
    (bitv
     (b-nand (b-nand *288 *292) (b-nand *290 *251))
     (bitv
      (b-nand (b-nand *288 *293) (b-nand *290 *254))
      (bitv
       (b-nand (b-nand *288 *294) (b-nand *290 *257))
       (bitv
        (b-nand (b-nand *288 *295) (b-nand *290 *260))
        (bitv
         (b-nand (b-nand *288 *296) (b-nand *290 *263))
         (bitv
          (b-nand (b-nand *288 *297) (b-nand *290 *266))
          (bitv
           (b-nand (b-nand *288 *298) (b-nand *290 *269))
           (bitv
            (b-nand (b-nand *288 *299) (b-nand *290 *272))
            (bitv (b-nand (b-nand *288 *300) (b-nand *290 *275))
                  (bitv (b-nand (b-nand *288 *301)
                                (b-nand *290 *278))
                        (bitv (b-nand (b-nand *288 *302)
                                      (b-nand *290 *281))
                              (bitv (b-nand (b-nand *288 *303)
                                            (b-nand *290 *284))
                                    (bitv (b-nand (b-nand *288 *304)
                                                  (b-nand *290 *287))
                                          (btm)))))))))))))))))))
```

C-FLAG (1 bit):

```
(update-v
```

```
*316 c-flag
(b-nand
 (b-nand *24
         (b-not (b-nand *28
                        (b-nand (b-nand *19 (b-not *305))
                                (b-nand *22 (b-nand *306 *305))))))
  (b-nand *34
   (b-nand
    (b-nand *21
     (b-nand
      (b-nand *19
       (b-nand (b-nand *18
                       (b-not (b-or *308
                                    (b-or (b-and *220 *307)
                                          (b-and b-reg-16 *307)))))
               (b-nand *20
                       (b-not (b-or *308
                                    (b-or (b-and *220 *309)
                                          (b-and b-reg-16 *309)))))))
      (b-nand *22
              (b-nand (b-nand *18
                              (b-not
                               (b-or a-reg-16
                                     (b-or *310 (b-and a-reg-16 *310)))))
                      (b-nand *20 (b-not (b-and *220 *311))))))
     (b-nand *28
             (b-nand
              (b-nand *19
                      (b-nand
                       (b-nand *18
                               (b-or *312
                                     (b-or (b-and a-reg-16 *313)
                                           (b-and b-reg-16 *313))))
                       (b-nand *20
                               (b-or *312
                                     (b-or (b-and a-reg-16 *314)
                                           (b-and b-reg-16 *314))))))
              (b-nand *22
                      (b-not (b-nand *18 (b-and a-reg-16 *315)))))))))))
```

V-FLAG (1 bit):
```
(update-v
 *316 v-flag
 (b-not
  (b-nand *34
   (b-nand
    (b-nand *21
     (b-nand (b-nand *19
```

```
                    (b-nand (b-nand *18
                                    (b-and *318 (b-xor *220 *317)))
                            (b-nand *20
                                    (b-and *318 (b-xor *220 *319)))))
              (b-nand *22
                      (b-nand (b-nand *18
                                      (b-and a-reg-16 (b-not *320)))
                              (b-nand *20
                                      (b-and (b-not *220)
                                             (b-xor *220 *321)))))))
      (b-nand *28
       (b-nand
        (b-nand *19
                (b-nand (b-nand *18
                                (b-and *323 (b-xor a-reg-16 *322)))
                        (b-nand *20
                                (b-and *323 (b-xor a-reg-16 *324)))))
        (b-nand *22
                (b-not (b-nand *18
                               (b-and *220
                                      (b-xor a-reg-16 *325)))))))))))
```

Z-FLAG (1 bit):
```
(update-v
 *316 z-flag
 (b-not
  (b-or *326
   (b-or *327
    (b-or *328
     (b-or *329
      (b-or *330
       (b-or *331
        (b-or *332
         (b-or *333
          (b-or *334
           (b-or *335
            (b-or *336
                 (b-or *337
                      (b-or *338
                           (b-or *339
                                (b-or *340 *341))))))))))))))))))
```

N-FLAG (1 bit):
```
(update-v *316 n-flag *341)
```

A-REG (16 bits):
```
(update-v
 (bitn *1 11)
```

```
a-reg
(bitv
 (b-nand (b-nand *342 *244) (b-nand *343 visual-mem-1))
 (bitv
  (b-nand (b-nand *342 *247) (b-nand *343 visual-mem-2))
  (bitv
   (b-nand (b-nand *342 *249) (b-nand *343 visual-mem-3))
   (bitv
    (b-nand (b-nand *342 *251) (b-nand *343 visual-mem-4))
    (bitv
     (b-nand (b-nand *342 *254) (b-nand *343 visual-mem-5))
     (bitv
      (b-nand (b-nand *342 *257) (b-nand *343 visual-mem-6))
      (bitv
       (b-nand (b-nand *342 *260) (b-nand *343 visual-mem-7))
       (bitv
        (b-nand (b-nand *342 *263) (b-nand *343 visual-mem-8))
        (bitv
         (b-nand (b-nand *342 *266) (b-nand *343 visual-mem-9))
         (bitv
          (b-nand (b-nand *342 *269) (b-nand *343 visual-mem-10))
          (bitv
             (b-nand (b-nand *342 *272) (b-nand *343 visual-mem-11))
             (bitv (b-nand (b-nand *342 *275)
                           (b-nand *343 visual-mem-12))
               (bitv (b-nand (b-nand *342 *278)
                             (b-nand *343 visual-mem-13))
                (bitv (b-nand (b-nand *342 *281)
                              (b-nand *343 visual-mem-14))
                  (bitv (b-nand (b-nand *342 *284)
                                (b-nand *343 visual-mem-15))
                    (bitv (b-nand (b-nand *342 *287)
                                  (b-nand *343 visual-mem-16))
                      (btm)))))))))))))))))))
```

B-REG (16 bits):

```
(update-v
 (bitn *1 13)
 b-reg
 (bitv (b-nand (b-nand *233 *244) (b-nand *344 visual-mem-1))
  (bitv (b-nand (b-nand *233 *247) (b-nand *344 visual-mem-2))
   (bitv (b-nand (b-nand *233 *249) (b-nand *344 visual-mem-3))
    (bitv (b-nand (b-nand *233 *251) (b-nand *344 visual-mem-4))
     (bitv (b-nand (b-nand *233 *254) (b-nand *344 visual-mem-5))
      (bitv (b-nand (b-nand *233 *257) (b-nand *344 visual-mem-6))
       (bitv (b-nand (b-nand *233 *260) (b-nand *344 visual-mem-7))
        (bitv (b-nand (b-nand *233 *263) (b-nand *344 visual-mem-8))
         (bitv (b-nand (b-nand *233 *266) (b-nand *344 visual-mem-9))
```

```
        (bitv (b-nand (b-nand *233 *269) (b-nand *344 visual-mem-10))
         (bitv (b-nand (b-nand *233 *272) (b-nand *344 visual-mem-11))
          (bitv (b-nand (b-nand *233 *275)
                        (b-nand *344 visual-mem-12))
           (bitv (b-nand (b-nand *233 *278)
                         (b-nand *344 visual-mem-13))
            (bitv (b-nand (b-nand *233 *281)
                          (b-nand *344 visual-mem-14))
             (bitv (b-nand (b-nand *233 *284)
                           (b-nand *344 visual-mem-15))
              (bitv (b-nand (b-nand *233 *287)
                            (b-nand *344 visual-mem-16))
               (btm)))))))))))))))))))
```

I-REG (16 bits):
```
(update-v (bitn *1 15)
          i-reg visual-mem)
```

```
where:
visual-mem-1:   (bitn visual-mem 1)
visual-mem-2:   (bitn visual-mem 2)
visual-mem-3:   (bitn visual-mem 3)
visual-mem-4:   (bitn visual-mem 4)
visual-mem-5:   (bitn visual-mem 5)
visual-mem-6:   (bitn visual-mem 6)
visual-mem-7:   (bitn visual-mem 7)
visual-mem-8:   (bitn visual-mem 8)
visual-mem-9:   (bitn visual-mem 9)
visual-mem-10:  (bitn visual-mem 10)
visual-mem-11:  (bitn visual-mem 11)
visual-mem-12:  (bitn visual-mem 12)
visual-mem-13:  (bitn visual-mem 13)
visual-mem-14:  (bitn visual-mem 14)
visual-mem-15:  (bitn visual-mem 15)
visual-mem-16:  (bitn visual-mem 16)
i-reg-1:        (bitn i-reg 1)
i-reg-2:        (bitn i-reg 2)
i-reg-3:        (bitn i-reg 3)
i-reg-4:        (bitn i-reg 4)
i-reg-5:        (bitn i-reg 5)
i-reg-6:        (bitn i-reg 6)
i-reg-7:        (bitn i-reg 7)
i-reg-8:        (bitn i-reg 8)
i-reg-9:        (bitn i-reg 9)
i-reg-10:       (bitn i-reg 10)
i-reg-11:       (bitn i-reg 11)
i-reg-12:       (bitn i-reg 12)
i-reg-13:       (bitn i-reg 13)
```

```
i-reg-14:      (bitn i-reg 14)
i-reg-15:      (bitn i-reg 15)
i-reg-16:      (bitn i-reg 16)
b-reg-1:       (bitn b-reg 1)
b-reg-2:       (bitn b-reg 2)
b-reg-3:       (bitn b-reg 3)
b-reg-4:       (bitn b-reg 4)
b-reg-5:       (bitn b-reg 5)
b-reg-6:       (bitn b-reg 6)
b-reg-7:       (bitn b-reg 7)
b-reg-8:       (bitn b-reg 8)
b-reg-9:       (bitn b-reg 9)
b-reg-10:      (bitn b-reg 10)
b-reg-11:      (bitn b-reg 11)
b-reg-12:      (bitn b-reg 12)
b-reg-13:      (bitn b-reg 13)
b-reg-14:      (bitn b-reg 14)
b-reg-15:      (bitn b-reg 15)
b-reg-16:      (bitn b-reg 16)
a-reg-1:       (bitn a-reg 1)
a-reg-2:       (bitn a-reg 2)
a-reg-3:       (bitn a-reg 3)
a-reg-4:       (bitn a-reg 4)
a-reg-5:       (bitn a-reg 5)
a-reg-6:       (bitn a-reg 6)
a-reg-7:       (bitn a-reg 7)
a-reg-8:       (bitn a-reg 8)
a-reg-9:       (bitn a-reg 9)
a-reg-10:      (bitn a-reg 10)
a-reg-11:      (bitn a-reg 11)
a-reg-12:      (bitn a-reg 12)
a-reg-13:      (bitn a-reg 13)
a-reg-14:      (bitn a-reg 14)
a-reg-15:      (bitn a-reg 15)
a-reg-16:      (bitn a-reg 16)
addr-out-1:    (bitn addr-out 1)
addr-out-2:    (bitn addr-out 2)
addr-out-3:    (bitn addr-out 3)
addr-out-4:    (bitn addr-out 4)
addr-out-5:    (bitn addr-out 5)
addr-out-6:    (bitn addr-out 6)
addr-out-7:    (bitn addr-out 7)
addr-out-8:    (bitn addr-out 8)
addr-out-9:    (bitn addr-out 9)
addr-out-10:   (bitn addr-out 10)
addr-out-11:   (bitn addr-out 11)
addr-out-12:   (bitn addr-out 12)
addr-out-13:   (bitn addr-out 13)
```

```
addr-out-14:    (bitn addr-out 14)
addr-out-15:    (bitn addr-out 15)
addr-out-16:    (bitn addr-out 16)
data-out-1:     (bitn data-out 1)
data-out-2:     (bitn data-out 2)
data-out-3:     (bitn data-out 3)
data-out-4:     (bitn data-out 4)
data-out-5:     (bitn data-out 5)
data-out-6:     (bitn data-out 6)
data-out-7:     (bitn data-out 7)
data-out-8:     (bitn data-out 8)
data-out-9:     (bitn data-out 9)
data-out-10:    (bitn data-out 10)
data-out-11:    (bitn data-out 11)
data-out-12:    (bitn data-out 12)
data-out-13:    (bitn data-out 13)
data-out-14:    (bitn data-out 14)
data-out-15:    (bitn data-out 15)
data-out-16:    (bitn data-out 16)
mar-1:          (bitn mar 1)
mar-2:          (bitn mar 2)
mar-3:          (bitn mar 3)
mar-4:          (bitn mar 4)
*1:             (v-nth mar (micro-store))
*2:             (bitn *1 5)
*3:             mar
*4:             (b-not reset)
*5:             (b-nand (b-nand *2 *343)
                        (b-nand *234 *344))
*6:             (bitn *1 4)
*7:             (b-and *11 *9)
*8:             (b-not i-reg-13)
*9:             (b-and (b-not i-reg-15) *12)
*10:            (b-and i-reg-14 *9)
*11:            (b-not i-reg-14)
*12:            (b-not i-reg-16)
*13:            (b-and *11 *14)
*14:            (b-and i-reg-15 *12)
*15:            (b-and i-reg-14 *14)
*16:            (bitn *1 14)
*17:            (b-not i-reg-12)
*18:            (b-not (b-nand *17 i-reg-13))
*19:            (b-not (b-nand *17 i-reg-14))
*20:            (b-not *18)
*21:            (b-not (b-nand *17 i-reg-15))
*22:            (b-not *19)
*23:            (b-nand *20 a-reg-2)
*24:            (b-not (b-nand *17 i-reg-16))
```

```
*25:        (b-not a-reg-1)
*26:        (b-not c-flag)
*27:        (b-xor *25 b-reg-1)
*28:        (b-not *21)
*29:        (b-nand *18 *30)
*30:        (b-xor a-reg-1 b-reg-1)
*31:        (b-nand *18 *25)
*32:        (b-nand *18 a-reg-2)
*33:        (b-nand *20 a-reg-3)
*34:        (b-not *24)
*35:        (b-not a-reg-2)
*36:        (b-and *25 b-reg-1)
*37:        (b-xor *35 b-reg-2)
*38:        (b-and a-reg-1 b-reg-1)
*39:        (b-xor a-reg-2 b-reg-2)
*40:        (b-nand *18 a-reg-3)
*41:        (b-nand *20 a-reg-4)
*42:        (b-or *36 (b-or *25 b-reg-1))
*43:        (b-not a-reg-3)
*44:        (b-and *35 b-reg-2)
*45:        (b-or *36 (b-or (b-and *25 *26) (b-and b-reg-1 *26)))
*46:        (b-xor *43 b-reg-3)
*47:        (b-and a-reg-2 b-reg-2)
*48:        (b-xor a-reg-3 b-reg-3)
*49:        (b-or *38 (b-or (b-and a-reg-1 c-flag)
                            (b-and b-reg-1 c-flag)))
*50:        (b-and a-reg-2 a-reg-1)
*51:        (b-nand *18 a-reg-4)
*52:        (b-nand *20 a-reg-5)
*53:        (b-or *44 (b-or (b-and *35 *42) (b-and b-reg-2 *42)))
*54:        (b-not a-reg-4)
*55:        (b-and *43 b-reg-3)
*56:        (b-or *44 (b-or (b-and *35 *45) (b-and b-reg-2 *45)))
*57:        (b-xor *54 b-reg-4)
*58:        (b-or a-reg-2 (b-or a-reg-1 *50))
*59:        (b-and *35 *25)
*60:        (b-and a-reg-3 b-reg-3)
*61:        (b-or *47 (b-or (b-and a-reg-2 *38) (b-and b-reg-2 *38)))
*62:        (b-xor a-reg-4 b-reg-4)
*63:        (b-or *47 (b-or (b-and a-reg-2 *49) (b-and b-reg-2 *49)))
*64:        (b-nand *18 a-reg-5)
*65:        (b-nand *20 a-reg-6)
*66:        (b-or *55 (b-or (b-and *43 *53) (b-and b-reg-3 *53)))
*67:        (b-not a-reg-5)
*68:        (b-and *54 b-reg-4)
*69:        (b-or *55 (b-or (b-and *43 *56) (b-and b-reg-3 *56)))
*70:        (b-xor *67 b-reg-5)
*71:        (b-or a-reg-3 (b-or *58 (b-and a-reg-3 *58)))
```

```
*72:        (b-and *43 *59)
*73:        (b-and a-reg-4 b-reg-4)
*74:        (b-or *60 (b-or (b-and a-reg-3 *61) (b-and b-reg-3 *61)))
*75:        (b-xor a-reg-5 b-reg-5)
*76:        (b-or *60 (b-or (b-and a-reg-3 *63) (b-and b-reg-3 *63)))
*77:        (b-and a-reg-3 *50)
*78:        (b-nand *18 a-reg-6)
*79:        (b-nand *20 a-reg-7)
*80:        (b-or *68 (b-or (b-and *54 *66) (b-and b-reg-4 *66)))
*81:        (b-not a-reg-6)
*82:        (b-and *67 b-reg-5)
*83:        (b-or *68 (b-or (b-and *54 *69) (b-and b-reg-4 *69)))
*84:        (b-xor *81 b-reg-6)
*85:        (b-or a-reg-4 (b-or *71 (b-and a-reg-4 *71)))
*86:        (b-and *54 *72)
*87:        (b-and a-reg-5 b-reg-5)
*88:        (b-or *73 (b-or (b-and a-reg-4 *74) (b-and b-reg-4 *74)))
*89:        (b-xor a-reg-6 b-reg-6)
*90:        (b-or *73 (b-or (b-and a-reg-4 *76) (b-and b-reg-4 *76)))
*91:        (b-and a-reg-4 *77)
*92:        (b-nand *18 a-reg-7)
*93:        (b-nand *20 a-reg-8)
*94:        (b-or *82 (b-or (b-and *67 *80) (b-and b-reg-5 *80)))
*95:        (b-not a-reg-7)
*96:        (b-and *81 b-reg-6)
*97:        (b-or *82 (b-or (b-and *67 *83) (b-and b-reg-5 *83)))
*98:        (b-xor *95 b-reg-7)
*99:        (b-or a-reg-5 (b-or *85 (b-and a-reg-5 *85)))
*100:       (b-and *67 *86)
*101:       (b-and a-reg-6 b-reg-6)
*102:       (b-or *87 (b-or (b-and a-reg-5 *88) (b-and b-reg-5 *88)))
*103:       (b-xor a-reg-7 b-reg-7)
*104:       (b-or *87 (b-or (b-and a-reg-5 *90) (b-and b-reg-5 *90)))
*105:       (b-and a-reg-5 *91)
*106:       (b-nand *18 a-reg-8)
*107:       (b-nand *20 a-reg-9)
*108:       (b-or *96 (b-or (b-and *81 *94) (b-and b-reg-6 *94)))
*109:       (b-not a-reg-8)
*110:       (b-and *95 b-reg-7)
*111:       (b-or *96 (b-or (b-and *81 *97) (b-and b-reg-6 *97)))
*112:       (b-xor *109 b-reg-8)
*113:       (b-or a-reg-6 (b-or *99 (b-and a-reg-6 *99)))
*114:       (b-and *81 *100)
*115:       (b-and a-reg-7 b-reg-7)
*116:       (b-or *101 (b-or (b-and a-reg-6 *102)
                            (b-and b-reg-6 *102)))
*117:       (b-xor a-reg-8 b-reg-8)
*118:       (b-or *101 (b-or (b-and a-reg-6 *104)
```

```
                             (b-and b-reg-6 *104)))
*119:        (b-and a-reg-6 *105)
*120:        (b-nand *18 a-reg-9)
*121:        (b-nand *20 a-reg-10)
*122:        (b-or *110 (b-or (b-and *95 *108) (b-and b-reg-7 *108)))
*123:        (b-not a-reg-9)
*124:        (b-and *109 b-reg-8)
*125:        (b-or *110 (b-or (b-and *95 *111) (b-and b-reg-7 *111)))
*126:        (b-xor *123 b-reg-9)
*127:        (b-or a-reg-7 (b-or *113 (b-and a-reg-7 *113)))
*128:        (b-and *95 *114)
*129:        (b-and a-reg-8 b-reg-8)
*130:        (b-or *115 (b-or (b-and a-reg-7 *116)
                             (b-and b-reg-7 *116)))
*131:        (b-xor a-reg-9 b-reg-9)
*132:        (b-or *115 (b-or (b-and a-reg-7 *118)
                             (b-and b-reg-7 *118)))
*133:        (b-and a-reg-7 *119)
*134:        (b-nand *18 a-reg-10)
*135:        (b-nand *20 a-reg-11)
*136:        (b-or *124 (b-or (b-and *109 *122) (b-and b-reg-8 *122)))
*137:        (b-not a-reg-10)
*138:        (b-and *123 b-reg-9)
*139:        (b-or *124 (b-or (b-and *109 *125) (b-and b-reg-8 *125)))
*140:        (b-xor *137 b-reg-10)
*141:        (b-or a-reg-8 (b-or *127 (b-and a-reg-8 *127)))
*142:        (b-and *109 *128)
*143:        (b-and a-reg-9 b-reg-9)
*144:        (b-or *129 (b-or (b-and a-reg-8 *130)
                             (b-and b-reg-8 *130)))
*145:        (b-xor a-reg-10 b-reg-10)
*146:        (b-or *129 (b-or (b-and a-reg-8 *132)
                             (b-and b-reg-8 *132)))
*147:        (b-and a-reg-8 *133)
*148:        (b-nand *18 a-reg-11)
*149:        (b-nand *20 a-reg-12)
*150:        (b-or *138 (b-or (b-and *123 *136) (b-and b-reg-9 *136)))
*151:        (b-not a-reg-11)
*152:        (b-and *137 b-reg-10)
*153:        (b-or *138 (b-or (b-and *123 *139) (b-and b-reg-9 *139)))
*154:        (b-xor *151 b-reg-11)
*155:        (b-or a-reg-9 (b-or *141 (b-and a-reg-9 *141)))
*156:        (b-and *123 *142)
*157:        (b-and a-reg-10 b-reg-10)
*158:        (b-or *143 (b-or (b-and a-reg-9 *144)
                             (b-and b-reg-9 *144)))
*159:        (b-xor a-reg-11 b-reg-11)
*160:        (b-or *143 (b-or (b-and a-reg-9 *146)
```

```
                               (b-and b-reg-9 *146)))
*161:        (b-and a-reg-9 *147)
*162:        (b-nand *18 a-reg-12)
*163:        (b-nand *20 a-reg-13)
*164:        (b-or *152 (b-or (b-and *137 *150) (b-and b-reg-10 *150)))
*165:        (b-not a-reg-12)
*166:        (b-and *151 b-reg-11)
*167:        (b-or *152 (b-or (b-and *137 *153) (b-and b-reg-10 *153)))
*168:        (b-xor *165 b-reg-12)
*169:        (b-or a-reg-10 (b-or *155 (b-and a-reg-10 *155)))
*170:        (b-and *137 *156)
*171:        (b-and a-reg-11 b-reg-11)
*172:        (b-or *157 (b-or (b-and a-reg-10 *158)
                             (b-and b-reg-10 *158)))
*173:        (b-xor a-reg-12 b-reg-12)
*174:        (b-or *157 (b-or (b-and a-reg-10 *160)
                             (b-and b-reg-10 *160)))
*175:        (b-and a-reg-10 *161)
*176:        (b-nand *18 a-reg-13)
*177:        (b-nand *20 a-reg-14)
*178:        (b-or *166 (b-or (b-and *151 *164) (b-and b-reg-11 *164)))
*179:        (b-not a-reg-13)
*180:        (b-and *165 b-reg-12)
*181:        (b-or *166 (b-or (b-and *151 *167) (b-and b-reg-11 *167)))
*182:        (b-xor *179 b-reg-13)
*183:        (b-or a-reg-11 (b-or *169 (b-and a-reg-11 *169)))
*184:        (b-and *151 *170)
*185:        (b-and a-reg-12 b-reg-12)
*186:        (b-or *171 (b-or (b-and a-reg-11 *172)
                             (b-and b-reg-11 *172)))
*187:        (b-xor a-reg-13 b-reg-13)
*188:        (b-or *171 (b-or (b-and a-reg-11 *174)
                             (b-and b-reg-11 *174)))
*189:        (b-and a-reg-11 *175)
*190:        (b-nand *18 a-reg-14)
*191:        (b-nand *20 a-reg-15)
*192:        (b-or *180 (b-or (b-and *165 *178) (b-and b-reg-12 *178)))
*193:        (b-not a-reg-14)
*194:        (b-and *179 b-reg-13)
*195:        (b-or *180 (b-or (b-and *165 *181) (b-and b-reg-12 *181)))
*196:        (b-xor *193 b-reg-14)
*197:        (b-or a-reg-12 (b-or *183 (b-and a-reg-12 *183)))
*198:        (b-and *165 *184)
*199:        (b-and a-reg-13 b-reg-13)
*200:        (b-or *185 (b-or (b-and a-reg-12 *186)
                             (b-and b-reg-12 *186)))
*201:        (b-xor a-reg-14 b-reg-14)
*202:        (b-or *185 (b-or (b-and a-reg-12 *188)
```

```
                              (b-and b-reg-12 *188)))
*203:          (b-and a-reg-12 *189)
*204:          (b-nand *18 a-reg-15)
*205:          (b-nand *20 a-reg-16)
*206:          (b-or *194 (b-or (b-and *179 *192) (b-and b-reg-13 *192)))
*207:          (b-not a-reg-15)
*208:          (b-and *193 b-reg-14)
*209:          (b-or *194 (b-or (b-and *179 *195) (b-and b-reg-13 *195)))
*210:          (b-xor *207 b-reg-15)
*211:          (b-or a-reg-13 (b-or *197 (b-and a-reg-13 *197)))
*212:          (b-and *179 *198)
*213:          (b-and a-reg-14 b-reg-14)
*214:          (b-or *199 (b-or (b-and a-reg-13 *200)
                                (b-and b-reg-13 *200)))
*215:          (b-xor a-reg-15 b-reg-15)
*216:          (b-or *199 (b-or (b-and a-reg-13 *202)
                                (b-and b-reg-13 *202)))
*217:          (b-and a-reg-13 *203)
*218:          (b-nand *18 a-reg-16)
*219:          (b-or *208 (b-or (b-and *193 *206) (b-and b-reg-14 *206)))
*220:          (b-not a-reg-16)
*221:          (b-and *207 b-reg-15)
*222:          (b-or *208 (b-or (b-and *193 *209) (b-and b-reg-14 *209)))
*223:          (b-xor *220 b-reg-16)
*224:          (b-or a-reg-14 (b-or *211 (b-and a-reg-14 *211)))
*225:          (b-and *193 *212)
*226:          (b-and a-reg-15 b-reg-15)
*227:          (b-or *213 (b-or (b-and a-reg-14 *214)
                                (b-and b-reg-14 *214)))
*228:          (b-xor a-reg-16 b-reg-16)
*229:          (b-or *213 (b-or (b-and a-reg-14 *216)
                                (b-and b-reg-14 *216)))
*230:          (b-and a-reg-14 *217)
*231:          (bitn *1 16)
*232:          (b-not no-store)
*233:          (b-nor i-reg-9 i-reg-10)
*234:          (b-not *2)
*235:          (bitn *1 6)
*236:          (b-not (b-or reset *235))
*237:          (b-or (bitn *1 1) reset)
*238:          (bitn *1 2)
*239:          (b-nand (b-nand *2 (b-and i-reg-4 i-reg-5))
                       (b-nand *234 (b-and i-reg-9 i-reg-10)))
*240:          (bitv
                (b-not (b-nand *236
                               (b-nand (b-nand *2 i-reg-1)
                                       (b-nand *234 i-reg-6))))
                (bitv (b-not (b-nand *236
```

```
                                (b-nand (b-nand *2 i-reg-2)
                                        (b-nand *234 i-reg-7))))
                    (bitv (b-not (b-nand *236
                                        (b-nand (b-nand *2 i-reg-3)
                                                (b-nand *234 i-reg-8))))
                        (btm))))
*241:       (b-or *238 *239)
*242:       (b-not *244)
*243:       (b-not *237)
*244:       (bitn *245 1)
*245:       (v-nth *240 reg-file)
*246:       (b-not *241)
*247:       (bitn *245 2)
*248:       (b-and *247 *244)
*249:       (bitn *245 3)
*250:       (b-or *247 (b-or *244 *248))
*251:       (bitn *245 4)
*252:       (b-and *249 *248)
*253:       (b-or *249 (b-or *250 (b-and *249 *250)))
*254:       (bitn *245 5)
*255:       (b-and *251 *252)
*256:       (b-or *251 (b-or *253 (b-and *251 *253)))
*257:       (bitn *245 6)
*258:       (b-and *254 *255)
*259:       (b-or *254 (b-or *256 (b-and *254 *256)))
*260:       (bitn *245 7)
*261:       (b-and *257 *258)
*262:       (b-or *257 (b-or *259 (b-and *257 *259)))
*263:       (bitn *245 8)
*264:       (b-and *260 *261)
*265:       (b-or *260 (b-or *262 (b-and *260 *262)))
*266:       (bitn *245 9)
*267:       (b-and *263 *264)
*268:       (b-or *263 (b-or *265 (b-and *263 *265)))
*269:       (bitn *245 10)
*270:       (b-and *266 *267)
*271:       (b-or *266 (b-or *268 (b-and *266 *268)))
*272:       (bitn *245 11)
*273:       (b-and *269 *270)
*274:       (b-or *269 (b-or *271 (b-and *269 *271)))
*275:       (bitn *245 12)
*276:       (b-and *272 *273)
*277:       (b-or *272 (b-or *274 (b-and *272 *274)))
*278:       (bitn *245 13)
*279:       (b-and *275 *276)
*280:       (b-or *275 (b-or *277 (b-and *275 *277)))
*281:       (bitn *245 14)
*282:       (b-and *278 *279)
```

```
*283:        (b-or *278 (b-or *280 (b-and *278 *280)))
*284:        (bitn *245 15)
*285:        (b-and *281 *282)
*286:        (b-or *281 (b-or *283 (b-and *281 *283)))
*287:        (bitn *245 16)
*288:        (b-and (bitn *1 8)
                  (b-nand (b-nand *2
                                  (b-and (b-not i-reg-4) i-reg-5))
                          (b-nand *234
                                  (b-and (b-not i-reg-9) i-reg-10))))
*289:        (b-xor *244 (b-not *247))
*290:        (b-not *288)
*291:        (b-xor *250 (b-not *249))
*292:        (b-xor *253 (b-not *251))
*293:        (b-xor *256 (b-not *254))
*294:        (b-xor *259 (b-not *257))
*295:        (b-xor *262 (b-not *260))
*296:        (b-xor *265 (b-not *263))
*297:        (b-xor *268 (b-not *266))
*298:        (b-xor *271 (b-not *269))
*299:        (b-xor *274 (b-not *272))
*300:        (b-xor *277 (b-not *275))
*301:        (b-xor *280 (b-not *278))
*302:        (b-xor *283 (b-not *281))
*303:        (b-xor *286 (b-not *284))
*304:        (b-xor (b-or *284 (b-or *286 (b-and *284 *286)))
                  (b-not *287))
*305:        (b-nand *20 a-reg-1)
*306:        (b-nand *18 a-reg-1)
*307:        (b-or *221 (b-or (b-and *207 *219) (b-and b-reg-15 *219)))
*308:        (b-and *220 b-reg-16)
*309:        (b-or *221 (b-or (b-and *207 *222) (b-and b-reg-15 *222)))
*310:        (b-or a-reg-15 (b-or *224 (b-and a-reg-15 *224)))
*311:        (b-and *207 *225)
*312:        (b-and a-reg-16 b-reg-16)
*313:        (b-or *226
                  (b-or (b-and a-reg-15 *227)
                        (b-and b-reg-15 *227)))
*314:        (b-or *226
                  (b-or (b-and a-reg-15 *229)
                        (b-and b-reg-15 *229)))
*315:        (b-and a-reg-15 *230)
*316:        (b-and *16 i-reg-11)
*317:        (b-xor *307 *223)
*318:        (b-equv *220 b-reg-16)
*319:        (b-xor *309 *223)
*320:        (b-xor *310 *220)
*321:        (b-xor *311 *220)
```

```
*322:          (b-xor *313 *228)
*323:          (b-equv a-reg-16 b-reg-16)
*324:          (b-xor *314 *228)
*325:          (b-xor *315 a-reg-16)
*326:          (b-nand
                (b-nand *24
                 (b-nand
                  (b-nand *21
                   (b-nand
                    (b-nand *19
                          (b-nand *306 (b-nand *20 *25)))
                     (b-nand *22
                          (b-nand (b-nand *18 *38)
                               (b-nand *20
                                    (b-or a-reg-1 b-reg-1))))))
                   (b-nand *28
                        (b-nand (b-nand *19 (b-nand *29 *23))
                             (b-nand *22 (b-nand *32 *23))))))
                (b-nand *34
                 (b-nand
                  (b-nand *21
                   (b-nand (b-nand *19
                               (b-nand (b-nand *18 (b-not *27))
                                    (b-nand *20 (b-xor *26 *27))))
                        (b-nand *22
                             (b-nand *31
                                  (b-nand *20 (b-not *25))))))
                   (b-nand *28
                    (b-nand
                     (b-nand *19
                          (b-nand *29
                               (b-nand *20 (b-xor c-flag *30))))
                      (b-nand *22 (b-nand *31 *305)))))))
*327:          (b-nand
                (b-nand *24
                 (b-nand
                  (b-nand *21
                   (b-nand
                    (b-nand *19 (b-nand *32 (b-nand *20 *35)))
                     (b-nand *22
                      (b-nand (b-nand *18 *47)
                           (b-nand *20 (b-or a-reg-2 b-reg-2))))))
                   (b-nand *28
                        (b-nand (b-nand *19
                                    (b-nand (b-nand *18 *39) *33))
                             (b-nand *22 (b-nand *40 *33))))))
                (b-nand *34
                 (b-nand
```

```
        (b-nand *21
         (b-nand
          (b-nand *19
                  (b-nand (b-nand *18 (b-xor *42 *37))
                          (b-nand *20 (b-xor *45 *37))))
           (b-nand *22
                  (b-nand (b-nand *18 (b-xor a-reg-1 *35))
                          (b-nand *20 (b-xor *25 *35)))))))
          (b-nand *28
           (b-nand
            (b-nand *19
                  (b-nand (b-nand *18 (b-xor *38 *39))
                          (b-nand *20 (b-xor *49 *39))))
           (b-nand *22
                  (b-nand (b-nand *18 (b-xor a-reg-1 a-reg-2))
                          *23)))))))
*328:         (b-nand
          (b-nand *24
           (b-nand
            (b-nand *21
             (b-nand
              (b-nand *19
                  (b-nand *40 (b-nand *20 *43)))
              (b-nand *22
                  (b-nand (b-nand *18 *60)
                          (b-nand *20
                                  (b-or a-reg-3 b-reg-3))))))
            (b-nand *28
                  (b-nand (b-nand *19
                                  (b-nand (b-nand *18 *48) *41))
                          (b-nand *22 (b-nand *51 *41))))))
          (b-nand *34
           (b-nand
            (b-nand *21
             (b-nand
              (b-nand *19
                  (b-nand (b-nand *18 (b-xor *53 *46))
                          (b-nand *20 (b-xor *56 *46))))
              (b-nand *22
                  (b-nand (b-nand *18 (b-xor *58 *43))
                          (b-nand *20 (b-xor *59 *43))))))
            (b-nand *28
             (b-nand
              (b-nand *19
                  (b-nand (b-nand *18 (b-xor *61 *48))
                          (b-nand *20 (b-xor *63 *48))))
              (b-nand *22
                  (b-nand (b-nand *18 (b-xor *50 a-reg-3))
```

```
                                     *33))))))
*329:              (b-nand
                   (b-nand *24
                    (b-nand
                     (b-nand *21
                      (b-nand
                       (b-nand *19
                              (b-nand *51 (b-nand *20 *54)))
                        (b-nand *22
                              (b-nand (b-nand *18 *73)
                                     (b-nand *20
                                            (b-or a-reg-4 b-reg-4))))))
                       (b-nand *28
                             (b-nand (b-nand *19
                                            (b-nand (b-nand *18 *62) *52))
                                    (b-nand *22 (b-nand *64 *52))))))
                    (b-nand *34
                     (b-nand
                      (b-nand *21
                       (b-nand
                        (b-nand *19
                               (b-nand (b-nand *18 (b-xor *66 *57))
                                      (b-nand *20 (b-xor *69 *57))))
                         (b-nand *22
                               (b-nand (b-nand *18 (b-xor *71 *54))
                                      (b-nand *20 (b-xor *72 *54))))))
                       (b-nand *28
                        (b-nand
                         (b-nand *19
                                (b-nand (b-nand *18 (b-xor *74 *62))
                                       (b-nand *20 (b-xor *76 *62))))
                          (b-nand *22
                                (b-nand (b-nand *18 (b-xor *77 a-reg-4))
                                       *41)))))))
*330:              (b-nand
                   (b-nand *24
                    (b-nand
                     (b-nand *21
                      (b-nand
                       (b-nand *19
                              (b-nand *64 (b-nand *20 *67)))
                        (b-nand *22
                              (b-nand (b-nand *18 *87)
                                     (b-nand *20
                                            (b-or a-reg-5 b-reg-5))))))
                       (b-nand *28
                             (b-nand (b-nand *19
                                            (b-nand (b-nand *18 *75) *65))
```

```
                              (b-nand *22 (b-nand *78 *65))))))
              (b-nand *34
               (b-nand
                (b-nand *21
                 (b-nand
                  (b-nand *19
                         (b-nand (b-nand *18 (b-xor *80 *70))
                                 (b-nand *20 (b-xor *83 *70))))
                  (b-nand *22
                         (b-nand (b-nand *18 (b-xor *85 *67))
                                 (b-nand *20 (b-xor *86 *67))))))
                (b-nand *28
                 (b-nand
                  (b-nand *19
                         (b-nand (b-nand *18 (b-xor *88 *75))
                                 (b-nand *20 (b-xor *90 *75))))
                  (b-nand *22
                         (b-nand (b-nand *18 (b-xor *91 a-reg-5))
                                 *52)))))))
*331:         (b-nand
              (b-nand *24
               (b-nand
                (b-nand *21
                 (b-nand
                  (b-nand *19
                         (b-nand *78 (b-nand *20 *81)))
                  (b-nand *22
                         (b-nand (b-nand *18 *101)
                                 (b-nand *20
                                         (b-or a-reg-6 b-reg-6))))))
                (b-nand *28
                       (b-nand (b-nand *19
                                      (b-nand (b-nand *18 *89) *79))
                               (b-nand *22 (b-nand *92 *79))))))
              (b-nand *34
               (b-nand
                (b-nand *21
                 (b-nand
                  (b-nand *19
                         (b-nand (b-nand *18 (b-xor *94 *84))
                                 (b-nand *20 (b-xor *97 *84))))
                  (b-nand *22
                         (b-nand (b-nand *18 (b-xor *99 *81))
                                 (b-nand *20 (b-xor *100 *81))))))
                (b-nand *28
                 (b-nand
                  (b-nand *19
                         (b-nand (b-nand *18 (b-xor *102 *89))
```

```
                              (b-nand *20 (b-xor *104 *89))))
                  (b-nand *22
                         (b-nand (b-nand *18 (b-xor *105 a-reg-6))
                                 *65)))))))
*332:          (b-nand
            (b-nand *24
             (b-nand
              (b-nand *21
               (b-nand
                (b-nand *19 (b-nand *92 (b-nand *20 *95)))
                (b-nand *22
                       (b-nand (b-nand *18 *115)
                               (b-nand *20
                                      (b-or a-reg-7 b-reg-7))))))
               (b-nand *28
                      (b-nand (b-nand *19
                                     (b-nand (b-nand *18 *103) *93))
                              (b-nand *22 (b-nand *106 *93))))))
              (b-nand *34
               (b-nand
                (b-nand *21
                 (b-nand
                  (b-nand *19
                         (b-nand (b-nand *18 (b-xor *108 *98))
                                 (b-nand *20 (b-xor *111 *98))))
                  (b-nand *22
                         (b-nand (b-nand *18 (b-xor *113 *95))
                                 (b-nand *20 (b-xor *114 *95))))))
                (b-nand *28
                 (b-nand
                  (b-nand *19
                         (b-nand (b-nand *18 (b-xor *116 *103))
                                 (b-nand *20 (b-xor *118 *103))))
                  (b-nand *22
                         (b-nand (b-nand *18 (b-xor *119 a-reg-7))
                                 *79)))))))
*333:          (b-nand
            (b-nand *24
             (b-nand
              (b-nand *21
               (b-nand
                (b-nand *19
                       (b-nand *106 (b-nand *20 *109)))
                (b-nand *22
                       (b-nand (b-nand *18 *129)
                               (b-nand *20
                                      (b-or a-reg-8 b-reg-8))))))
               (b-nand *28
```

```
                        (b-nand (b-nand *19
                                        (b-nand (b-nand *18 *117) *107))
                              (b-nand *22 (b-nand *120 *107))))))
                (b-nand *34
                 (b-nand
                  (b-nand *21
                   (b-nand
                    (b-nand *19
                            (b-nand (b-nand *18 (b-xor *122 *112))
                                    (b-nand *20 (b-xor *125 *112))))
                    (b-nand *22
                            (b-nand (b-nand *18 (b-xor *127 *109))
                                    (b-nand *20 (b-xor *128 *109))))))
                   (b-nand *28
                    (b-nand
                     (b-nand *19
                             (b-nand (b-nand *18 (b-xor *130 *117))
                                     (b-nand *20 (b-xor *132 *117))))
                     (b-nand *22
                             (b-nand (b-nand *18 (b-xor *133 a-reg-8))
                                     *93)))))))
*334:          (b-nand
                (b-nand *24
                 (b-nand
                  (b-nand *21
                   (b-nand
                    (b-nand *19
                            (b-nand *120 (b-nand *20 *123)))
                    (b-nand *22
                            (b-nand (b-nand *18 *143)
                                    (b-nand *20
                                            (b-or a-reg-9 b-reg-9))))))
                   (b-nand *28
                           (b-nand (b-nand *19
                                           (b-nand (b-nand *18 *131) *121))
                                 (b-nand *22 (b-nand *134 *121))))))
                (b-nand *34
                 (b-nand
                  (b-nand *21
                   (b-nand
                    (b-nand *19
                            (b-nand (b-nand *18 (b-xor *136 *126))
                                    (b-nand *20 (b-xor *139 *126))))
                    (b-nand *22
                            (b-nand (b-nand *18 (b-xor *141 *123))
                                    (b-nand *20 (b-xor *142 *123))))))
                   (b-nand *28
                    (b-nand
```

```
                     (b-nand *19
                            (b-nand (b-nand *18 (b-xor *144 *131))
                                    (b-nand *20 (b-xor *146 *131))))
                     (b-nand *22
                            (b-nand (b-nand *18 (b-xor *147 a-reg-9))
                                    *107)))))))
*335:           (b-nand
                 (b-nand *24
                  (b-nand
                   (b-nand *21
                    (b-nand
                     (b-nand *19
                            (b-nand *134 (b-nand *20 *137)))
                     (b-nand *22
                            (b-nand (b-nand *18 *157)
                                    (b-nand *20
                                           (b-or a-reg-10 b-reg-10))))))
                   (b-nand *28
                          (b-nand (b-nand *19
                                         (b-nand (b-nand *18 *145) *135))
                                 (b-nand *22 (b-nand *148 *135))))))
                 (b-nand *34
                  (b-nand
                   (b-nand *21
                    (b-nand
                     (b-nand *19
                            (b-nand (b-nand *18 (b-xor *150 *140))
                                    (b-nand *20 (b-xor *153 *140))))
                     (b-nand *22
                            (b-nand (b-nand *18 (b-xor *155 *137))
                                    (b-nand *20 (b-xor *156 *137))))))
                   (b-nand *28
                    (b-nand
                     (b-nand *19
                            (b-nand (b-nand *18 (b-xor *158 *145))
                                    (b-nand *20 (b-xor *160 *145))))
                     (b-nand *22
                            (b-nand (b-nand *18 (b-xor *161 a-reg-10))
                                    *121)))))))
*336:           (b-nand
                 (b-nand *24
                  (b-nand
                   (b-nand *21
                    (b-nand
                     (b-nand *19
                            (b-nand *148 (b-nand *20 *151)))
                     (b-nand *22
                            (b-nand (b-nand *18 *171)
```

```
                                  (b-nand *20
                                          (b-or a-reg-11 b-reg-11))))))
                (b-nand *28
                     (b-nand (b-nand *19
                                     (b-nand (b-nand *18 *159) *149))
                             (b-nand *22 (b-nand *162 *149))))))
                (b-nand *34
                 (b-nand
                  (b-nand *21
                   (b-nand
                    (b-nand *19
                            (b-nand (b-nand *18 (b-xor *164 *154))
                                    (b-nand *20 (b-xor *167 *154))))
                    (b-nand *22
                            (b-nand (b-nand *18 (b-xor *169 *151))
                                    (b-nand *20 (b-xor *170 *151))))))
                  (b-nand *28
                   (b-nand
                    (b-nand *19
                            (b-nand (b-nand *18 (b-xor *172 *159))
                                    (b-nand *20 (b-xor *174 *159))))
                    (b-nand *22
                            (b-nand (b-nand *18 (b-xor *175 a-reg-11))
                                    *135)))))))
*337:           (b-nand
                 (b-nand *24
                  (b-nand
                   (b-nand *21
                    (b-nand
                     (b-nand *19
                             (b-nand *162 (b-nand *20 *165)))
                     (b-nand *22
                             (b-nand (b-nand *18 *185)
                                     (b-nand *20
                                             (b-or a-reg-12 b-reg-12))))))
                   (b-nand *28
                        (b-nand (b-nand *19
                                        (b-nand (b-nand *18 *173) *163))
                                (b-nand *22 (b-nand *176 *163))))))
                 (b-nand *34
                  (b-nand
                   (b-nand *21
                    (b-nand
                     (b-nand *19
                             (b-nand (b-nand *18 (b-xor *178 *168))
                                     (b-nand *20 (b-xor *181 *168))))
                     (b-nand *22
                             (b-nand (b-nand *18 (b-xor *183 *165))
```

```
                             (b-nand *20 (b-xor *184 *165))))))
                (b-nand *28
                 (b-nand
                  (b-nand *19
                        (b-nand (b-nand *18 (b-xor *186 *173))
                                (b-nand *20 (b-xor *188 *173))))
                  (b-nand *22
                        (b-nand (b-nand *18 (b-xor *189 a-reg-12))
                                *149)))))))
*338:           (b-nand
                 (b-nand *24
                  (b-nand
                   (b-nand *21
                    (b-nand
                     (b-nand *19
                           (b-nand *176 (b-nand *20 *179)))
                     (b-nand *22
                           (b-nand (b-nand *18 *199)
                                   (b-nand *20
                                         (b-or a-reg-13 b-reg-13))))))
                   (b-nand *28
                         (b-nand (b-nand *19
                                       (b-nand (b-nand *18 *187) *177))
                                 (b-nand *22 (b-nand *190 *177))))))
                 (b-nand *34
                  (b-nand
                   (b-nand *21
                    (b-nand
                     (b-nand *19
                           (b-nand (b-nand *18 (b-xor *192 *182))
                                   (b-nand *20 (b-xor *195 *182))))
                     (b-nand *22
                           (b-nand (b-nand *18 (b-xor *197 *179))
                                   (b-nand *20 (b-xor *198 *179))))))
                   (b-nand *28
                    (b-nand
                     (b-nand *19
                           (b-nand (b-nand *18 (b-xor *200 *187))
                                   (b-nand *20 (b-xor *202 *187))))
                     (b-nand *22
                           (b-nand (b-nand *18 (b-xor *203 a-reg-13))
                                   *163)))))))
*339:           (b-nand
                 (b-nand *24
                  (b-nand
                   (b-nand *21
                    (b-nand
                     (b-nand *19
```

```
                             (b-nand *190 (b-nand *20 *193)))
                  (b-nand *22
                          (b-nand (b-nand *18 *213)
                                  (b-nand *20
                                          (b-or a-reg-14 b-reg-14))))))
            (b-nand *28
                    (b-nand (b-nand *19
                                    (b-nand (b-nand *18 *201) *191))
                            (b-nand *22 (b-nand *204 *191))))))
         (b-nand *34
          (b-nand
           (b-nand *21
            (b-nand
             (b-nand *19
                     (b-nand (b-nand *18 (b-xor *206 *196))
                             (b-nand *20 (b-xor *209 *196))))
             (b-nand *22
                     (b-nand (b-nand *18 (b-xor *211 *193))
                             (b-nand *20 (b-xor *212 *193))))))
           (b-nand *28
            (b-nand
             (b-nand *19
                     (b-nand (b-nand *18 (b-xor *214 *201))
                             (b-nand *20 (b-xor *216 *201))))
             (b-nand *22
                     (b-nand (b-nand *18 (b-xor *217 a-reg-14))
                             *177)))))))
*340:       (b-nand
             (b-nand *24
              (b-nand
               (b-nand *21
                (b-nand
                 (b-nand *19
                         (b-nand *204 (b-nand *20 *207)))
                 (b-nand *22
                         (b-nand (b-nand *18 *226)
                                 (b-nand *20
                                         (b-or a-reg-15 b-reg-15))))))
               (b-nand *28
                       (b-nand (b-nand *19
                                       (b-nand (b-nand *18 *215) *205))
                               (b-nand *22 (b-nand *218 *205))))))
             (b-nand *34
              (b-nand
               (b-nand *21
                (b-nand
                 (b-nand *19
                         (b-nand (b-nand *18 (b-xor *219 *210))
```

```
                                   (b-nand *20 (b-xor *222 *210))))
                    (b-nand *22
                            (b-nand (b-nand *18 (b-xor *224 *207))
                                    (b-nand *20 (b-xor *225 *207))))))
                 (b-nand *28
                  (b-nand
                   (b-nand *19
                           (b-nand (b-nand *18 (b-xor *227 *215))
                                   (b-nand *20 (b-xor *229 *215))))
                    (b-nand *22
                            (b-nand (b-nand *18 (b-xor *230 a-reg-15))
                                    *191)))))))
*341:            (b-nand
                 (b-nand *24
                  (b-nand
                   (b-nand *21
                    (b-nand
                     (b-nand *19
                             (b-nand *218 (b-nand *20 *220)))
                      (b-nand *22
                              (b-nand (b-nand *18 *312)
                                      (b-nand *20
                                              (b-or a-reg-16 b-reg-16))))))
                   (b-nand *28
                    (b-nand (b-nand *19 (b-not (b-nand *18 *228)))
                            (b-nand *22
                                    (b-nand *218 (b-nand *20 c-flag)))))))
                  (b-nand *34
                   (b-nand
                    (b-nand *21
                            (b-nand (b-nand *19
                                            (b-nand (b-nand *18 *317)
                                                    (b-nand *20 *319)))
                                    (b-nand *22
                                            (b-nand (b-nand *18 *320)
                                                    (b-nand *20 *321)))))
                    (b-nand *28
                            (b-nand (b-nand *19
                                            (b-nand (b-nand *18 *322)
                                                    (b-nand *20 *324)))
                                    (b-nand *22
                                            (b-nand (b-nand *18 *325)
                                                    *205)))))))
*342:            (b-nor i-reg-4 i-reg-5)
*343:            (b-not *342)
*344:            (b-not *233)
```

Chapter 15

Conclusions

Formal mathematics will play an ever-increasing role in the design of computing systems. The operation of a computing system must be deterministic in the sense that users must know what the system does. To insure computing system determinancy, the specification of all aspects of computer system operation must have an unambigious mathematical basis and systems should be verified to satisfy their specifications. Because "to err is human" we believe we need all the help we can get when verifying the correspondence between implementations and specifications. Thus we advocate the use of formal, mathematical specification languages, formal hardware and software descriptions and semantics, and mechanical deduction engines to check the correspondence.

The accurate specification of computing system operation begins with the hardware itself. Several aspects of the FM8501 formalization are:

- arbitrary sized combinational logic descriptions

- characterization of hardware devices within a formal theory

- mathematically constructed datatypes for bit-vectors, natural numbers, and integers

- formal representation of microcode

- mathematical characterization of individual microcode states, transitions, and timing considerations

- mathematical specification of von Neumann like devices

- mechanically checked equivalence of two large and complex von Neumann machines

I find the ability to prove that circuits have mathematical properties most interesting. Consider for example the adder verified. The axiomatization for natural numbers began with a Peano-like definition, where addition is merely concatenation. These concepts are simple, believable, compact and abstract. We then defined a function for binary addition and we proved that it implemented the abstract operation of addition. We then expanded the function into a gate graph that is not simple, believable, compact or abstract–but it is correct.

The verification of FM8501 is interesting as all proofs were performed by a heuristically guided mechanical theorem-prover. The theorem-prover allowed a very large number of proofs to be performed, certainly many more than I could have proved by hand. Additionally, the theorem-prover assisted me in formalizing the FM8501: many typograpical errors were found as theorem-prover commands were invoked, bugs in false "theorems" were quickly located, and the ability to execute hardware definitions assisted in the development of formal hardware descriptions and specifications.

A number of things could be improved with regard to FM8501. A better mechanism for representing clocks is needed. A great deal of energy was spent insuring the correspondence between the low-level and the high-level clocks. The ability to have quantified expressions would have allowed for a more compact presentation with respect to the FM8501 clocking.

I am also unhappy about the characterization of external devices, such as `real-mem`, since we have not written down a formal characterization of the behavior assumed of the devices. Because we have no independent specification of memory, for example, it is unclear how one might go about proving that a particular memory design meets the requirements of the FM8501. Additionally, the characterization of external devices are wrapped up in the same function which specifies the microprocessor. Since all storage devices are represented at the "top-level," it is difficult to glue together separate synchronous machines and we must externally select which formal function parameters are to be implemented with hardware. Also, since external devices are included in the "top-level" specification, it is difficult to know what exactly what is external (or internal). More work is needed here.

This work does not address real world considerations of layout, fan-in, and fan-out. The common subexpressions generated when expanding a circuit may be used so many times that implementation may require buffering or subexpression duplication. Further work is needed to ensure a mechanical conversion of expanded circuits into manufacturable devices.

A good deal of meta-knowledge is required when using the Boyer-Moore theorem-prover. This mechanical theorem-prover is an experts' system, written by experts and for use by experts. Without J Moore to "train" the theorem-prover, it would have been impossible to prove all of the theorems listed in the Appendix. The future is bright; as theorem-prover's become "smarter" the amount of required user meta-knowledge will lessen.

We speculate that formal verification can encourage the production of faster, more efficient hardware. There are two reasons for this. First, by permitting the designer to describe arbitrarily sized circuits, we remove him from the combinatorial explosion encountered when one considers particular sizes. Second, by giving the designer a mechanical assistant capable of confirming the correctness of circuits, we permit the designer to introduce efficiencies (i.e., complexities) of which he would otherwise be afraid.

The methods used in the verification of FM8501 can be extended into the areas of automatic design. A library of commonly used functions was created during the process of creating FM8501. It should be possible to take (some) specifications and mechanically convert them into circuits.

Testing presents another exciting avenue to explore. During the verification of FM8501, the semantics of the logical functions were assumed. Composition was also assumed to work. Neither of these may actually be true with an implementation. Gates may be flawed, and wires may be broken. The ability to do test generation can be enhanced with the tools used here. The theorem-prover could be used to help determine what kinds of tests would be necessary for various circuits. Test is certainly an important problem. Verification of the circuit is only the first half of the job; it also has to work after it is manufactured.

The verification of FM8501 was hard work, but it was worth the effort. The ability to specify something as complicated as a microprocessor with only several pages of formulae is clearly a step forward. The specification of FM8501 presented is unambigious and mathematical. This must certainly be the course of the future.

Appendix:
FM8501 Formulas

This appendix presents the formulas defined and proved in the construction
of FM8501. Before presenting the formulas, the work required to generate the
formulas is dimensioned.

The effort expended in defining and proving the formulas in this appendix
was approximately 13 man months. This includes the definition and proof of a
simple DMA-like device on which we experimented with the use of oracles. Five
man months were spent in the deveolpment of the ALU and the remainder was
on the sequential logic part. Roughly 80 hours of Symbolics 3600 CPU time was
required to develop the ALU, and twice that much was used in the development
of sequential logic. To process the final set of formulas presented in the appendix
takes less than two hours on a Symbolics 3600.

The list of definitions and theorems presented below represent the input to
the Boyer-Moore theorem-prover for defining and proving correct the FM8501
microprocessor. This formula list starts by proving a number of mathematical
lemmas about natural numbers and integers. The hardware primitives are then
defined and composed into the ALU, followed by the specification and verification
of the ALU. Next, the FM8501 hardware is defined, followed by the theorems
which demonstrate the operation of each microinstruction. The microinstruction
theorems are composed into a macroinstruction theorem. The presentation of
the FM8501 specification follows, with the proof of the theorems demonstrating
the correctness of FM8501.

```
;;;;;;;;;;;;;;;;;;;;;;;;;;;;;;;;;;;;;;;;;;;;;;;;;;;;;;;;;;;;;;;;;;;;;;;;
;;                                                                    ;;
;;                      Lemmas about PLUS                             ;;
;;                                                                    ;;
;;;;;;;;;;;;;;;;;;;;;;;;;;;;;;;;;;;;;;;;;;;;;;;;;;;;;;;;;;;;;;;;;;;;;;;;

(prove-lemma plus-1 (rewrite)
  (equal (plus 1 x) (add1 x)))

(prove-lemma plus-right-id (rewrite)
  (implies (not (numberp y))
           (equal (plus x y) (fix x))))

(prove-lemma plus-add1 (rewrite)
  (equal (plus x (add1 y))
         (if (numberp y)
             (add1 (plus x y))
             (add1 x))))

(prove-lemma commutativity2-of-plus (rewrite)
  (equal (plus x (plus y z))
         (plus y (plus x z))))

(prove-lemma commutativity-of-plus (rewrite)
  (equal (plus x y) (plus y x)))

(prove-lemma associativity-of-plus (rewrite)
  (equal (plus (plus x y) z)
         (plus x (plus y z))))

(prove-lemma plus-equal-0 (rewrite)
  (equal (equal (plus a b) 0)
         (and (zerop a) (zerop b))))

(prove-lemma plus-cancellation (rewrite)
  (equal (equal (plus a b) (plus a c))
         (equal (fix b) (fix c))))
```

```
;;;;;;;;;;;;;;;;;;;;;;;;;;;;;;;;;;;;;;;;;;;;;;;;;;;;;;;;;;;;;;;;;;;;;;;;;;;;
;;                                                                      ;;
;;                       Lemmas about TIMES                             ;;
;;                                                                      ;;
;;;;;;;;;;;;;;;;;;;;;;;;;;;;;;;;;;;;;;;;;;;;;;;;;;;;;;;;;;;;;;;;;;;;;;;;;;;;

(prove-lemma times-zero2 (rewrite)
  (implies (not (numberp y))
           (equal (times x y) 0)))

(prove-lemma distributivity-of-times-over-plus (rewrite)
  (equal (times x (plus y z))
         (plus (times x y) (times x z))))

(prove-lemma times-add1 (rewrite)
  (equal (times x (add1 y))
         (if (numberp y)
             (plus x (times x y))
             (fix x))))

(prove-lemma commutativity-of-times (rewrite)
  (equal (times x y) (times y x)))

(prove-lemma commutativity2-of-times (rewrite)
  (equal (times x (times y z))
         (times y (times x z))))

(prove-lemma associativity-of-times (rewrite)
  (equal (times (times x y) z)
         (times x (times y z))))

(prove-lemma equal-times-0 (rewrite)
  (equal (equal (times x y) 0)
         (or (zerop x) (zerop y))))

(prove-lemma times-1 (rewrite)
  (equal (times 1 x) (fix x)))

(prove-lemma equal-bools (rewrite)
  (implies (and (or (equal bool1 t) (equal bool1 f))
                (or (equal bool2 t) (equal bool2 f)))
           (equal (equal bool1 bool2)
                  (and (implies bool1 bool2)
                       (implies bool2 bool1)))))

(disable equal-bools)

(prove-lemma lessp-times (rewrite)
  (equal (lessp (times y x) (times x z))
         (and (not (zerop x))
```

```
           (lessp y z)))

  ((enable equal-bools)))

(prove-lemma times-2-not-1 (rewrite)
  (not (equal (times 2 x) 1)))

(prove-lemma lessp-crock1 (rewrite)
  (equal (lessp (plus z (times 2 v w)) w)
         (and (zerop v) (lessp z w))))
```

```
;;;;;;;;;;;;;;;;;;;;;;;;;;;;;;;;;;;;;;;;;;;;;;;;;;;;;;;;;;;;;;;;;;;;;;;;
;;                                                                    ;;
;;                       Lemmas about EXP                             ;;
;;                                                                    ;;
;;;;;;;;;;;;;;;;;;;;;;;;;;;;;;;;;;;;;;;;;;;;;;;;;;;;;;;;;;;;;;;;;;;;;;;;

(defn exp (i j)
  (if (zerop j)
      1
      (times i (exp i (sub1 j)))))

(prove-lemma exp-plus (rewrite)
  (equal (exp i (plus j k))
         (times (exp i j) (exp i k))))

(prove-lemma exp-of-0 (rewrite)
  (equal (exp 0 k) (if (zerop k) 1 0)))

(prove-lemma exp-of-1 (rewrite)
  (equal (exp 1 k) 1))

(prove-lemma exp-by-0 (rewrite)
  (equal (exp x 0) 1))

(prove-lemma exp-times (rewrite)
  (equal (exp (times i j) k)
         (times (exp i k) (exp j k))))

(prove-lemma exp-2-never-0 (rewrite)
  (lessp 0 (exp 2 i)))
```

```
;;;;;;;;;;;;;;;;;;;;;;;;;;;;;;;;;;;;;;;;;;;;;;;;;;;;;;;;;;;;;;;;;;;;;;;;;;;
;;                                                                       ;;
;;                    Lemmas about DIFFERENCE                            ;;
;;                                                                       ;;
;;;;;;;;;;;;;;;;;;;;;;;;;;;;;;;;;;;;;;;;;;;;;;;;;;;;;;;;;;;;;;;;;;;;;;;;;;;

(prove-lemma difference-elim (elim)
  (implies (and (numberp y) (not (lessp y x)))
           (equal (plus x (difference y x)) y)))

(prove-lemma difference-2 (rewrite)
  (equal (difference x 2)
         (sub1 (sub1 x))))

(prove-lemma difference-x-x (rewrite)
  (equal (difference x x) 0))

(prove-lemma difference-plus (rewrite)
  (equal (difference (plus j x) j)
         (fix x)))

(prove-lemma difference-plus-cancellation (rewrite)
  (equal (difference (plus a x) (plus a y))
         (difference x y)))

(prove-lemma pathological-difference (rewrite)
  (implies (lessp x y) (equal (difference x y) 0)))

(prove-lemma difference-crock1 (rewrite)
  (equal (difference (plus x (difference y z)) y)
         (if (lessp y z)
             (difference x y)
             (difference x z))))

(prove-lemma difference-difference (rewrite)
  (equal (difference (difference x y) z)
         (difference x (plus y z))))

(prove-lemma lessp-difference (rewrite)
  (equal (lessp (difference x y) x)
         (and (not (zerop x)) (not (zerop y)))))

(prove-lemma difference-add1 nil
  (equal (difference (add1 x) y)
         (if (lessp y (add1 x))
             (add1 (difference x y))
             0)))
```

```
;;;;;;;;;;;;;;;;;;;;;;;;;;;;;;;;;;;;;;;;;;;;;;;;;;;;;;;;;;;;;;;;;;;;;;;;;
;;                                                                     ;;
;;                Lemmas about QUOTIENT and REMAINDER                  ;;
;;                                                                     ;;
;;;;;;;;;;;;;;;;;;;;;;;;;;;;;;;;;;;;;;;;;;;;;;;;;;;;;;;;;;;;;;;;;;;;;;;;;

(prove-lemma remainder-quotient (rewrite)
  (equal (plus (remainder x y)
               (times y (quotient x y)))
         (fix x)))

(prove-lemma remainder-by-1 (rewrite)
  (equal (remainder y 1) 0))

(prove-lemma remainder-by-nonnumber (rewrite)
  (implies (not (numberp x))
           (equal (remainder y x) (fix y))))

(prove-lemma lessp-remainder (rewrite generalize)
  (equal (lessp (remainder x y) y)
         (not (zerop y))))

(prove-lemma remainder-quotient-elim (elim)
  (implies (and (not (zerop y)) (numberp x))
           (equal (plus (remainder x y)
                        (times y (quotient x y)))
                  x)))

(prove-lemma remainder-x-x (rewrite)
  (equal (remainder x x) 0))

(prove-lemma remainder-plus (rewrite)
  (equal (remainder (plus j x) j)
         (remainder x j)))

(prove-lemma remainder-plus-times (rewrite)
  (equal (remainder (plus x (times i j)) j)
         (remainder x j)))

(prove-lemma remainder-plus-times-commuted (rewrite)
  (equal (remainder (plus x (times j i)) j)
         (remainder x j)))

(prove-lemma remainder-times (rewrite)
  (equal (remainder (times j i) j)
         0)
  ((use (remainder-plus-times (x 0)))
   (disable remainder-plus-times)))
```

```
(prove-lemma remainder-add1-times (rewrite)
  (equal (remainder (add1 (times j i)) j)
         (remainder 1 j))
  ((use (remainder-plus-times (x 1)))
   (disable remainder-plus-times)))

(prove-lemma quotient-plus-times (rewrite)
  (equal (quotient (plus x (times i j)) j)
         (if (zerop j)
             0
             (plus i (quotient x j)))))

(prove-lemma quotient-plus-times-commuted (rewrite)
  (equal (quotient (plus x (times j i)) j)
         (if (zerop j)
             0
             (plus i (quotient x j)))))

(prove-lemma quotient-times (rewrite)
  (equal (quotient (times j i) j)
         (if (zerop j) 0 (fix i)))
  ((use (quotient-plus-times (x 0)))
   (disable quotient-plus-times)))

(prove-lemma quotient-add1-times (rewrite)
  (equal (quotient (add1 (times j i)) j)
         (if (zerop j) 0 (plus i (quotient 1 j))))
  ((use (quotient-plus-times (x 1)))
   (disable quotient-plus-times)))

(disable times)

(prove-lemma times-distributes-over-remainder (rewrite)
  (equal (remainder (times x y) (times x z))
         (times x (remainder y z)))
  ((expand (remainder (times v x) (times x z)))))

(prove-lemma remainder-of-1 (rewrite)
  (equal (remainder 1 x)
         (if (equal x 1) 0 1))
  ((expand (remainder 1 x))))

(prove-lemma remainder-crock1 (rewrite)
  (implies (and (numberp x)
                (lessp x z)
                (numberp v)
                (numberp z)
                (not (equal z 0)))
           (equal (remainder (add1 (plus (times 2 x) (times 2 v z)))
```

```
                                   (times 2 z))
                         (add1 (times 2 x))))
  ((use (remainder-plus-times (x (add1 (times 2 x)))
                              (i v)
                              (j (times 2 z))))
   (disable remainder-plus-times)))

(prove-lemma times-2-distributes-over-remainder-add1 (rewrite)
  (equal (remainder (add1 (times 2 y)) (times 2 z))
         (add1 (times 2 (remainder y z)))))

(prove-lemma remainder-crock2 (rewrite)
  (implies (lessp v (exp 2 (sub1 size)))
           (equal (remainder (plus (times 2 v)
                                   (times 2 w (exp 2 (sub1 size))))
                             (times 2 (exp 2 (sub1 size))))
                  (times 2 v)))
  ((use (remainder-plus-times (x (times 2 v))
                              (i w)
                              (j (times 2 (exp 2 (sub1 size))))))
   (disable remainder-plus-times)))

(prove-lemma remainder-crock3 (rewrite)
  (equal (remainder (plus x (difference y z)) y)
         (if (lessp (plus x (difference y z)) y)
             (plus x (difference y z))
             (if (lessp y z)
                 (remainder x y)
                 (remainder (difference x z) y)))))

(prove-lemma remainder-of-0 (rewrite)
  (equal (remainder 0 x) 0))

(prove-lemma remainder-crock4 (rewrite)
  (equal (remainder (add1 (plus x (difference y z))) y)
         (if (lessp (add1 (plus x (difference y z))) y)
             (add1 (plus x (difference y z)))
             (if (lessp y z)
                 (remainder (add1 x) y)
                 (if (lessp z (add1 x))
                     (remainder (add1 (difference x z)) y)
                     0)))))
  ((use (remainder-crock3 (x (add1 x)))
        (difference-add1 (x x) (y z)))
   (disable remainder-crock3 difference lessp remainder)))

(prove-lemma quotient-2i-by-2 (rewrite)
  (and (equal (quotient (add1 (plus i i)) 2) (fix i))
       (equal (quotient (plus i i) 2) (fix i))))
```

```
(prove-lemma remainder-2i-by-2 (rewrite)
  (and (equal (remainder (add1 (plus i i)) 2) 1)
       (equal (remainder (plus i i) 2) 0)))
```

```
;;;;;;;;;;;;;;;;;;;;;;;;;;;;;;;;;;;;;;;;;;;;;;;;;;;;;;;;;;;;;;;;;;;;;;;;
;;                                                                  ;;
;;                    Boolean Operations                           ;;
;;                                                                  ;;
;;;;;;;;;;;;;;;;;;;;;;;;;;;;;;;;;;;;;;;;;;;;;;;;;;;;;;;;;;;;;;;;;;;;;;;;

(defn xor (x y)
  (if x (if y f t) (if y t f)))

(defn b-not (x)
  (if x f t))

(defn b-nand (x y)
  (if x (if y f t) t))

(defn b-nor (x y)
  (if x f (if y f t)))

(defn b-and (x y)
  (and x y))

(defn b-or (x y)
  (or x y))

(defn b-xor (x y)
  (if x (if y f t) (if y t f)))

(defn b-equv (x y)
  (if x (if y t f) (if y f t)))

(defn boolp (x)
  (or (truep x) (falsep x)))
```

```
;;;;;;;;;;;;;;;;;;;;;;;;;;;;;;;;;;;;;;;;;;;;;;;;;;;;;;;;;;;;;;;;;;;;;;;;;;;;;
;;                                                                         ;;
;;                 Primitive Bit Vector Operations                        ;;
;;                                                                         ;;
;;;;;;;;;;;;;;;;;;;;;;;;;;;;;;;;;;;;;;;;;;;;;;;;;;;;;;;;;;;;;;;;;;;;;;;;;;;;;

(add-shell bitv btm bitvp
           ((bit (one-of truep falsep) false)
            (vec (one-of bitvp) btm)))

(prove-lemma boolp-bit (generalize)
  (boolp (bit x)))

(defn fix-bv (x)
  (if (bitvp x) x (btm)))

(defn carry (c)
  (if c 1 0))

(defn size (a)
  (if (bitvp a)
      (if (equal a (btm))
          0
          (add1 (size (vec a))))
      0))

(defn trunc (a n)
  (if (zerop n)
      (btm)
      (bitv (bit a) (trunc (vec a) (sub1 n)))))

(defn compl (x)
  (if (bitvp x)
      (if (equal x (btm))
          (btm)
          (bitv (not (bit x)) (compl (vec x))))
      (btm)))

(defn incr (c x)
  (if (bitvp x)
      (if (equal x (btm))
          (btm)
          (bitv (xor c (bit x))
                (incr (and c (bit x)) (vec x))))
      (btm)))

(defn bitn (x n)
  (if (zerop n)
      f
```

```
      (if (equal n 1)
          (bit x)
          (bitn (vec x) (sub1 n)))))

(defn btmp (a)
  (if (bitvp a) (equal a (btm)) t))

(defn all-zerosp (a)
  (if (bitvp a)
      (if (equal a (btm))
          t
          (and (not (bit a)) (all-zerosp (vec a))))
      t))

(defn all-onesp (a)
  (if (bitvp a)
      (if (equal a (btm))
          t
          (and (bit a) (all-onesp (vec a))))
      t))

(prove-lemma size-of-trunc (rewrite)
  (equal (size (trunc a n)) (fix n)))

(prove-lemma size-of-compl (rewrite)
  (equal (size (compl a)) (size a)))

(prove-lemma size-of-incr (rewrite)
  (equal (size (incr c a)) (size a)))

(prove-lemma incr-f-noop (rewrite)
  (equal (incr f a) (fix-bv a)))

(prove-lemma size-0 (rewrite)
  (equal (equal (size x) 0) (btmp x)))
```

```
;;;;;;;;;;;;;;;;;;;;;;;;;;;;;;;;;;;;;;;;;;;;;;;;;;;;;;;;;;;;;;;;;;;;;;
;;                                                                  ;;
;;            Definitions about Logical Functions                   ;;
;;                                                                  ;;
;;;;;;;;;;;;;;;;;;;;;;;;;;;;;;;;;;;;;;;;;;;;;;;;;;;;;;;;;;;;;;;;;;;;;;


(defn v-not (a)                 ; Vector not
  (if (bitvp a)
      (if (equal a (btm))
          (btm)
          (bitv (not (bit a))
                (v-not (vec a))))
      (btm)))

(defn v-or (a b)                ; Vector or
  (if (bitvp a)
      (if (equal a (btm))
          (btm)
          (bitv (or (bit a) (bit b))
                (v-or (vec a) (vec b))))
      (btm)))

(defn v-and (a b)               ; Vector and
  (if (bitvp a)
      (if (equal a (btm))
          (btm)
          (bitv (and (bit a) (bit b))
                (v-and (vec a) (vec b))))
      (btm)))

(defn v-xor (a b)               ; Vector exclusive or
  (if (bitvp a)
      (if (equal a (btm))
          (btm)
          (bitv (xor (bit a) (bit b))
                (v-xor (vec a) (vec b))))
      (btm)))

(defn bv-not (a)                ; Bit vector not
  (if (bitvp a)
      (if (equal a (btm))
          (btm)
          (bitv (b-not (bit a))
                (bv-not (vec a))))
      (btm)))

(defn bv-or (a b)               ; Bit vector or
  (if (bitvp a)
```

```
     (if (equal a (btm))
         (btm)
         (bitv (b-or (bit a) (bit b))
               (bv-or (vec a) (vec b))))
     (btm)))

(defn bv-and (a b)              ; Bit vector and
  (if (bitvp a)
      (if (equal a (btm))
          (btm)
          (bitv (b-and (bit a) (bit b))
                (bv-and (vec a) (vec b))))
      (btm)))

(defn bv-xor (a b)              ; Bit vector exclusive or
  (if (bitvp a)
      (if (equal a (btm))
          (btm)
          (bitv (b-xor (bit a) (bit b))
                (bv-xor (vec a) (vec b))))
      (btm)))
```

```
;;;;;;;;;;;;;;;;;;;;;;;;;;;;;;;;;;;;;;;;;;;;;;;;;;;;;;;;;;;;;;;;;;;;;;;
;;                                                                   ;;
;;                TC Numbers and their Operations                    ;;
;;                                                                   ;;
;;;;;;;;;;;;;;;;;;;;;;;;;;;;;;;;;;;;;;;;;;;;;;;;;;;;;;;;;;;;;;;;;;;;;;;

(defn tcp (x)
  (or (numberp x)
      (and (negativep x)
           (not (zerop (negative-guts x))))))

(defn tc-in-rangep (x n)
  (if (zerop n)
      f
      (if (negativep x)
          (not (lessp (exp 2 (sub1 n))
                      (negative-guts x)))
          (lessp x (exp 2 (sub1 n))))))

(defn add (x y)
  (if (negativep x)
      (if (negativep y)
          (minus (plus (negative-guts x) (negative-guts y)))
          (if (lessp y (negative-guts x))
              (minus (difference (negative-guts x) y))
              (difference y (negative-guts x))))
      (if (negativep y)
          (if (lessp x (negative-guts y))
              (minus (difference (negative-guts y) x))
              (difference x (negative-guts y)))
          (plus x y))))

(prove-lemma commutativity2-of-add (rewrite)
  (equal (add x (add y z)) (add y (add x z))))

(prove-lemma commutativity-of-add (rewrite)
  (equal (add x y) (add y x)))

(prove-lemma associativity-of-add (rewrite)
  (equal (add (add x y) z) (add x (add y z)))
  ((disable add)))

(prove-lemma add-with-carry-of-negatives-is-negative nil
  (implies (and (tcp x)
                (tcp y)
                (negativep x)
                (negativep y))
           (negativep (add x (add y (carry c)))))))
```

```
(prove-lemma add-with-carry-of-non-negatives-is-non-negative nil
  (implies (and (tcp x)
                (tcp y)
                (not (negativep x))
                (not (negativep y)))
           (not (negativep (add x (add y (carry c)))))))

(prove-lemma overflow-lemma1 (rewrite)
  (implies (and (tcp x)
                (tcp y)
                (tc-in-rangep x n)
                (tc-in-rangep y n)
                (negativep (add x (add y (carry c)))))
           (not (negativep (add x (add y (add (carry c) (exp 2 n))))))))

(prove-lemma overflow-lemma2 (rewrite)
  (implies (and (tcp x)
                (tcp y)
                (tc-in-rangep x n)
                (tc-in-rangep y n)
                (not (negativep (add x (add y (carry c))))))
           (negativep (add x (add y (add (carry c)
                                         (minus (exp 2 n))))))))

(prove-lemma opposite-signs-implies-tc-in-rangep (rewrite)
  (implies (and (tcp x)
                (tcp y)
                (tc-in-rangep x n)
                (tc-in-rangep y n)
                (negativep x)
                (not (negativep y)))
           (tc-in-rangep (add x (add y (carry c))) n)))

(prove-lemma opposite-signs-implies-tc-in-rangep-commuted (rewrite)
  (implies (and (tcp x)
                (tcp y)
                (tc-in-rangep x n)
                (tc-in-rangep y n)
                (negativep x)
                (not (negativep y)))
           (tc-in-rangep (add y (add x (carry c))) n))
  ((disable tcp add tc-in-rangep carry)))
```

```
;;;;;;;;;;;;;;;;;;;;;;;;;;;;;;;;;;;;;;;;;;;;;;;;;;;;;;;;;;;;;;;;;;;;;;;;;
;;                                                                     ;;
;;          Mapping Functions between BV, NAT, and TC                  ;;
;;                                                                     ;;
;;;;;;;;;;;;;;;;;;;;;;;;;;;;;;;;;;;;;;;;;;;;;;;;;;;;;;;;;;;;;;;;;;;;;;;;;


(defn nat-to-bv (n size)                 ; Natural number to bit vector
  (if (zerop size)
      (btm)
      (bitv (if (zerop (remainder n 2)) f t)
            (nat-to-bv (quotient n 2)
                       (sub1 size)))))

(defn bv-to-nat (x)                      ; Bit vector to natural number
  (if (bitvp x)
      (if (equal x (btm))
          0
          (plus (if (bit x) 1 0)
                (times 2 (bv-to-nat (vec x)))))
      0))

(defn tc-to-bv (x size)        ; Two's complement number to bit vector
  (if (negativep x)
      (incr t
            (compl (nat-to-bv (negative-guts x) size)))
      (nat-to-bv x size)))

(defn bv-to-tc (x)             ; Bit vector to two's complement number
  (if (bitn x (size x))
      (minus (bv-to-nat (incr t (compl x))))
      (bv-to-nat x)))

(defn nat-to-tc (n size)       ; Natural number to two's complement number
  (if (lessp n (exp 2 (sub1 size)))
      n
      (minus (difference (exp 2 size) n))))

(defn tc-to-nat (n size)       ; Two's complement number to natural number
  (if (negativep n)
      (difference (exp 2 size)
                  (negative-guts n))
      n))
```

```
;;;;;;;;;;;;;;;;;;;;;;;;;;;;;;;;;;;;;;;;;;;;;;;;;;;;;;;;;;;;;;;;;;;;;;;;;;
;;                                                                      ;;
;;          Elementary Properties of Mapping Functions                  ;;
;;                                                                      ;;
;;;;;;;;;;;;;;;;;;;;;;;;;;;;;;;;;;;;;;;;;;;;;;;;;;;;;;;;;;;;;;;;;;;;;;;;;;

(prove-lemma size-of-nat-to-bv (rewrite)
  (equal (size (nat-to-bv n size)) (fix size)))

(prove-lemma size-of-tc-to-bv (rewrite)
  (equal (size (tc-to-bv x size)) (fix size)))

(prove-lemma bv-to-nat-of-incr (rewrite)
  (equal (bv-to-nat (incr t a))
         (if (all-onesp a)
             0
             (add1 (bv-to-nat a)))))

(prove-lemma bitn-implies-compl-not-all-onesp (rewrite)
  (implies (bitn a i) (not (all-onesp (compl a)))))

(prove-lemma upper-bound-on-bv-to-nat (rewrite)
  (lessp (bv-to-nat a) (exp 2 (size a))))

(prove-lemma bv-to-nat-of-compl (rewrite)
  (equal (bv-to-nat (compl a))
         (difference (sub1 (exp 2 (size a))) (bv-to-nat a))))

(prove-lemma bv-to-nat-to-tc-lemma1 nil
  (implies (bitn a (size a))
           (equal (bv-to-nat (incr t (compl a)))
                  (difference (exp 2 (size a))
                              (bv-to-nat a)))))

(prove-lemma bv-to-nat-to-tc-lemma2 nil
  (equal (bitn a (size a))
         (if (zerop (size a))
             f
             (not (lessp (bv-to-nat a) (exp 2 (sub1 (size a))))))))

(prove-lemma bv-to-nat-of-trunc (rewrite)
  (equal (bv-to-nat (trunc a n)) (remainder (bv-to-nat a) (exp 2 n))))

(prove-lemma all-onesp-of-compl (rewrite)
  (equal (all-onesp (compl a))
         (equal (bv-to-nat a) 0)))

(prove-lemma tcp-bv-to-tc (rewrite)
  (tcp (bv-to-tc a)))
```

```
(prove-lemma upper-bound-on-non-negative-bv-to-nat (rewrite)
  (implies (and (bitvp a)
                (not (equal a (btm)))
                (not (bitn a (size a))))
           (lessp (bv-to-nat a) (exp 2 (sub1 (size a)))))))

(prove-lemma lower-bound-on-negative-bv-to-nat (rewrite)
  (implies (and (bitvp a)
                (not (equal a (btm)))
                (bitn a (size a)))
           (not (lessp (bv-to-nat a) (exp 2 (sub1 (size a))))))))

(prove-lemma tc-in-rangep-of-bv-to-tc (rewrite)
  (implies (equal n (size a))
           (equal (tc-in-rangep (bv-to-tc a) n)
                  (and (bitvp a) (not (equal a (btm)))))))

(prove-lemma bitn-means-negativep (rewrite)
  (implies (equal n (size a))
           (equal (bitn a n)
                  (negativep (bv-to-tc a)))))

(disable bitn-means-negativep)
```

```
;;;;;;;;;;;;;;;;;;;;;;;;;;;;;;;;;;;;;;;;;;;;;;;;;;;;;;;;;;;;;;;;;;;;;;;;
;;                                                                    ;;
;;          Relationship between TC and NAT Addition                  ;;
;;                                                                    ;;
;;;;;;;;;;;;;;;;;;;;;;;;;;;;;;;;;;;;;;;;;;;;;;;;;;;;;;;;;;;;;;;;;;;;;;;;

(prove-lemma plus-to-add nil
  (implies (and (tcp x)
                (tcp y)
                (tc-in-rangep x n)
                (tc-in-rangep y n))
           (equal (nat-to-tc (remainder (plus (carry c)
                                              (tc-to-nat x n)
                                              (tc-to-nat y n))
                                        (exp 2 n))
                             n)
                  (if (tc-in-rangep (add x (add y (carry c)))
                                    n)
                      (add x (add y (carry c)))
                      (if (negativep (add x (add y (carry c))))
                          (add x (add y (add (carry c) (exp 2 n))))
                          (add x (add y (add (carry c)
                                             (minus (exp 2 n)))))))))))
```

```
;;;;;;;;;;;;;;;;;;;;;;;;;;;;;;;;;;;;;;;;;;;;;;;;;;;;;;;;;;;;;;;;;;;;;;;;;
;;                                                                     ;;
;;      Fundamental Relationships between the Mapping Functions        ;;
;;                                                                     ;;
;;;;;;;;;;;;;;;;;;;;;;;;;;;;;;;;;;;;;;;;;;;;;;;;;;;;;;;;;;;;;;;;;;;;;;;;;

(prove-lemma bv-to-nat-to-bv (rewrite)
  (implies (equal size (size a))
           (equal (nat-to-bv (bv-to-nat a) size)
                  (fix-bv a))))

(prove-lemma bv-to-nat-to-tc (rewrite)
  (equal (bv-to-tc a) (nat-to-tc (bv-to-nat a) (size a)))
  ((use (bv-to-nat-to-tc-lemma1)
        (bv-to-nat-to-tc-lemma2))))

(disable bv-to-nat-to-tc)

(prove-lemma nat-to-bv-to-nat (rewrite)
  (equal (bv-to-nat (nat-to-bv n size))
         (remainder n (exp 2 size))))

(prove-lemma tc-to-bv-to-nat (rewrite)
  (implies (and (tcp x)
                (tc-in-rangep x n))
           (equal (tc-to-nat x n) (bv-to-nat (tc-to-bv x n)))))

(disable tc-to-bv-to-nat)

(prove-lemma bv-to-tc-to-nat (rewrite)
  (implies (equal n (size a))
           (equal (tc-to-nat (bv-to-tc a) n)
                  (bv-to-nat a))))

(disable bv-to-tc-to-nat)

(prove-lemma incr-compl-nat-to-bv-0 (rewrite)
  (equal (incr t (compl (nat-to-bv 0 (size x))))
         (nat-to-bv 0 (size x))))

(prove-lemma bitn-on-implies-non-0 (rewrite)
  (implies (bitn a n) (not (equal (bv-to-nat a) 0))))

(prove-lemma bv-to-tc-to-bv (rewrite)
  (implies (equal size (size a))
           (equal (tc-to-bv (bv-to-tc a) size)
                  (fix-bv a)))
  ((disable bv-to-nat-of-incr bv-to-nat-of-compl)))
```

```
;;;;;;;;;;;;;;;;;;;;;;;;;;;;;;;;;;;;;;;;;;;;;;;;;;;;;;;;;;;;;;;;;;;;;;;;;;;;
;;                                                                        ;;
;;                         Bridge Lemmas                                  ;;
;;                                                                        ;;
;;;;;;;;;;;;;;;;;;;;;;;;;;;;;;;;;;;;;;;;;;;;;;;;;;;;;;;;;;;;;;;;;;;;;;;;;;;;

(prove-lemma embed-in-nat-to-bv nil
  (implies (equal x y) (equal (nat-to-bv x n) (nat-to-bv y n))))

(prove-lemma embed-in-tc-to-bv nil
  (implies (equal x y) (equal (tc-to-bv x n) (tc-to-bv y n))))
```

```
;;;;;;;;;;;;;;;;;;;;;;;;;;;;;;;;;;;;;;;;;;;;;;;;;;;;;;;;;;;;;;;;;;;;;;;
;;                                                                   ;;
;;                           BV-ADDER                                ;;
;;                                                                   ;;
;;;;;;;;;;;;;;;;;;;;;;;;;;;;;;;;;;;;;;;;;;;;;;;;;;;;;;;;;;;;;;;;;;;;;;;

(defn bv-adder (c a b)
  (if (bitvp a)
      (if (equal a (btm))
          (bitv c (btm))
          (bitv (b-xor c (b-xor (bit a) (bit b)))
                (bv-adder (b-or (b-and (bit a) (bit b))
                                (b-or (b-and (bit a) c)
                                      (b-and (bit b) c)))
                          (vec a)
                          (vec b))))
      (bitv c (btm))))

(defn bv-adder-output (c a b)
  (trunc (bv-adder c a b) (size a)))

(defn bv-adder-carry-out (c a b)
  (bitn (bv-adder c a b) (add1 (size a))))

(defn bv-adder-overflowp (c a b)
  (b-and (b-equv (bitn a (size a)) (bitn b (size b)))
         (b-xor (bitn a (size a))
                (bitn (bv-adder-output c a b)
                      (size a)))))
```

```
;;;;;;;;;;;;;;;;;;;;;;;;;;;;;;;;;;;;;;;;;;;;;;;;;;;;;;;;;;;;;;;;;;;;;;;;
;;                                                                    ;;
;;              Fundamental Properties of BV-ADDER                    ;;
;;                                                                    ;;
;;;;;;;;;;;;;;;;;;;;;;;;;;;;;;;;;;;;;;;;;;;;;;;;;;;;;;;;;;;;;;;;;;;;;;;;

(prove-lemma size-of-bv-adder (rewrite)
  (equal (size (bv-adder c a b))
         (add1 (size a))))

(prove-lemma bv-to-nat-of-bv-adder (rewrite)
  (implies (and (bitvp a)
                (bitvp b)
                (equal (size a) (size b))
                (boolp c))
           (equal (bv-to-nat (bv-adder c a b))
                  (plus (bv-to-nat a)
                        (bv-to-nat b)
                        (carry c)))))

; From here on we use only the above two lemmas about BV-ADDER
; The definition of BV-ADDER is disabled and henceforth any adder
; with the two properties above would suffice.

(disable bv-adder)

(prove-lemma bv-adder-non-btm (rewrite)
  (not (equal (bv-adder c a b) (btm)))
  ((use (size-of-bv-adder))
   (disable size-of-bv-adder)))

(prove-lemma size-bv-adder-output (rewrite)
  (equal (size (bv-adder-output c a b))
         (size a)))
```

```
;;;;;;;;;;;;;;;;;;;;;;;;;;;;;;;;;;;;;;;;;;;;;;;;;;;;;;;;;;;;;;;;;;;;;;;;;;;
;;                                                                       ;;
;;                      NAT view of BV-ADDER                             ;;
;;                                                                       ;;
;;;;;;;;;;;;;;;;;;;;;;;;;;;;;;;;;;;;;;;;;;;;;;;;;;;;;;;;;;;;;;;;;;;;;;;;;;;

(prove-lemma nat-interpretation-of-bv-adder-output (rewrite)
  (implies (and (bitvp a)
                (bitvp b)
                (equal (size a) (size b))
                (boolp c))
           (equal (bv-to-nat (bv-adder-output c a b))
                  (if (lessp (plus (bv-to-nat a) (bv-to-nat b) (carry c))
                             (exp 2 (size a)))
                      (plus (bv-to-nat a) (bv-to-nat b) (carry c))
                      (remainder (plus (bv-to-nat a)
                                       (bv-to-nat b)
                                       (carry c))
                                 (exp 2 (size a)))))))

(disable nat-interpretation-of-bv-adder-output)

(prove-lemma nat-bv-adder-output-seen-as-bit-vector (rewrite)
  (implies (and (bitvp a)
                (bitvp b)
                (equal (size a) (size b))
                (boolp c))
           (equal (bv-adder-output c a b)
                  (if (lessp (plus (bv-to-nat a) (bv-to-nat b) (carry c))
                             (exp 2 (size a)))
                      (nat-to-bv (plus (bv-to-nat a)
                                       (bv-to-nat b)
                                       (carry c))
                                 (size a))
                      (nat-to-bv
                        (remainder (plus (bv-to-nat a)
                                         (bv-to-nat b)
                                         (carry c))
                                   (exp 2 (size a)))
                        (size a)))))
  ((use (embed-in-nat-to-bv
          (x (bv-to-nat (bv-adder-output c a b)))
          (y (if (lessp (plus (bv-to-nat a) (bv-to-nat b) (carry c))
                        (exp 2 (size a)))
                 (plus (bv-to-nat a) (bv-to-nat b) (carry c))
                 (remainder (plus (bv-to-nat a) (bv-to-nat b) (carry c))
                            (exp 2 (size a)))))
          (n (size a)))
        (nat-interpretation-of-bv-adder-output))
```

```
    (disable boolp bv-adder-output carry)))

(disable nat-bv-adder-output-seen-as-bit-vector)

(prove-lemma nat-interpretation-of-bv-adder-carry-out (rewrite)
  (implies (and (bitvp a)
                (bitvp b)
                (equal (size a) (size b))
                (boolp c))
           (equal (bv-adder-carry-out c a b)
                  (not (lessp (plus (bv-to-nat a)
                                    (bv-to-nat b)
                                    (carry c))
                              (exp 2 (size a)))))))
  ((use (upper-bound-on-non-negative-bv-to-nat
         (a (bv-adder c a b)))
        (lower-bound-on-negative-bv-to-nat
         (a (bv-adder c a b))))
   (disable bitn carry upper-bound-on-non-negative-bv-to-nat
            lower-bound-on-negative-bv-to-nat)))

(disable nat-interpretation-of-bv-adder-carry-out)
```

```
;;;;;;;;;;;;;;;;;;;;;;;;;;;;;;;;;;;;;;;;;;;;;;;;;;;;;;;;;;;;;;;;;;;;;;;;;
;;                                                                     ;;
;;                      TC View of BV-ADDER                            ;;
;;                                                                     ;;
;;;;;;;;;;;;;;;;;;;;;;;;;;;;;;;;;;;;;;;;;;;;;;;;;;;;;;;;;;;;;;;;;;;;;;;;;

(prove-lemma tc-interpretation-of-bv-adder-output-lemma1 (rewrite)
  (implies (and (bitvp a)
                (bitvp b)
                (equal (size a) (size b))
                (boolp c))
           (equal (bv-to-tc (trunc (bv-adder c a b)
                                   (size a)))
                  (nat-to-tc (remainder (plus (carry c)
                                              (bv-to-nat a)
                                              (bv-to-nat b))
                                        (exp 2 (size a)))
                             (size a))))
  ((enable bv-to-nat-to-tc)
   (disable bv-to-tc tc-to-bv nat-to-tc tc-to-nat exp)))

(prove-lemma tc-interpretation-of-bv-adder-output (rewrite)
  (implies (and (bitvp a)
                (bitvp b)
                (not (equal a (btm)))
                (not (equal b (btm)))
                (equal (size a) (size b))
                (boolp c))
           (equal (bv-to-tc (bv-adder-output c a b))
                  (if (tc-in-rangep (add (bv-to-tc a)
                                         (add (bv-to-tc b) (carry c)))
                                    (size a))
                      (add (bv-to-tc a) (add (bv-to-tc b) (carry c)))
                      (if (negativep (add (bv-to-tc a)
                                          (add (bv-to-tc b) (carry c))))
                          (add (bv-to-tc a)
                               (add (bv-to-tc b)
                                    (add (carry c) (exp 2 (size a)))))
                          (add (bv-to-tc a)
                               (add (bv-to-tc b)
                                    (add (carry c)
                                         (minus (exp 2 (size a)))))))))))
  ((use (plus-to-add (x (bv-to-tc a))
                     (y (bv-to-tc b))
                     (n (size a))))
   (enable bv-to-tc-to-nat)
   (disable boolp bv-to-tc trunc bv-adder size
            tc-in-rangep add carry exp
```

```
                    nat-to-tc tc-to-nat tcp)))

(disable tc-interpretation-of-bv-adder-output-lemma1)

(disable tc-interpretation-of-bv-adder-output)

(prove-lemma tc-bv-adder-output-seen-as-bit-vector-lemma1 (rewrite)
  (implies (and (bitvp a)
                (bitvp b)
                (not (equal a (btm)))
                (not (equal b (btm)))
                (equal (size a) (size b))
                (boolp c))
           (equal (tc-to-bv (bv-to-tc (bv-adder-output c a b))
                            (size (bv-adder-output c a b)))
                  (tc-to-bv
                    (if (tc-in-rangep (add (bv-to-tc a)
                                           (add (bv-to-tc b)
                                                (carry c)))
                                      (size a))
                        (add (bv-to-tc a) (add (bv-to-tc b)
                                               (carry c)))
                        (if (negativep (add (bv-to-tc a)
                                            (add (bv-to-tc b)
                                                 (carry c))))
                            (add (bv-to-tc a)
                                 (add (bv-to-tc b)
                                      (add (carry c)
                                           (exp 2 (size a)))))
                            (add (bv-to-tc a)
                                 (add (bv-to-tc b)
                                      (add (carry c)
                                           (minus (exp 2 (size a))))))))
                    (size a))))
  ((use (embed-in-tc-to-bv
         (x (bv-to-tc (bv-adder-output c a b)))
         (y (if (tc-in-rangep (add (bv-to-tc a)
                                   (add (bv-to-tc b) (carry c)))
                              (size a))
                (add (bv-to-tc a) (add (bv-to-tc b) (carry c)))
                (if (negativep (add (bv-to-tc a)
                                    (add (bv-to-tc b) (carry c))))
                    (add (bv-to-tc a)
                         (add (bv-to-tc b)
                              (add (carry c) (exp 2 (size a)))))
                    (add (bv-to-tc a)
                         (add (bv-to-tc b)
                              (add (carry c)
                                   (minus (exp 2 (size a))))))))))))
```

```
              (n (size (bv-adder-output c a b))))
          (size-bv-adder-output))
    (enable tc-interpretation-of-bv-adder-output)
    (disable bv-adder-output bv-to-tc tc-to-bv tc-in-rangep
             carry add exp boolp size-bv-adder-output)
    (hands-off bv-adder-output add tc-in-rangep)))

(disable tc-bv-adder-output-seen-as-bit-vector-lemma1)

(prove-lemma tc-bv-adder-output-seen-as-bit-vector (rewrite)
  (implies (and (bitvp a)
                (bitvp b)
                (not (equal a (btm)))
                (not (equal b (btm)))
                (equal (size a) (size b))
                (boolp c))
           (equal (bv-adder-output c a b)
                  (tc-to-bv
                   (if (tc-in-rangep
                         (add (bv-to-tc a)
                              (add (bv-to-tc b) (carry c)))
                         (size a))
                       (add (bv-to-tc a) (add (bv-to-tc b) (carry c)))
                       (if (negativep (add (bv-to-tc a)
                                           (add (bv-to-tc b) (carry c))))
                           (add (bv-to-tc a)
                                (add (bv-to-tc b)
                                     (add (carry c) (exp 2 (size a)))))
                           (add (bv-to-tc a)
                                (add (bv-to-tc b)
                                     (add (carry c)
                                          (minus (exp 2 (size a)))))))))
                   (size a))))
    ((use (bv-to-tc-to-bv (a (bv-adder-output c a b))
                          (size (size (bv-adder-output c a b))))
          (tc-bv-adder-output-seen-as-bit-vector-lemma1))
     (disable bv-adder-output bv-to-tc tc-to-bv
              tc-in-rangep carry add exp boolp
              size-bv-adder-output bv-to-tc-to-bv)
     (hands-off bv-adder-output add tc-in-rangep tc-to-bv if)))

(disable tc-bv-adder-output-seen-as-bit-vector)

(prove-lemma tc-interpretation-of-bv-adder-overflowp (rewrite)
  (implies (and (bitvp a)
                (bitvp b)
                (equal (size a) (size b))
                (boolp c)
                (not (equal a (btm)))
```

```
                        (not (equal b (btm))))
                (equal (bv-adder-overflowp c a b)
                        (not (tc-in-rangep (add (bv-to-tc a)
                                                (add (bv-to-tc b) (carry c)))
                                           (size a)))))
          ((use (add-with-carry-of-negatives-is-negative
                (x (bv-to-tc a)) (y (bv-to-tc b)) (n (size a)))
                (add-with-carry-of-non-negatives-is-non-negative
                (x (bv-to-tc a)) (y (bv-to-tc b)) (n (size a))))
          (enable bitn-means-negativep tc-interpretation-of-bv-adder-output)
          (disable tc-in-rangep add bv-to-tc size carry boolp
                  bv-adder-output)))

(disable tc-interpretation-of-bv-adder-overflowp)
```

```
;;;;;;;;;;;;;;;;;;;;;;;;;;;;;;;;;;;;;;;;;;;;;;;;;;;;;;;;;;;;;;;;;;;;;;;;;;
;;                                                                      ;;
;;      Definitions and Lemmas about Subtraction Functions             ;;
;;                                                                      ;;
;;;;;;;;;;;;;;;;;;;;;;;;;;;;;;;;;;;;;;;;;;;;;;;;;;;;;;;;;;;;;;;;;;;;;;;;;;

(defn bv-subtracter-output (c a b)
  (bv-adder-output (b-not c) (bv-not a) b))

(defn bv-subtracter-carry-out (c a b)
  (b-not (bv-adder-carry-out (b-not c) (bv-not a) b)))

(defn bv-subtracter-overflowp (c a b)
  (bv-adder-overflowp (b-not c)
                      (bv-not a)
                      b))

(prove-lemma bv-not-is-compl (rewrite)
  (equal (bv-not a) (compl a)))

(prove-lemma subtract-lemma1 (rewrite)
  (implies (equal (size b) (size a))
           (equal (lessp (difference (bv-to-nat b) (bv-to-nat a))
                         (exp 2 (size a)))
                  t)))

(prove-lemma subtract-lemma2 (rewrite)
  (implies (and (not (zerop b))
                (not (lessp (sub1 b) a)))
           (equal (lessp (plus b (difference (sub1 n) a))
                         n)
                  f)))

(prove-lemma subtract-lemma3 (rewrite)
  (implies (and (not (zerop b))
                (not (lessp (sub1 b) a))
                (lessp a n))
           (equal (difference (plus b (difference (sub1 n) a)) n)
                  (difference (sub1 b) a))))

(prove-lemma subtract-lemma4 (rewrite)
  (implies (equal (size b) (size a))
           (equal (lessp (difference (sub1 (bv-to-nat b)) (bv-to-nat a))
                         (exp 2 (size a)))
                  t)))

(prove-lemma size-bv-subtracter-output (rewrite)
  (equal (size (bv-subtracter-output c a b))
         (size a)))
```

```
;;;;;;;;;;;;;;;;;;;;;;;;;;;;;;;;;;;;;;;;;;;;;;;;;;;;;;;;;;;;;;;;;;;;;;;;
;;                                                                    ;;
;;                NAT View of BV-SUBTRACTER                           ;;
;;                                                                    ;;
;;;;;;;;;;;;;;;;;;;;;;;;;;;;;;;;;;;;;;;;;;;;;;;;;;;;;;;;;;;;;;;;;;;;;;;;

(prove-lemma nat-interpretation-of-bv-subtracter-output (rewrite)
  (implies (and (bitvp a)
                (bitvp b)
                (equal (size a) (size b))
                (boolp c))
           (equal (bv-to-nat (bv-subtracter-output c a b))
                  (if (not (lessp (bv-to-nat b)
                                  (plus (bv-to-nat a) (carry c))))
                      (difference (bv-to-nat b)
                                  (plus (bv-to-nat a) (carry c)))
                      (difference (exp 2 (size a))
                                  (difference (plus (bv-to-nat a)
                                                    (carry c))
                                              (bv-to-nat b)))))))

(disable nat-interpretation-of-bv-subtracter-output)

(prove-lemma nat-bv-subtracter-output-seen-as-bit-vector (rewrite)
  (implies (and (bitvp a)
                (bitvp b)
                (equal (size a) (size b))
                (boolp c))
           (equal (bv-subtracter-output c a b)
                  (if (not (lessp (bv-to-nat b)
                                  (plus (bv-to-nat a) (carry c))))
                      (nat-to-bv (difference (bv-to-nat b)
                                             (plus (bv-to-nat a)
                                                   (carry c)))
                                 (size a))
                      (nat-to-bv (difference (exp 2 (size a))
                                             (difference
                                              (plus (bv-to-nat a)
                                                    (carry c))
                                              (bv-to-nat b)))
                                 (size a)))))
  ((use (embed-in-nat-to-bv
         (x (bv-to-nat (bv-subtracter-output c a b)))
         (y (if (not (lessp (bv-to-nat b)
                            (plus (bv-to-nat a) (carry c))))
                (difference (bv-to-nat b)
                            (plus (bv-to-nat a) (carry c)))
                (difference (exp 2 (size a))
                            (difference (plus (bv-to-nat a)
```

```
                                             (carry c))
                                    (bv-to-nat b)))))
            (n (size a)))
         (nat-interpretation-of-bv-subtracter-output))
    (disable boolp bv-subtracter-output carry exp difference)))

(disable nat-bv-subtracter-output-seen-as-bit-vector)

(prove-lemma equal-lessp-hack (rewrite)
  (equal (equal (lessp x y) z)
         (if (lessp x y)
             (equal z t)
             (equal z f))))

(prove-lemma nat-interpretation-of-bv-subtracter-carry-out (rewrite)
  (implies (and (bitvp a)
                (bitvp b)
                (equal (size a) (size b))
                (boolp c))
           (equal (bv-subtracter-carry-out c a b)
                  (lessp (bv-to-nat b)
                         (plus (bv-to-nat a) (carry c)))))
  ((enable nat-to-bv-to-nat nat-interpretation-of-bv-adder-carry-out)
   (disable size-bv-subtracter-output)))

(disable nat-interpretation-of-bv-subtracter-carry-out)
```

```
;;;;;;;;;;;;;;;;;;;;;;;;;;;;;;;;;;;;;;;;;;;;;;;;;;;;;;;;;;;;;;;;;;;;;;;;;
;;                                                                   ;;
;;                  TC View of BV-SUBTRACTER                         ;;
;;                                                                   ;;
;;;;;;;;;;;;;;;;;;;;;;;;;;;;;;;;;;;;;;;;;;;;;;;;;;;;;;;;;;;;;;;;;;;;;;;;;

(defn tc-minus (x)
  (if (negativep x)
      (negative-guts x)
      (if (zerop x) 0 (minus x))))

(prove-lemma tc-minus-add (rewrite)
  (equal (tc-minus (add x y)) (add (tc-minus x) (tc-minus y))))

(prove-lemma bitn-compl (rewrite)
  (implies (and (not (zerop n))
                (not (lessp (size a) n)))
           (equal (bitn (compl a) n) (not (bitn a n)))))

(prove-lemma equal-difference-0 (rewrite)
  (equal (equal (difference x y) 0)
         (not (lessp y x))))

(prove-lemma top-bit-off-implies-smaller (rewrite)
  (implies (and (bitvp a)
                (not (equal a (btm)))
                (not (bitn a (size a))))
           (lessp (bv-to-nat a) (sub1 (exp 2 (size a))))))

(prove-lemma tc-minus-bv-to-tc (rewrite)
  (implies (and (bitvp a)
                (not (equal a (btm))))
           (equal (tc-minus (bv-to-tc a))
                  (if (equal (bv-to-tc a) 0)
                      0
                      (add 1 (bv-to-tc (compl a)))))))

(defn tc-fix (x)
  (if (tcp x) x 0))

(prove-lemma tcp-add (rewrite)
  (and (implies (tcp x) (tcp (add x y)))
       (implies (tcp y) (tcp (add x y)))))

(prove-lemma add-0 (rewrite)
  (equal (add 0 x) (tc-fix x)))

(prove-lemma add-1-1 (rewrite)
  (equal (add 1 (add -1 x)) (tc-fix x)))
```

```
(prove-lemma bv-to-tc-compl-0 (rewrite)
  (implies (and (bitvp a)
                (not (equal a (btm)))
                (equal (bv-to-tc a) 0))
           (equal (bv-to-tc (compl a)) -1)))

(prove-lemma tc-minus-add-carry (rewrite)
  (implies (and (bitvp a)
                (not (equal a (btm))))
           (equal (tc-minus (add (bv-to-tc a) (carry c)))
                  (add (bv-to-tc (compl a)) (carry (not c)))))
  ((disable add bv-to-tc tc-minus tcp)))

(prove-lemma boolp-b-not (rewrite)
  (boolp (b-not x)))

(prove-lemma compl-not-btm (rewrite)
  (equal (equal (compl a) (btm))
         (or (not (bitvp a)) (equal a (btm)))))

(prove-lemma tc-interpretation-of-bv-subtracter-output (rewrite)
  (implies (and (bitvp a)
                (bitvp b)
                (not (equal a (btm)))
                (not (equal b (btm)))
                (equal (size a) (size b))
                (boolp c))
           (equal (bv-to-tc (bv-subtracter-output c a b))
                  (if (tc-in-rangep (add (bv-to-tc b)
                                         (tc-minus (add (bv-to-tc a)
                                                        (carry c))))
                                    (size a))
                      (add (bv-to-tc b) (tc-minus (add (bv-to-tc a)
                                                       (carry c))))
                      (if (negativep (add (bv-to-tc b)
                                          (tc-minus (add (bv-to-tc a)
                                                         (carry c)))))
                          (add (bv-to-tc b)
                               (add (exp 2 (size a))
                                    (tc-minus (add (bv-to-tc a)
                                                   (carry c)))))
                          (add (bv-to-tc b)
                               (add (minus (exp 2 (size a)))
                                    (tc-minus (add (bv-to-tc a)
                                                   (carry c)))))
                          ))))
  ((disable add carry boolp tc-minus bv-to-tc
            tc-in-rangep bv-adder-output
            tc-minus-add tc-minus-bv-to-tc)
   (enable tc-interpretation-of-bv-adder-output)))
```

```
(disable tc-interpretation-of-bv-subtracter-output)

(prove-lemma tc-bv-subtracter-output-seen-as-bit-vector-lemma1 (rewrite)
  (implies (and (bitvp a)
                (bitvp b)
                (not (equal a (btm)))
                (not (equal b (btm)))
                (equal (size a) (size b))
                (boolp c))
           (equal (tc-to-bv (bv-to-tc (bv-subtracter-output c a b))
                            (size (bv-subtracter-output c a b)))
                  (tc-to-bv
                   (if (tc-in-rangep (add (bv-to-tc b)
                                          (tc-minus (add (bv-to-tc a)
                                                         (carry c))))
                                     (size a))
                       (add (bv-to-tc b) (tc-minus (add (bv-to-tc a)
                                                        (carry c))))
                       (if (negativep (add (bv-to-tc b)
                                           (tc-minus (add (bv-to-tc a)
                                                          (carry c)))))
                           (add (bv-to-tc b)
                                (add (exp 2 (size a))
                                     (tc-minus (add (bv-to-tc a)
                                                    (carry c)))))
                           (add (bv-to-tc b)
                                (add (minus (exp 2 (size a)))
                                     (tc-minus (add (bv-to-tc a)
                                                    (carry c)))))))
                   (size a))))
  ((use (embed-in-tc-to-bv
         (x (bv-to-tc (bv-subtracter-output c a b)))
         (y (if (tc-in-rangep (add (bv-to-tc b)
                                   (tc-minus (add (bv-to-tc a)
                                                  (carry c))))
                              (size a))
                (add (bv-to-tc b) (tc-minus (add (bv-to-tc a)
                                                 (carry c))))
                (if (negativep (add (bv-to-tc b)
                                    (tc-minus (add (bv-to-tc a)
                                                   (carry c)))))
                    (add (bv-to-tc b)
                         (add (exp 2 (size a))
                              (tc-minus (add (bv-to-tc a)
                                             (carry c)))))
                    (add (bv-to-tc b)
                         (add (minus (exp 2 (size a)))
                              (tc-minus (add (bv-to-tc a)
```

```
                                        (carry c)))))))))
            (n (size (bv-subtracter-output c a b))))
          (size-bv-subtracter-output))
    (enable tc-interpretation-of-bv-subtracter-output)
    (disable add carry boolp tc-minus bv-to-tc
             tc-in-rangep bv-adder-output
             tc-minus-add tc-minus-bv-to-tc)
    (hands-off bv-subtracter-output add tc-in-rangep)))

(disable tc-bv-subtracter-output-seen-as-bit-vector-lemma1)

(prove-lemma tc-bv-subtracter-output-seen-as-bit-vector (rewrite)
  (implies (and (bitvp a)
                (bitvp b)
                (not (equal a (btm)))
                (not (equal b (btm)))
                (equal (size a) (size b))
                (boolp c))
           (equal (bv-subtracter-output c a b)
                  (if (tc-in-rangep (add (bv-to-tc b)
                                         (tc-minus (add (bv-to-tc a)
                                                        (carry c))))
                                    (size a))
                      (tc-to-bv (add (bv-to-tc b)
                                     (tc-minus (add (bv-to-tc a)
                                                    (carry c))))
                                (size a))
                      (if (negativep (add (bv-to-tc b)
                                          (tc-minus (add (bv-to-tc a)
                                                         (carry c)))))
                          (tc-to-bv
                           (add (bv-to-tc b)
                                (add (exp 2 (size a))
                                     (tc-minus (add (bv-to-tc a)
                                                    (carry c)))))
                           (size a))
                          (tc-to-bv
                           (add (bv-to-tc b)
                                (add (minus (exp 2 (size a)))
                                     (tc-minus (add (bv-to-tc a)
                                                    (carry c)))))
                           (size a))))))
  ((use (tc-bv-subtracter-output-seen-as-bit-vector-lemma1))
   (disable add carry boolp tc-minus bv-to-tc
            tc-in-rangep bv-subtracter-output
            tc-minus-add tc-minus-bv-to-tc
            tc-to-bv tc-minus-add-carry)))

(disable tc-bv-subtracter-output-seen-as-bit-vector)
```

```
(prove-lemma tc-interpretation-of-bv-subtracter-overflowp (rewrite)
  (implies (and (bitvp a)
                (bitvp b)
                (not (equal a (btm)))
                (not (equal b (btm)))
                (equal (size a) (size b))
                (boolp c))
           (equal (bv-subtracter-overflowp c a b)
                  (not (tc-in-rangep (add (bv-to-tc b)
                                          (tc-minus (add (bv-to-tc a)
                                                         (carry c))))
                                     (size a)))))
  ((disable add carry boolp tc-minus bv-to-tc
            tc-in-rangep bv-adder-output
            tc-minus-add tc-minus-bv-to-tc)
   (enable tc-interpretation-of-bv-adder-overflowp)))

(disable tc-interpretation-of-bv-subtracter-overflowp)
```

```
;;;;;;;;;;;;;;;;;;;;;;;;;;;;;;;;;;;;;;;;;;;;;;;;;;;;;;;;;;;;;;;;;;;;;;;;;;;;;
;;                                                                         ;;
;;      Definitions and Lemmas for Shift and Rotate Functions              ;;
;;                                                                         ;;
;;;;;;;;;;;;;;;;;;;;;;;;;;;;;;;;;;;;;;;;;;;;;;;;;;;;;;;;;;;;;;;;;;;;;;;;;;;;;
(defn v-append (a b)                       ; Append two bit vectors
  (if (bitvp a)
      (if (equal a (btm))
          b
          (bitv (bit a)
                (v-append (vec a) b)))
      b))
(defn v-lsr (a)                           ; Vector logical shift right
  (if (bitvp a)
      (if (equal a (btm))
          (btm)
          (v-append (vec a) (bitv f (btm))))
      (btm)))
(defn v-lsl (a)                           ; Vector logical shift left
  (if (bitvp a)
      (if (equal a (btm))
          (btm)
          (v-append (bitv f (btm)) (trunc a (sub1 (size a)))))
      (btm)))
(defn v-asr (a)                           ; Vector arithmetic shift right
  (if (bitvp a)
      (if (equal a (btm))
          (btm)
          (v-append (vec a) (bitv (bitn a (size a)) (btm))))
      (btm)))
(defn v-asl (a)                           ; Vector arithmetric shift left
  (v-lsl a))
(defn v-ror (a c)                         ; Vector rotate right
  (if (bitvp a)
      (if (equal a (btm))
          (btm)
          (v-append (vec a) (bitv c (btm))))
      (btm)))
(defn v-rol (a c)                         ; Vector rotate left
  (if (bitvp a)
      (if (equal a (btm))
          (btm)
          (v-append (bitv c (btm)) (trunc a (sub1 (size a)))))
      (btm)))
```

```
(defn bv-append (a b) (v-append a b))

(defn bv-lsr (a) (v-lsr a))

(defn bv-asr (a) (v-asr a))

(defn bv-ror (a c) (v-ror a c))
```

```
;;;;;;;;;;;;;;;;;;;;;;;;;;;;;;;;;;;;;;;;;;;;;;;;;;;;;;;;;;;;;;;;;;;;;;;;;;;;
;;                                                                      ;;
;;      Natural and Two's Complement Interpretation of Shifters         ;;
;;                                                                      ;;
;;;;;;;;;;;;;;;;;;;;;;;;;;;;;;;;;;;;;;;;;;;;;;;;;;;;;;;;;;;;;;;;;;;;;;;;;;;;

(prove-lemma bv-to-nat-v-append (rewrite)
  (equal (bv-to-nat (v-append a b))
         (plus (bv-to-nat a) (times (bv-to-nat b) (exp 2 (size a))))))

(prove-lemma bv-lsr-divides-by-two-lemma (rewrite)
  (equal (v-lsr a)
         (nat-to-bv (quotient (bv-to-nat a) 2)
                    (size a))))

(defn mod2 (x)
  (if (negativep x)
      (minus (quotient (add1 (negative-guts x)) 2))
      (quotient x 2)))

(prove-lemma bitvp-v-append (rewrite)
  (equal (bitvp (v-append a b))
         (if (bitvp a)
             (or (not (equal a (btm))) (bitvp b))
             (bitvp b))))

(prove-lemma bitn-v-append (rewrite)
  (equal (bitn (v-append a b) n)
         (if (lessp (size a) n)
             (bitn b (difference n (size a)))
             (bitn a n))))

(prove-lemma size-v-append (rewrite)
  (equal (size (v-append a b)) (plus (size a) (size b))))

(prove-lemma difference-x-x-1 (rewrite)
  (equal (difference x (sub1 x))
         (if (zerop x) 0 1)))

(prove-lemma bv-to-nat-of-twos-compl (rewrite)
  (equal (bv-to-nat (incr t (compl a)))
         (if (equal (bv-to-nat a) 0)
             0
             (difference (exp 2 (size a)) (bv-to-nat a)))))

(prove-lemma difference-2x-x (rewrite)
  (equal (difference (times 2 y) (plus x y))
         (difference y x)))
```

```
(prove-lemma quotient-crock1 (rewrite)
  (equal (quotient (add1 (difference (times 2 y) (times 2 x))) 2)
         (difference y x)))

(prove-lemma add1-difference-sub1 (rewrite)
  (equal (add1 (difference (sub1 x) y))
         (if (lessp y x)
             (difference x y)
             1)))

(prove-lemma quotient-crock2 (rewrite)
  (equal (quotient (difference (times 2 y) (times 2 x)) 2)
         (difference y x)))

(prove-lemma bv-asr-divides-by-two (rewrite)
  (equal (bv-to-tc (bv-asr a))
         (mod2 (bv-to-tc a))))
```

```
;;;;;;;;;;;;;;;;;;;;;;;;;;;;;;;;;;;;;;;;;;;;;;;;;;;;;;;;;;;;;;;;;;;;;;;;;;;
;;                                                                     ;;
;;          Definitions and Lemmas about Hardware IF                   ;;
;;               and Constructor for ALU Result                       ;;
;;                                                                     ;;
;;;;;;;;;;;;;;;;;;;;;;;;;;;;;;;;;;;;;;;;;;;;;;;;;;;;;;;;;;;;;;;;;;;;;;;;;;;

(defn b-if (c a b)                ; Binary if
 (b-nand (b-nand c a)
         (b-nand (b-not c) b)))

(defn bv-if (c a b)              ; Bit-vector if
  (if (bitvp a)
      (if (equal a (btm))
          (btm)
          (bitv (b-if c (bit a) (bit b))
                (bv-if c (vec a) (vec b))))
      (btm)))

(prove-lemma bv-if-works (rewrite)
  (equal (bv-if c a b)
         (if c (if (bitvp a) a (btm)) (trunc b (size a)))))

(add-shell bv-cv nil bv-cvp ((bv (one-of bitvp) btm)
                             (c (one-of truep falsep) false)
                             (v (one-of truep falsep) false)))

(defn bv-cv-if (c a b)          ; Bit-vector, carry, and overflow if
  (bv-cv (bv-if c (bv a) (bv b))
         (b-if c (c a) (c b))
         (b-if c (v a) (v b))))

(prove-lemma trunc-size (rewrite)
  (implies (and (bitvp b)
                (equal (size b) (size a)))
           (equal (trunc b (size a)) b))
  ((induct (bv-and a b))))

(prove-lemma bv-cv-if-works (rewrite)
  (implies (and (bv-cvp a)
                (bv-cvp b)
                (equal (size (bv a)) (size (bv b))))
           (and (equal (bv-cv-if t a b) a)
                (equal (bv-cv-if f a b) b))))
```

```
;;;;;;;;;;;;;;;;;;;;;;;;;;;;;;;;;;;;;;;;;;;;;;;;;;;;;;;;;;;;;;;;;;;;;;;;;;;;;;
;;                                                                        ;;
;;                          SIZE Lemmas                                   ;;
;;                                                                        ;;
;;;;;;;;;;;;;;;;;;;;;;;;;;;;;;;;;;;;;;;;;;;;;;;;;;;;;;;;;;;;;;;;;;;;;;;;;;;;;;

(prove-lemma size-bv-bv-cv-if (rewrite)
  (equal (size (bv (bv-cv-if c a b))) (size (bv a))))

; We rewrite "bv-not" to "v-not", etc., and so we need these size lemmas
; about the v-functions.

(prove-lemma size-v-not (rewrite)
  (equal (size (v-not a)) (size a)))

(prove-lemma size-v-and (rewrite)
  (equal (size (v-and a b)) (size a)))

(prove-lemma size-v-or (rewrite)
  (equal (size (v-or a b)) (size a)))

(prove-lemma size-v-xor (rewrite)
  (equal (size (v-xor a b)) (size a)))

(prove-lemma size-v-append-1 (rewrite)
  (equal (size
           (if (bitvp a)
               (if (equal a (btm))
                   (btm)
                   (v-append (vec a) (bitv x (btm))))
               (btm)))
         (size a)))

(prove-lemma size-v-append-2 (rewrite)
  (equal (size (v-append (vec a) (bitv x (btm))))
         (if (bitvp a)
             (if (equal a (btm))
                 1
                 (size a))
             1)))

; We have already proved (SIZE (BV-ADDER-OUTPUT C A B)) = (SIZE A) and
;                        (SIZE (BV-SUBTRACTER-OUTPUT C A B)) = (SIZE A).
```

```
;;;;;;;;;;;;;;;;;;;;;;;;;;;;;;;;;;;;;;;;;;;;;;;;;;;;;;;;;;;;;;;;;;;;;;;;;;;;;
;;                                                                         ;;
;;                        ALU Definition                                   ;;
;;                                                                         ;;
;;;;;;;;;;;;;;;;;;;;;;;;;;;;;;;;;;;;;;;;;;;;;;;;;;;;;;;;;;;;;;;;;;;;;;;;;;;;;

(disable bv-cv-if)

(defn bv-alu-cv (a b c op-code)
  (bv-cv-if (bitn op-code 4)
    (bv-cv-if (bitn op-code 3)
      (bv-cv-if (bitn op-code 2)
        (bv-cv-if (bitn op-code 1)
                  (bv-cv a                          ; Op-code 15 - move
                         f
                         f)
                  (bv-cv (bv-not a)                 ; Op-code 14 - not
                         f
                         f))
          (bv-cv-if (bitn op-code 1)
                  (bv-cv (bv-and a b)               ; Op-code 13 - and
                         f
                         f)
                  (bv-cv (bv-or a b)                ; Op-code 12 - or
                         f
                         f)))
        (bv-cv-if (bitn op-code 2)
          (bv-cv-if (bitn op-code 1)
                  (bv-cv (bv-xor a b)               ; Op-code 11 - xor
                         f
                         f)
                  (bv-cv (bv-lsr a)                 ; Op-code 10 - lsr
                         (bitn a 1)
                         f))
          (bv-cv-if (bitn op-code 1)
                  (bv-cv (bv-asr a)                 ; Op-code 9 - asr
                         (bitn a 1)
                         f)
                  (bv-cv (bv-ror a c)               ; Op-code 8 - ror
                         (if (zerop (size a))
                             c
                             (bitn a 1))
                         f)))))
    (bv-cv-if (bitn op-code 3)
      (bv-cv-if (bitn op-code 2)
        (bv-cv-if
          (bitn op-code 1)
          (bv-cv (bv-subtracter-output f a b)       ; Op-code 7 - sub
```

```
                    (bv-subtracter-carry-out f a b)
                    (bv-subtracter-overflowp f a b))
        (bv-cv (bv-subtracter-output c a b)          ; Op-code 6 - subb
                    (bv-subtracter-carry-out c a b)
                    (bv-subtracter-overflowp c a b)))
      (bv-cv-if
        (bitn op-code 1)                             ; Op-code 5 - dec
        (bv-cv (bv-subtracter-output t (nat-to-bv 0 (size a)) a)
                    (bv-subtracter-carry-out t (nat-to-bv 0 (size a)) a)
                    (bv-subtracter-overflowp t (nat-to-bv 0 (size a)) a))
                                                     ; Op-code 4 - neg
        (bv-cv (bv-subtracter-output f a (nat-to-bv 0 (size a)))
                    (bv-subtracter-carry-out f a (nat-to-bv 0 (size a)))
                    (bv-subtracter-overflowp f a (nat-to-bv 0 (size a)))))))
    (bv-cv-if (bitn op-code 2)
      (bv-cv-if
        (bitn op-code 1)
        (bv-cv (bv-adder-output f a b)               ; Op-code 3 - add
                    (bv-adder-carry-out f a b)
                    (bv-adder-overflowp f a b))
        (bv-cv (bv-adder-output c a b)               ; Op-code 2 - addc
                    (bv-adder-carry-out c a b)
                    (bv-adder-overflowp c a b)))
      (bv-cv-if
        (bitn op-code 1)                             ; Op-code 1 - inc
        (bv-cv (bv-adder-output t a (nat-to-bv 0 (size a)))
                    (bv-adder-carry-out t a (nat-to-bv 0 (size a)))
                    (bv-adder-overflowp t a (nat-to-bv 0 (size a))))
        (bv-cv a                                     ; Op-code 0 - nop, move
                    f
                    f)))))))

(prove-lemma v-not-is-compl (rewrite)
  (equal (v-not a) (compl a)))

(prove-lemma bv-and-is-v-and (rewrite)
  (equal (bv-and a b) (v-and a b)))

(prove-lemma bv-or-is-v-or (rewrite)
  (equal (bv-or a b) (v-or a b)))

(prove-lemma bv-xor-is-v-xor (rewrite)
  (equal (bv-xor a b) (v-xor a b)))

(prove-lemma bv-cv-if-reduce (rewrite)
  (equal (bv-cv-if c
                    (bv-cv x y z)
                    (bv-cv x y z))
          (bv-cv x y z))
  ((enable bv-cv-if)))
```

```
;;;;;;;;;;;;;;;;;;;;;;;;;;;;;;;;;;;;;;;;;;;;;;;;;;;;;;;;;;;;;;;;;;;;;;;;;;;
;;                                                                       ;;
;;    BV-ALU with Theorem-Prover "IFs".  This was done to speed the      ;;
;;        rewriting when proving the large lemmas that follow.           ;;
;;                                                                       ;;
;;;;;;;;;;;;;;;;;;;;;;;;;;;;;;;;;;;;;;;;;;;;;;;;;;;;;;;;;;;;;;;;;;;;;;;;;;;

(prove-lemma bv-alu-cv-with-ifs (rewrite)
  (implies
    (and (bitvp a)
         (bitvp b)
         (equal (size a) (size b)))
    (equal
      (bv-alu-cv a b c op-code)
      (if (bitn op-code 4)
          (if (bitn op-code 3)
              (if (bitn op-code 2)
                  (if (bitn op-code 1)
                      (bv-cv a                   ; Op-code 15 - move
                             f
                             f)
                      (bv-cv (bv-not a)          ; Op-code 14 - not
                             f
                             f))
                  (if (bitn op-code 1)
                      (bv-cv (bv-and a b)        ; Op-code 13 - and
                             f
                             f)
                      (bv-cv (bv-or a b)         ; Op-code 12 - or
                             f
                             f)))
              (if (bitn op-code 2)
                  (if (bitn op-code 1)
                      (bv-cv (bv-xor a b)        ; Op-code 11 - xor
                             f
                             f)
                      (bv-cv (bv-lsr a)          ; Op-code 10 - lsr
                             (bitn a 1)
                             f))
                  (if (bitn op-code 1)
                      (bv-cv (bv-asr a)          ; Op-code 9 - asr
                             (bitn a 1)
                             f)
                      (bv-cv (bv-ror a c)        ; Op-code 8 - ror
                             (if (zerop (size a))
                                 c
                                 (bitn a 1))
                             f)))))
```

```
     (if (bitn op-code 3)
         (if (bitn op-code 2)
             (if (bitn op-code 1)
                                            ; Op-code 7 - sub
                 (bv-cv (bv-subtracter-output f a b)
                        (bv-subtracter-carry-out f a b)
                        (bv-subtracter-overflowp f a b))
                                            ; Op-code 6 - subb
                 (bv-cv (bv-subtracter-output c a b)
                        (bv-subtracter-carry-out c a b)
                        (bv-subtracter-overflowp c a b)))
                                            ; Op-code 5 - dec
             (if (bitn op-code 1)
                 (bv-cv (bv-subtracter-output
                            t (nat-to-bv 0 (size a)) a)
                        (bv-subtracter-carry-out
                            t (nat-to-bv 0 (size a)) a)
                        (bv-subtracter-overflowp
                            t (nat-to-bv 0 (size a)) a))
                                            ; Op-code 4 - neg
                 (bv-cv (bv-subtracter-output
                            f a (nat-to-bv 0 (size a)))
                        (bv-subtracter-carry-out
                            f a (nat-to-bv 0 (size a)))
                        (bv-subtracter-overflowp
                            f a (nat-to-bv 0 (size a))))))
             (if (bitn op-code 2)
                 (if (bitn op-code 1)
                                              ; Op-code 3 - add
                     (bv-cv (bv-adder-output f a b)
                            (bv-adder-carry-out f a b)
                            (bv-adder-overflowp f a b))
                                              ; Op-code 2 - addc
                     (bv-cv (bv-adder-output c a b)
                            (bv-adder-carry-out c a b)
                            (bv-adder-overflowp c a b)))
                 (if (bitn op-code 1)          ; Op-code 1 - inc
                     (bv-cv (bv-adder-output t a (nat-to-bv 0 (size a)))
                            (bv-adder-carry-out
                               t a (nat-to-bv 0 (size a)))
                            (bv-adder-overflowp
                               t a (nat-to-bv 0 (size a))))
                     (bv-cv a                  ; Op-code 0 - nop, move
                            f f)))))))
((disable bv-adder-output bv-adder-carry-out bv-adder-overflowp
          bv-subtracter-output bv-subtracter-carry-out
          bv-subtracter-overflowp nat-to-bv-to-nat
          remainder-of-0 carry)))
```

```
;;;;;;;;;;;;;;;;;;;;;;;;;;;;;;;;;;;;;;;;;;;;;;;;;;;;;;;;;;;;;;;;;;;;;;;;
;;                                                                    ;;
;;                    Boolean ALU Help Lemmas                         ;;
;;                                                                    ;;
;;;;;;;;;;;;;;;;;;;;;;;;;;;;;;;;;;;;;;;;;;;;;;;;;;;;;;;;;;;;;;;;;;;;;;;;

(prove-lemma nat-to-bv-of-2i (rewrite)
  (implies (boolp c)
           (equal (nat-to-bv (plus (carry c) (plus i i)) n)
                  (if (zerop n)
                      (btm)
                      (bitv c (nat-to-bv i (sub1 n)))))))

(prove-lemma nat-to-bv-to-nat-wrong-size (rewrite)
  (equal (nat-to-bv (bv-to-nat a) n)
         (trunc a n)))

(prove-lemma nat-to-bv-ignores-remainder (rewrite)
  (equal (nat-to-bv (remainder i (exp 2 n)) n)
         (nat-to-bv i n)))

(disable nat-to-bv-ignores-remainder)

(prove-lemma bv-adder-as-shifter (rewrite)
  (implies (and (bitvp a) (boolp c))
           (equal (bv-adder c a a)
                  (nat-to-bv (plus (bv-to-nat a)
                                   (bv-to-nat a)
                                   (carry c))
                             (add1 (size a)))))
  ((use (embed-in-nat-to-bv (x (bv-to-nat (bv-adder c a a)))
                            (y (plus (bv-to-nat a)
                                     (bv-to-nat a)
                                     (carry c)))
                            (n (add1 (size a))))
        (bv-to-nat-of-bv-adder (b a)))
   (disable nat-to-bv-to-nat-wrong-size bv-to-nat-of-bv-adder)))

(prove-lemma bv-adder-output-used-as-asl (rewrite)
  (implies (and (bitvp a)
                (boolp c))
           (equal (bv-adder-output c a a)
                  (if (equal a (btm))
                      (btm)
                      (bitv c (trunc a (sub1 (size a))))))))

(disable bv-adder-output-used-as-asl)
```

```
(prove-lemma bitn-equiv-lessp (rewrite)
  (implies (bitvp a)
           (equal (bitn a (size a))
                  (not (lessp (bv-to-nat a) (exp 2 (sub1 (size a))))))))

(prove-lemma bv-adder-carry-out-used-as-asl (rewrite)
  (implies (and (bitvp a)
                (boolp c))
           (equal (bv-adder-carry-out c a a)
                  (if (zerop (size a))
                      c
                      (bitn a (size a))))))

(disable bv-adder-carry-out-used-as-asl)

(disable bv-adder-as-shifter)
```

```
;;;;;;;;;;;;;;;;;;;;;;;;;;;;;;;;;;;;;;;;;;;;;;;;;;;;;;;;;;;;;;;;;;;;;;;;;;;
;;                                                                       ;;
;;                 Boolean Operation of ALU                             ;;
;;                                                                       ;;
;;;;;;;;;;;;;;;;;;;;;;;;;;;;;;;;;;;;;;;;;;;;;;;;;;;;;;;;;;;;;;;;;;;;;;;;;;;

(prove-lemma bv-alu-cv-correct-boolean nil
  (implies (and (bitvp a)
                (bitvp b)
                (equal (size a) (size b))
                (boolp c))

        (and (equal (bv-alu-cv a b c (nat-to-bv 15 4))        ; Move
                    (bv-cv a f f))

             (equal (bv-alu-cv a b c (nat-to-bv 14 4))        ; Not
                    (bv-cv (v-not a) f f))

             (equal (bv-alu-cv a b c (nat-to-bv 13 4))        ; And
                    (bv-cv (v-and a b) f f))

             (equal (bv-alu-cv a b c (nat-to-bv 12 4))        ; Or
                    (bv-cv (v-or a b) f f))

             (equal (bv-alu-cv a b c (nat-to-bv 11 4))        ; Xor
                    (bv-cv (v-xor a b) f f))

             (equal (bv-alu-cv a b c (nat-to-bv 10 4))        ; Lsr
                    (bv-cv (v-lsr a)
                           (bitn a 1)
                           f))

             (equal (bv-alu-cv a b c (nat-to-bv 9 4))         ; Asr
                    (bv-cv (v-asr a)
                           (bitn a 1)
                           f))

             (equal (bv-alu-cv a b c (nat-to-bv 8 4))         ; Ror
                    (bv-cv (v-ror a c)
                           (if (zerop (size a))
                               c
                               (bitn a 1))
                           f))

             (implies (equal a b)                             ; Lsl
                      (and (equal (bv (bv-alu-cv a b c
                                                 (nat-to-bv 3 4)))
                                  (v-lsl a))
```

```
                    (equal (c (bv-alu-cv a b c
                                         (nat-to-bv 3 4)))
                           (bitn a (size a)))))

        (implies (equal a b)                            ; Asl
                 (and (equal (bv (bv-alu-cv a b c
                                            (nat-to-bv 3 4)))
                             (v-asl a))
                      (equal (c (bv-alu-cv a b c
                                           (nat-to-bv 3 4)))
                             (bitn a (size a)))))

        (implies (equal a b)                            ; Rol
                 (and (equal (bv (bv-alu-cv a b c
                                            (nat-to-bv 2 4)))
                             (v-rol a c))
                      (equal (c (bv-alu-cv a b c
                                           (nat-to-bv 2 4)))
                             (if (zerop (size a))
                                 c
                                 (bitn a (size a)))))))))
((disable bv-adder-output bv-adder-carry-out bv-adder-overflowp
          bv-subtracter-output bv-subtracter-carry-out
          bv-subtracter-overflowp)
 (enable bv-adder-output-used-as-asl bv-adder-carry-out-used-as-asl)))
```

```
;;;;;;;;;;;;;;;;;;;;;;;;;;;;;;;;;;;;;;;;;;;;;;;;;;;;;;;;;;;;;;;;;;;;;;;;;;;;;
;;                                                                       ;;
;;                 Natural Number ALU Help Lemmas                        ;;
;;                                                                       ;;
;;;;;;;;;;;;;;;;;;;;;;;;;;;;;;;;;;;;;;;;;;;;;;;;;;;;;;;;;;;;;;;;;;;;;;;;;;;;;

(prove-lemma v-append-quotient (rewrite)
  (implies (and (bitvp a)
                (not (equal a (btm))))
           (equal (nat-to-bv (quotient (bv-to-nat a) 2)
                             (size a))
                  (v-append (vec a)
                            (bitv f (btm)))))))

(prove-lemma bit-interpretation-of-even-and-odd (rewrite)
  (equal (equal (remainder (bv-to-nat a) 2) 0)
         (not (bit a))))

(prove-lemma nat-to-bv-to-nat-hidden-to-accomodate-hands-off (rewrite)
  (equal (difference x
                     (bv-to-nat (nat-to-bv 0 n)))
         (fix x)))

(prove-lemma zero-not-less-than-anything (rewrite)
  (not (lessp (sub1 (bv-to-nat a))
              (bv-to-nat (nat-to-bv 0 (size a))))))

(prove-lemma nat-interpretation-of-inc-bit-vector (rewrite)
  (implies (bitvp a)
           (equal (bv-adder-output t a (nat-to-bv 0 (size a)))
                  (if (lessp (add1 (bv-to-nat a))
                             (exp 2 (size a)))
                      (nat-to-bv (add1 (bv-to-nat a)) (size a))
                      (nat-to-bv 0 (size a)))))
  ((disable pathological-difference boolp v-lsr
            bv-adder-output bv-adder-carry-out bv-adder-overflowp
            bv-subtracter-output bv-subtracter-carry-out
            bv-subtracter-overflowp)
   (enable nat-bv-adder-output-seen-as-bit-vector)))

(disable nat-interpretation-of-inc-bit-vector)

(prove-lemma nat-interpretation-of-inc-carry-out (rewrite)
  (implies (bitvp a)
           (equal (bv-adder-carry-out t a (nat-to-bv 0 (size a)))
                  (not (lessp (add1 (bv-to-nat a))
                              (exp 2 (size a))))))
  ((disable pathological-difference boolp v-lsr
            bv-adder-output bv-adder-carry-out bv-adder-overflowp
```

```
          bv-subtracter-output bv-subtracter-carry-out
          bv-subtracter-overflowp)
  (enable nat-interpretation-of-bv-adder-carry-out)))

(disable nat-interpretation-of-inc-carry-out)
```

```
;;;;;;;;;;;;;;;;;;;;;;;;;;;;;;;;;;;;;;;;;;;;;;;;;;;;;;;;;;;;;;;;;;;;;;;;;;;
;;                                                                       ;;
;;                 Natural Number Operation of ALU                      ;;
;;                                                                       ;;
;;;;;;;;;;;;;;;;;;;;;;;;;;;;;;;;;;;;;;;;;;;;;;;;;;;;;;;;;;;;;;;;;;;;;;;;;;;

(prove-lemma bv-alu-cv-correct-natural-number nil
  (implies
   (and (bitvp a)
        (bitvp b)
        (equal (size a) (size b))
        (boolp c))

   (and (equal (bv-alu-cv a b c (nat-to-bv 10 4)) ; Lsr
               (bv-cv (nat-to-bv (quotient (bv-to-nat a) 2)
                                 (size a))
                      (not (zerop (remainder (bv-to-nat a) 2)))
                      f))

        (equal (bv (bv-alu-cv a b c (nat-to-bv 7 4))) ; Sub - bv
               (if (not (lessp (bv-to-nat b)
                               (bv-to-nat a)))
                   (nat-to-bv (difference (bv-to-nat b)
                                          (bv-to-nat a))
                              (size a))
                   (nat-to-bv (difference (exp 2 (size a))
                                          (difference (bv-to-nat a)
                                                      (bv-to-nat b)))
                              (size a))))

        (equal (c (bv-alu-cv a b c (nat-to-bv 7 4))) ; Sub - carry
               (lessp (bv-to-nat b) (bv-to-nat a)))

        (equal (bv (bv-alu-cv a b c (nat-to-bv 6 4))) ; Subb - bv
               (if (not (lessp (bv-to-nat b)
                               (plus (bv-to-nat a) (carry c))))
                   (nat-to-bv (difference (bv-to-nat b)
                                          (plus (bv-to-nat a) (carry c)))
                              (size a))
                   (nat-to-bv (difference (exp 2 (size a))
                                          (difference (plus (bv-to-nat a)
                                                            (carry c))
                                                      (bv-to-nat b)))
                              (size a))))

        (equal (c (bv-alu-cv a b c (nat-to-bv 6 4))) ; Subb - carry
               (lessp (bv-to-nat b)
                      (plus (bv-to-nat a) (carry c))))))
```

```
(equal (bv (bv-alu-cv a b c (nat-to-bv 5 4))) ; Dec - bv
       (if (zerop (bv-to-nat a))
           (nat-to-bv (sub1 (exp 2 (size a)))
                      (size a))
         (nat-to-bv (sub1 (bv-to-nat a))
                    (size a))))

(equal (c (bv-alu-cv a b c (nat-to-bv 5 4))) ; Dec - carry
       (zerop (bv-to-nat a)))

(equal (bv (bv-alu-cv a b c (nat-to-bv 3 4))) ; Add - bv
       (if (lessp (plus (bv-to-nat a) (bv-to-nat b))
                  (exp 2 (size a)))
           (nat-to-bv (plus (bv-to-nat a) (bv-to-nat b))
                      (size a))
         (nat-to-bv
          (remainder (plus (bv-to-nat a) (bv-to-nat b))
                     (exp 2 (size a)))
          (size a))))

(equal (c (bv-alu-cv a b c (nat-to-bv 3 4))) ; Add - carry
       (not (lessp (plus (bv-to-nat a) (bv-to-nat b))
                   (exp 2 (size a)))))

(equal (bv (bv-alu-cv a b c (nat-to-bv 2 4))) ; Addc - bv
       (if (lessp (plus (bv-to-nat a) (bv-to-nat b) (carry c))
                  (exp 2 (size a)))
           (nat-to-bv (plus (bv-to-nat a)
                            (bv-to-nat b)
                            (carry c))
                      (size a))
         (nat-to-bv
          (remainder (plus (bv-to-nat a) (bv-to-nat b) (carry c))
                     (exp 2 (size a)))
          (size a))))

(equal (c (bv-alu-cv a b c (nat-to-bv 2 4))) ; Addc - carry
       (not (lessp (plus (bv-to-nat a) (bv-to-nat b) (carry c))
                   (exp 2 (size a)))))

(equal (bv (bv-alu-cv a b c (nat-to-bv 1 4))) ; Inc - bv
       (if (lessp (add1 (bv-to-nat a))
                  (exp 2 (size a)))
           (nat-to-bv (add1 (bv-to-nat a)) (size a))
         (nat-to-bv 0 (size a))))
```

```
          (equal (c (bv-alu-cv a b c (nat-to-bv 1 4))) ; Inc - carry
                 (not (lessp (add1 (bv-to-nat a))
                             (exp 2 (size a)))))))))
  ((disable pathological-difference boolp v-lsr
            bv-adder-output bv-adder-carry-out bv-adder-overflowp
            bv-subtracter-output bv-subtracter-carry-out
            bv-subtracter-overflowp nat-to-bv-to-nat)
   (hands-off bv-to-nat nat-to-bv)
   (enable nat-interpretation-of-inc-carry-out
           nat-interpretation-of-inc-bit-vector
           nat-interpretation-of-bv-subtracter-carry-out
           nat-bv-subtracter-output-seen-as-bit-vector
           nat-interpretation-of-bv-adder-carry-out
           nat-bv-adder-output-seen-as-bit-vector)))
```

```
;;;;;;;;;;;;;;;;;;;;;;;;;;;;;;;;;;;;;;;;;;;;;;;;;;;;;;;;;;;;;;;;;;;;;;;;
;;                                                                    ;;
;;          Two's Complement ALU Help Lemmas                          ;;
;;                                                                    ;;
;;;;;;;;;;;;;;;;;;;;;;;;;;;;;;;;;;;;;;;;;;;;;;;;;;;;;;;;;;;;;;;;;;;;;;;;

(prove-lemma twos-complement-twos-complement (rewrite)
  (implies (bitvp a)
           (equal (incr t (compl (incr t (compl a))))
                  a)))

(prove-lemma tc-to-bv-to-tc-negative (rewrite)
  (implies (and (bitvp a)
                (equal (size a) n))
           (equal (tc-to-bv (bv-to-tc a) n)
                  a))
  ((disable bv-to-nat-of-twos-compl bitn-equiv-lessp bv-to-nat-of-incr
            bv-to-nat-of-compl all-onesp-of-compl
            bitn-on-implies-non-0)))

(prove-lemma v-asr-is-a-bitv (rewrite)
  (bitvp (v-asr a)))

(prove-lemma size-of-v-asr nil
  (equal (size (v-asr a))
         (size a)))

(prove-lemma bv-asr-divides-by-two-bridge (rewrite)
  (implies (bitvp a)
           (equal (tc-to-bv (mod2 (bv-to-tc a))
                            (size a))
                  (bv-asr a)))
  ((use (embed-in-tc-to-bv (x (bv-to-tc (bv-asr a)))
                           (y (mod2 (bv-to-tc a)))
                           (n (size a)))
        (bv-asr-divides-by-two)
        (size-of-v-asr))
   (disable bv-asr-divides-by-two tc-to-bv)
   (hands-off mod2 bv-to-tc v-asr)))

(prove-lemma bv-to-tc-to-bv-of-zero-is-zero (rewrite)
  (equal (bv-to-tc (tc-to-bv 0 n))
         0))

(prove-lemma tc-to-bv-is-not-btm-for-non-zero-size (rewrite)
  (implies (not (zerop n))
           (equal (equal (tc-to-bv 0 n)
                         (btm))
                  f)))
```

```
(prove-lemma nat-of-zero-is-tc-of-zero (rewrite)
  (equal (nat-to-bv 0 size)
         (tc-to-bv 0 size)))

(prove-lemma tc-fix-of-add (rewrite)
  (equal (tc-fix (add a b))
         (add (tc-fix a) b)))

(prove-lemma tc-to-bv-of-bitv-not-btm (rewrite)
  (implies (and (not (equal a (btm)))
                (bitvp a))
           (not (equal (tc-to-bv 0 (size a))
                              (btm)))))

(prove-lemma tc-interpretation-of-inc-bit-vector (rewrite)
  (implies (and (bitvp a)
                (not (equal a (btm))))
           (equal (bv-adder-output t a (nat-to-bv 0 (size a)))
                  (tc-to-bv
                    (if (tc-in-rangep (add (bv-to-tc a) 1)
                                      (size a))
                        (add (bv-to-tc a) 1)
                        (if (negativep (add (bv-to-tc a) 1))
                            (add (bv-to-tc a)
                                 (add 1
                                      (exp 2 (size a))))
                            (add (bv-to-tc a)
                                 (add 1
                                      (minus (exp 2 (size a)))))))
                    (size a))))
  ((disable bv-adder-output add tc-in-rangep negativep bv-to-tc tc-to-bv)
   (hands-off exp)
   (enable tc-bv-adder-output-seen-as-bit-vector)))

(disable tc-interpretation-of-inc-bit-vector)

(prove-lemma tc-interpretation-of-dec-bit-vector (rewrite)
  (implies (and (bitvp a)
                (not (equal a (btm))))
           (equal (bv-subtracter-output t (nat-to-bv 0 (size a)) a)
                  (tc-to-bv
                    (if (tc-in-rangep (add (bv-to-tc a) -1)
                                      (size a))
                        (add (bv-to-tc a) -1)
                        (if (negativep (add (bv-to-tc a) -1))
                            (add (bv-to-tc a)
                                 (add -1
                                      (exp 2 (size a))))
                            (add (bv-to-tc a)
```

```
                               (add -1
                                    (minus (exp 2 (size a)))))))
                    (size a))))
  ((disable bv-subtracter-output add tc-in-rangep
            negativep bv-to-tc tc-to-bv)
   (hands-off exp)
   (enable tc-bv-subtracter-output-seen-as-bit-vector)))

(disable tc-interpretation-of-dec-bit-vector)

(prove-lemma tc-interpretation-of-inc-overflowp (rewrite)
  (implies (and (bitvp a)
                (not (equal a (btm))))
           (equal (bv-adder-overflowp t a (nat-to-bv 0 (size a)))
                  (not (tc-in-rangep (add (bv-to-tc a) 1)
                                     (size a)))))
  ((disable bv-adder-overflowp add tc-in-rangep
            negativep bv-to-tc tc-to-bv)
   (hands-off exp)
   (enable tc-interpretation-of-bv-adder-overflowp)))

(disable tc-interpretation-of-inc-overflowp)

(prove-lemma tc-interpretation-of-dec-overflowp (rewrite)
  (implies (and (bitvp a)
                (not (equal a (btm))))
           (equal (bv-subtracter-overflowp t (nat-to-bv 0 (size a)) a)
                  (not (tc-in-rangep (add (bv-to-tc a) -1)
                                     (size a)))))
  ((disable bv-subtracter-overflowp add tc-in-rangep
            negativep bv-to-tc tc-to-bv)
   (hands-off exp)
   (enable tc-interpretation-of-bv-subtracter-overflowp)))

(disable tc-interpretation-of-dec-overflowp)

(prove-lemma tc-interpretation-of-negation-output (rewrite)
  (implies (and (bitvp a)
                (not (equal a (btm))))
           (equal (bv-subtracter-output f a (nat-to-bv 0 (size a)))
                  (tc-to-bv
                    (if (tc-in-rangep (tc-minus (bv-to-tc a))
                                      (size a))
                        (tc-minus (bv-to-tc a))
                        (if (negativep (tc-minus (bv-to-tc a)))
                            (add (exp 2 (size a))
                                 (tc-minus (bv-to-tc a)))
                            (add (minus (exp 2 (size a)))
                                 (tc-minus (bv-to-tc a)))))))
```

```
                     (size a))))
  ((disable bv-subtracter-output add tc-in-rangep
           negativep bv-to-tc tc-to-bv)
   (hands-off exp)
   (enable tc-bv-subtracter-output-seen-as-bit-vector)))

(disable tc-interpretation-of-negation-output)

(prove-lemma tc-interpretation-of-negation-overflowp (rewrite)
  (implies (and (bitvp a)
                (not (equal a (btm))))
           (equal (bv-subtracter-overflowp f a (nat-to-bv 0 (size a)))
                  (not (tc-in-rangep (tc-minus (bv-to-tc a))
                                     (size a)))))
  ((disable bv-subtracter-overflowp add tc-in-rangep
           negativep bv-to-tc tc-to-bv)
   (hands-off exp)
   (enable tc-interpretation-of-bv-subtracter-overflowp)))

(disable tc-interpretation-of-negation-overflowp)

(disable nat-of-zero-is-tc-of-zero)

(disable tc-fix-of-add)
```

```
;;;;;;;;;;;;;;;;;;;;;;;;;;;;;;;;;;;;;;;;;;;;;;;;;;;;;;;;;;;;;;;;;;;;;;;;;;;;;;
;;                                                                      ;;
;;          Two's Complement Operation of the ALU                       ;;
;;                                                                      ;;
;;;;;;;;;;;;;;;;;;;;;;;;;;;;;;;;;;;;;;;;;;;;;;;;;;;;;;;;;;;;;;;;;;;;;;;;;;;;;;

(prove-lemma alu-correct-twos-complement nil
  (implies
    (and (bitvp a)
         (not (equal a (btm)))
         (bitvp b)
         (not (equal b (btm)))
         (equal (size a) (size b))
         (boolp c))

    (and (equal (bv (bv-alu-cv a b c (nat-to-bv 9 4))) ; Asr - bv
                (tc-to-bv (mod2 (bv-to-tc a))
                          (size a)))
         (equal (v (bv-alu-cv a b c (nat-to-bv 9 4))) ; Asr - ovflow
                f)

         (equal (bv (bv-alu-cv a b c (nat-to-bv 7 4))) ; Sub - bv
                (tc-to-bv
                 (if (tc-in-rangep (add (bv-to-tc b)
                                        (tc-minus (bv-to-tc a)))
                                   (size a))
                     (add (bv-to-tc b)
                          (tc-minus (bv-to-tc a)))
                     (if (negativep (add (bv-to-tc b)
                                         (tc-minus (bv-to-tc a))))
                         (add (bv-to-tc b)
                              (add (exp 2 (size a))
                                   (tc-minus (bv-to-tc a))))
                         (add (bv-to-tc b)
                              (add (minus (exp 2 (size a)))
                                   (tc-minus (bv-to-tc a))))))
                 (size a)))
         (equal (v (bv-alu-cv a b c (nat-to-bv 7 4))) ; Sub - ovflow
                (not (tc-in-rangep (add (bv-to-tc b)
                                        (tc-minus (bv-to-tc a)))
                                   (size a))))


         (equal (bv (bv-alu-cv a b c (nat-to-bv 6 4))) ; Subb - bv
                (tc-to-bv
                 (if (tc-in-rangep (add (bv-to-tc b)
                                        (tc-minus (add (bv-to-tc a)
                                                       (carry c))))
```

```
                          (size a))
              (add (bv-to-tc b) (tc-minus (add (bv-to-tc a)
                                               (carry c))))
           (if (negativep (add (bv-to-tc b)
                              (tc-minus (add (bv-to-tc a)
                                            (carry c)))))
               (add (bv-to-tc b)
                    (add (exp 2 (size a))
                         (tc-minus (add (bv-to-tc a)
                                        (carry c)))))
               (add (bv-to-tc b)
                    (add (minus (exp 2 (size a)))
                         (tc-minus (add (bv-to-tc a)
                                        (carry c))))))))
           (size a)))
   (equal (v (bv-alu-cv a b c (nat-to-bv 6 4))) ; Subb - ovflow
          (not (tc-in-rangep (add (bv-to-tc b)
                                  (tc-minus (add (bv-to-tc a)
                                                 (carry c))))
                             (size a))))

   (equal (bv (bv-alu-cv a b c (nat-to-bv 5 4))) ; Dec - bv
          (tc-to-bv
           (if (tc-in-rangep (add (bv-to-tc a) -1)
                             (size a))
               (add (bv-to-tc a) -1)
               (if (negativep (add (bv-to-tc a) -1))
                   (add (bv-to-tc a)
                        (add -1
                             (exp 2 (size a))))
                   (add (bv-to-tc a)
                        (add -1
                             (minus (exp 2 (size a)))))))
           (size a)))
   (equal (v (bv-alu-cv a b c (nat-to-bv 5 4))) ; Dec - ovflow
          (not (tc-in-rangep (add (bv-to-tc a) -1)
                             (size a))))


   (equal (bv (bv-alu-cv a b c (nat-to-bv 4 4))) ; Neg - bv
          (tc-to-bv
           (if (tc-in-rangep (tc-minus (bv-to-tc a))
                             (size a))
               (tc-minus (bv-to-tc a))
               (if (negativep (tc-minus (bv-to-tc a)))
                   (add (exp 2 (size a))
                        (tc-minus (bv-to-tc a)))
                   (add (minus (exp 2 (size a)))
```

```
                    (tc-minus (bv-to-tc a)))))
          (size a)))
  (equal (v (bv-alu-cv a b c (nat-to-bv 4 4))) ; Neg - ovflow
         (not (tc-in-rangep (tc-minus (bv-to-tc a))
                            (size a))))


  (equal (bv (bv-alu-cv a b c (nat-to-bv 3 4))) ; Add -  bv
         (tc-to-bv
          (if (tc-in-rangep (add (bv-to-tc a)
                                 (bv-to-tc b))
                            (size a))
              (add (bv-to-tc a) (bv-to-tc b))
              (if (negativep (add (bv-to-tc a)
                                  (bv-to-tc b)))
                  (add (bv-to-tc a)
                       (add (bv-to-tc b)
                            (exp 2 (size a))))
                  (add (bv-to-tc a)
                       (add (bv-to-tc b)
                            (minus (exp 2 (size a)))))))
          (size a)))
  (equal (v (bv-alu-cv a b c (nat-to-bv 3 4))) ; Add - ovflow
         (not (tc-in-rangep (add (bv-to-tc a)
                                 (bv-to-tc b))
                            (size a))))


  (equal (bv (bv-alu-cv a b c (nat-to-bv 2 4))) ; Addc - bv
         (tc-to-bv
          (if (tc-in-rangep (add (bv-to-tc a)
                                 (add (bv-to-tc b)
                                      (carry c)))
                            (size a))
              (add (bv-to-tc a) (add (bv-to-tc b)
                                     (carry c)))
              (if (negativep (add (bv-to-tc a)
                                  (add (bv-to-tc b)
                                       (carry c))))
                  (add (bv-to-tc a)
                       (add (bv-to-tc b)
                            (add (carry c)
                                 (exp 2 (size a)))))
                  (add (bv-to-tc a)
                       (add (bv-to-tc b)
                            (add (carry c)
                                 (minus (exp 2 (size a))))))))
          (size a)))
  (equal (v (bv-alu-cv a b c (nat-to-bv 2 4))) ; Addc - ovflow
```

```
                (not (tc-in-rangep (add (bv-to-tc a)
                                        (add (bv-to-tc b) (carry c)))
                                   (size a))))

        (equal (bv (bv-alu-cv a b c (nat-to-bv 1 4))) ; Inc - bv
               (tc-to-bv
                (if (tc-in-rangep (add (bv-to-tc a) 1)
                                  (size a))
                    (add (bv-to-tc a) 1)
                  (if (negativep (add (bv-to-tc a) 1))
                      (add (bv-to-tc a)
                           (add 1 (exp 2 (size a))))
                    (add (bv-to-tc a)
                         (add 1 (minus (exp 2 (size a)))))))
                (size a)))
        (equal (v (bv-alu-cv a b c (nat-to-bv 1 4))) ; Inc - ovflow
               (not (tc-in-rangep (add (bv-to-tc a) 1)
                                  (size a))))))
  ((disable pathological-difference boolp v-lsr v-asr mod2
           bv-adder-output bv-adder-carry-out bv-adder-overflowp
           bv-subtracter-output bv-subtracter-carry-out
           bv-subtracter-overflowp
           nat-to-bv-to-nat add tc-in-rangep minus tc-to-bv)
   (hands-off nat-to-bv bv-to-nat bv-to-tc)
   (enable tc-interpretation-of-bv-subtracter-overflowp
          tc-bv-subtracter-output-seen-as-bit-vector
          tc-interpretation-of-bv-adder-overflowp
          tc-bv-adder-output-seen-as-bit-vector
          tc-interpretation-of-inc-bit-vector
          tc-interpretation-of-dec-bit-vector
          tc-interpretation-of-inc-overflowp
          tc-interpretation-of-dec-overflowp
          tc-interpretation-of-negation-output
          tc-interpretation-of-negation-overflowp)))
```

```
;;;;;;;;;;;;;;;;;;;;;;;;;;;;;;;;;;;;;;;;;;;;;;;;;;;;;;;;;;;;;;;;;;;;;;;;
;;                                                                    ;;
;;   The following contains definitions and lemmas concerning the     ;;
;;   hardware necessary to build "big-machine".                       ;;
;;                                                                    ;;
;;;;;;;;;;;;;;;;;;;;;;;;;;;;;;;;;;;;;;;;;;;;;;;;;;;;;;;;;;;;;;;;;;;;;;;;


;;;;;;;;;;;;;;;;;;;;;;;;;;;;;;;;;;;;;;;;;;;;;;;;;;;;;;;;;;;;;;;;;;;;;;;;
;;                                                                    ;;
;;                   Miscellaneous Lemmas                             ;;
;;                                                                    ;;
;;;;;;;;;;;;;;;;;;;;;;;;;;;;;;;;;;;;;;;;;;;;;;;;;;;;;;;;;;;;;;;;;;;;;;;;

(prove-lemma size-bv-bv-alu-cv (rewrite)
  (equal (size (bv (bv-alu-cv a b c op-code)))
         (size a))
  ((disable bv-adder-output bv-adder-carry-out bv-adder-overflowp
            bv-subtracter-output bv-subtracter-carry-out
            bv-subtracter-overflowp
            nat-to-bv-to-nat remainder-of-0 carry)))

(disable bv-alu-cv)

(disable bv-alu-cv-with-ifs)

(defn fix-bool (x) (if x t f))

(defn properp (x)
  (if (nlistp x) (equal x nil) (properp (cdr x))))

(prove-lemma assoc-of-append (rewrite)
  (equal (append (append a b) c) (append a (append b c))))

(prove-lemma length-0 (rewrite)
  (equal (equal (length x) 0) (nlistp x)))

(defn v-nat-dec (a)         ; Word width decrement
  (if (zerop (bv-to-nat a))
      (nat-to-bv (sub1 (exp 2 (size a)))
                 (size a))              ; This is not needed for plus.
      (nat-to-bv (sub1 (bv-to-nat a))   ; (sub1 0) is zero and no wrap-
                 (size a))))            ; around is possible.

(defn v-nat-inc (a)              ; Word width increment
  (nat-to-bv (add1 (bv-to-nat a)) (size a)))

(prove-lemma size-v-nat-dec (rewrite)
  (equal (size (v-nat-dec x))
         (size x)))

(prove-lemma size-v-nat-inc (rewrite)
  (equal (size (v-nat-inc x))
         (size x)))
```

```
;;;;;;;;;;;;;;;;;;;;;;;;;;;;;;;;;;;;;;;;;;;;;;;;;;;;;;;;;;;;;;;;;;;;;;;;;;
;;                                                                      ;;
;;                     Memory Accessors                                 ;;
;;                                                                      ;;
;;;;;;;;;;;;;;;;;;;;;;;;;;;;;;;;;;;;;;;;;;;;;;;;;;;;;;;;;;;;;;;;;;;;;;;;;;

(defn nth (n lst)
  (if (zerop n)
      (car lst)
      (nth (sub1 n) (cdr lst))))

(defn v-nth (v-n lst)
  (nth (bv-to-nat v-n) lst))

(defn update-v (c cell value)
  (if (truep c)
      value
      cell))

(defn update-nth (c n lst value)
  (if (and (truep c)
           (listp lst))
      (if (zerop n)
          (cons value (cdr lst))
          (cons (car lst) (update-nth c (sub1 n) (cdr lst) value)))
      lst))

(defn update-v-nth (c v-n lst value)
  (update-nth c (bv-to-nat v-n) lst value))

(prove-lemma length-update-nth (rewrite)
  (equal (length (update-nth c n lst value))
         (length lst)))

(prove-lemma length-update-v-nth (rewrite)
  (equal (length (update-v-nth c n lst value))
         (length lst)))

(prove-lemma listp-update-nth (rewrite)
  (equal (listp (update-nth c n lst value))
         (listp lst)))

(prove-lemma listp-update-v-nth (rewrite)
  (equal (listp (update-v-nth c n lst value))
         (listp lst)))
```

```
;;;;;;;;;;;;;;;;;;;;;;;;;;;;;;;;;;;;;;;;;;;;;;;;;;;;;;;;;;;;;;;;;;;;;;;;;;;;;;;;
;;                                                                          ;;
;;            Zero and Negative Flag Interpretation Lemmas                  ;;
;;                                                                          ;;
;;;;;;;;;;;;;;;;;;;;;;;;;;;;;;;;;;;;;;;;;;;;;;;;;;;;;;;;;;;;;;;;;;;;;;;;;;;;;;;;

(defn b-bv-nzerop (a)                ; Not zerop vector test
  (if (bitvp a)
      (if (equal a (btm))
          f
          (b-or (bit a)
                (b-bv-nzerop (vec a))))
      f))

(defn b-bv-zerop (a)
  (b-not (b-bv-nzerop a)))

(defn v-zerop (a)
  (if (bitvp a)
      (if (equal a (btm))
          t
          (and (equal (bit a) f)
               (v-zerop (vec a))))
      t))

(prove-lemma b-bv-zerop-equal-v-zerop (rewrite)
  (equal (b-bv-zerop a)
         (v-zerop a)))

; The following are the natural number and tc intepretation lemmas for
; the zero flag.

(prove-lemma v-zerop-equal-bv-to-nat-zero (rewrite)
  (equal (v-zerop a)
         (zerop (bv-to-nat a))))

(prove-lemma v-zerop-equal-bv-to-tc-zero (rewrite)
  (equal (v-zerop a)
         (equal 0 (bv-to-tc a))))

(disable v-zerop-equal-bv-to-nat-zero)

(disable v-zerop-equal-bv-to-tc-zero)

;  The following is the tc interpretation lemma for the negative flag.

(prove-lemma n-flag-equals-negativep (rewrite)
  (equal (bitn a (size a))
         (negativep (bv-to-tc a))))
```

```
(disable n-flag-equals-negativep)

(defn bv-equal (a b)                      ; Vector equal test
  (if (bitvp a)
      (if (equal a (btm))
          t
          (b-and (b-equv (bit a) (bit b))
                 (bv-equal (vec a) (vec b))))
      f))

(prove-lemma bv-equal-is-equal (rewrite)
  (implies (and (bitvp a)
                (bitvp b)
                (equal (size a) (size b)))
           (equal (bv-equal a b)
                  (equal a b))))

(disable bv-equal-is-equal)
```

```
;;;;;;;;;;;;;;;;;;;;;;;;;;;;;;;;;;;;;;;;;;;;;;;;;;;;;;;;;;;;;;;;;;;;;;;;
;;                                                                    ;;
;;          Assumptions made about the Various Registers              ;;
;;                                                                    ;;
;;;;;;;;;;;;;;;;;;;;;;;;;;;;;;;;;;;;;;;;;;;;;;;;;;;;;;;;;;;;;;;;;;;;;;;;

(defn nxsz nil 4)                    ; Width of micro address reg

(defn machine-size nil 16)           ; Word width of microprocessor
```

```
;;;;;;;;;;;;;;;;;;;;;;;;;;;;;;;;;;;;;;;;;;;;;;;;;;;;;;;;;;;;;;;;;;;;;;;;;;;;;
;;                                                                         ;;
;;              Register, RAMP, and ROMP Recognizers                       ;;
;;                                                                         ;;
;;    A RAM and ROM checker are presented below and are used to ensure     ;;
;;    that RAM and ROM (constant function) have certain properties.        ;;
;;                                                                         ;;
;;;;;;;;;;;;;;;;;;;;;;;;;;;;;;;;;;;;;;;;;;;;;;;;;;;;;;;;;;;;;;;;;;;;;;;;;;;;;

(defn sizep (register width)
  (equal (size register) width))

(defn every-member-sizep (lst n)
  (if (nlistp lst)
      t
      (and (sizep (car lst) n)
           (every-member-sizep (cdr lst) n))))

(defn ramp (ram width locations)
  (and (equal (length ram) locations)
       (every-member-sizep ram width)))

(defn romp (rom width locations)
  (and (equal (length rom) locations)
       (every-member-sizep rom width)))

(prove-lemma every-member-sizep-implies-size-nth (rewrite)
  (implies (and (lessp n (length lst))
                (every-member-sizep lst width))
           (equal (size (nth n lst)) width)))

(prove-lemma every-member-sizep-implies-size-nth-machine-size (rewrite)
  (implies (and (lessp n (length lst))
                (every-member-sizep lst (machine-size)))
           (equal (size (nth n lst)) (machine-size))))

(prove-lemma every-member-sizep-implies-size-nth-0 (rewrite)
  (implies (and (every-member-sizep lst width)
                (lessp 0 (length lst)))
           (equal (size (car lst)) width)))

(disable boolp)
```

```
;;;;;;;;;;;;;;;;;;;;;;;;;;;;;;;;;;;;;;;;;;;;;;;;;;;;;;;;;;;;;;;;;;;;;;
;;                                                                  ;;
;;                      Op-code Accessors                          ;;
;;                                                                  ;;
;;;;;;;;;;;;;;;;;;;;;;;;;;;;;;;;;;;;;;;;;;;;;;;;;;;;;;;;;;;;;;;;;;;;;;

(defn bv-op-code (i-reg)
  (bitv (bitn i-reg 13)
        (bitv (bitn i-reg 14)
              (bitv (bitn i-reg 15)
                    (bitv (bitn i-reg 16)
                          (btm))))))

(defn b-move-op (i-reg)
  (bitn i-reg 12))

(defn b-cc-set (i-reg)
  (bitn i-reg 11))

(defn b-direct-reg-b (i-reg)
  (b-nor (bitn i-reg 9)
         (bitn i-reg 10)))

(defn b-indirect-reg-b (i-reg)
  (b-and (bitn i-reg 9)
         (b-not (bitn i-reg 10))))

(defn b-indirect-reg-b-dec (i-reg)
  (b-and (b-not (bitn i-reg 9))
         (bitn i-reg 10)))

(defn b-indirect-reg-b-inc (i-reg)
  (b-and (bitn i-reg 9)
         (bitn i-reg 10)))

(defn bv-oprd-b (i-reg)
  (bitv (bitn i-reg 6)
        (bitv (bitn i-reg 7)
              (bitv (bitn i-reg 8)
                    (btm)))))

(defn b-direct-reg-a (i-reg)
  (b-nor (bitn i-reg 4)
         (bitn i-reg 5)))

(defn b-indirect-reg-a (i-reg)
  (b-and (bitn i-reg 4)
         (b-not (bitn i-reg 5))))
```

```
(defn b-indirect-reg-a-dec (i-reg)
  (b-and (b-not (bitn i-reg 4))
         (bitn i-reg 5)))

(defn b-indirect-reg-a-inc (i-reg)
  (b-and (bitn i-reg 4)
         (bitn i-reg 5)))

(defn bv-oprd-a (i-reg)
  (bitv (bitn i-reg 1)
        (bitv (bitn i-reg 2)
              (bitv (bitn i-reg 3)
                    (btm)))))
```

```
;;;;;;;;;;;;;;;;;;;;;;;;;;;;;;;;;;;;;;;;;;;;;;;;;;;;;;;;;;;;;;;;;;;;;;;;;
;;                                                                     ;;
;;                  Sub-functions for FM8501                           ;;
;;                                                                     ;;
;; NOTE:  Many definitions below are presented in pairs.  A hardware   ;;
;;        version is presented along with a version that is more       ;;
;;        agreeable to the theorem-prover.  The second of these        ;;
;;        paired definitions has a "WITH-IFS" ending.  Not all         ;;
;;        of the hardware functions have a "WITH-IFS" pair.            ;;
;;                                                                     ;;
;;;;;;;;;;;;;;;;;;;;;;;;;;;;;;;;;;;;;;;;;;;;;;;;;;;;;;;;;;;;;;;;;;;;;;;;;

(defn bv-alu-op-code (i-reg)
  (bv-if (b-move-op i-reg)
         (nat-to-bv 0 4)
         (bv-op-code i-reg)))

(defn b-store-alu-result (c-flag v-flag z-flag n-flag i-reg)
  (b-or (b-or (b-not (b-move-op i-reg))
              (bitn (bv-op-code i-reg) 4))
        (b-or (b-or (b-or (b-and (b-not c-flag)
                                 (bv-equal (bv-op-code i-reg)
                                           (nat-to-bv 0 4)))
                          (b-and c-flag
                                 (bv-equal (bv-op-code i-reg)
                                           (nat-to-bv 1 4))))
                    (b-or (b-and (b-not v-flag)
                                 (bv-equal (bv-op-code i-reg)
                                           (nat-to-bv 2 4)))
                          (b-and v-flag
                                 (bv-equal (bv-op-code i-reg)
                                           (nat-to-bv 3 4)))))
              (b-or (b-or (b-and (b-not z-flag)
                                 (bv-equal (bv-op-code i-reg)
                                           (nat-to-bv 4 4)))
                          (b-and z-flag
                                 (bv-equal (bv-op-code i-reg)
                                           (nat-to-bv 5 4))))
                    (b-or (b-and (b-not n-flag)
                                 (bv-equal (bv-op-code i-reg)
                                           (nat-to-bv 6 4)))
                          (b-and n-flag
                                 (bv-equal (bv-op-code i-reg)
                                           (nat-to-bv 7 4)))))))))

(defn b-store-alu-result-with-ifs (c-flag v-flag z-flag n-flag i-reg)
  (or (not (b-move-op i-reg))
      (bitn (bv-op-code i-reg) 4)
      (equal (bv-op-code i-reg)
```

```
              (nat-to-bv (if c-flag 1 0) 4))
      (equal (bv-op-code i-reg)
              (nat-to-bv (if v-flag 3 2) 4))
      (equal (bv-op-code i-reg)
              (nat-to-bv (if z-flag 5 4) 4))
      (equal (bv-op-code i-reg)
              (nat-to-bv (if n-flag 7 6) 4)))))

(prove-lemma b-store-alu-result-ifs (rewrite)
  (equal (b-store-alu-result c-flag v-flag z-flag n-flag i-reg)
         (b-store-alu-result-with-ifs
           c-flag v-flag z-flag n-flag i-reg)))

(disable b-store-alu-result)
```

```
;;;;;;;;;;;;;;;;;;;;;;;;;;;;;;;;;;;;;;;;;;;;;;;;;;;;;;;;;;;;;;;;;;;;;;;;;;;
;;                                                                       ;;
;;                          Micro-ROM                                    ;;
;;                                                                       ;;
;;;;;;;;;;;;;;;;;;;;;;;;;;;;;;;;;;;;;;;;;;;;;;;;;;;;;;;;;;;;;;;;;;;;;;;;;;;
```

```
(defn make-micro-word (1)
 (if (nlistp 1)
     (btm)
     (if (nlistp (cdr 1))
         (nat-to-bv (car 1) (nxsz))
         (bitv (if (equal (car 1) 't) t f)
             (make-micro-word (cdr 1)))))))

(defn make-micro-rom (1)
  (if (nlistp 1) nil (cons (make-micro-word (car 1))
                          (make-micro-rom (cdr 1))))))

(defn micro-store nil
;                 1 1 1 1 1 1 1 1
;     1 2 3 4 5 6 7 8 9 0 1 2 3 4 5 6 7
  (make-micro-rom '((f f f f f f f f t f f f f f f 1)          ;0

                    (f t f t f t f f f t f t f f f f 2)        ;1
                    (f f f t f f f f t f f f f f f f 3)        ;2
                    (f f f f f f f f f t f f f f t f 4)        ;3

                    (f f f f t f f t f t f t f f f f 5)        ;4
                    (f f f f t f f f t f f f f f f f 6)        ;5
                    (f f f f t f f f f t t f f f f f 7)        ;6

                    (f f f f f f f t f t f t f f f f 8)        ;7
                    (f f f f f f f f t f f f f f f f 9)        ;8
                    (f f f f f f f f t f f t f f f 10)         ;9

                    (f f f f f f f f f t f f f t f f 11)       ;10
                    (t f t f f f f f f f f f f f f t 12)       ;11

                    (f f f f t f t f f t f f f f f f 13)       ;12
                    (f f f f f f t f f t f f f f f f 1)        ;13
```

; The remaining lines send us to state 0 if mar ever gets beyond 13.
; This is provably impossible after resetting; however, if struck by
; alpha radiation this insures a reset. It also makes some of the proofs
; easier because we know that (next (micro-rom mar)) has size 4 provided
; mar has size 4.

```
                    (f f f f f f f f t f f f f f f 0)          ;14
                    (f f f f f f f f t t f f f f f 0)          ;15
```

```
                    )))
(defn micro-rom (addr)
  (v-nth addr (micro-store)))

;  Accessors for data in the ROM named "micro-store".

(defn b-dout-incdec    (x) (bitn x 1)) ; Data out reg or address unit

(defn b-force-inc      (x) (bitn x 2)) ; Force increment for address

(defn b-en-no-store    (x) (bitn x 3)) ; Let "NO-STORE" effect sequencer

(defn b-ir-mem-ref     (x) (bitn x 4)) ; Memory reference for instruction

(defn b-oprda-oprdb    (x) (bitn x 5)) ; Select operand A or operand B

(defn b-pc-regnum      (x) (bitn x 6)) ; Select PC or register in file

(defn b-postinc        (x) (bitn x 7)) ; Post-increment address mode

(defn b-predec         (x) (bitn x 8)) ; Pre-decrement address mode

(defn b-rd             (x) (bitn x 9)) ; Read cycle

(defn b-seq            (x) (bitn x 10)) ; Sequence micro-address register

(defn b-we-a-reg       (x) (bitn x 11)) ; Write enable A register

(defn b-we-addr-out    (x) (bitn x 12)) ; Write enable address-out reg

(defn b-we-b-reg       (x) (bitn x 13)) ; Write enable B register

(defn b-we-alu-result  (x) (bitn x 14)) ; WE DATA-OUT, CC-REG, NO-STORE

(defn b-we-ir          (x) (bitn x 15)) ; Write enable instruction reg

(defn b-wr             (x) (bitn x 16)) ; Write cycle

(defn bv-next          (x) (bitv (bitn x 17)           ; Next micro address
                                 (bitv (bitn x 18)
                                       (bitv (bitn x 19)
                                             (bitv (bitn x 20)
                                                   (btm)))))))

(defn right-bv-next-size (lst)
  (if (nlistp lst)
      t
      (and (equal (size (bv-next (car lst))) (nxsz))
           (right-bv-next-size (cdr lst)))))

(prove-lemma size-bv-next-micro-rom-lemma (rewrite)
  (equal (size (bv-next x)) 4))

(disable micro-rom)
```

```
;;;;;;;;;;;;;;;;;;;;;;;;;;;;;;;;;;;;;;;;;;;;;;;;;;;;;;;;;;;;;;;;;;;;;;
;;                                                                  ;;
;;    Hardware Variable and Constant Assumptions for FM8501         ;;
;;                                                                  ;;
;;  The following definition describes the assumptions about the    ;;
;;  various registers (variables) and the ROM used in the           ;;
;;  construction of the FM8501 microprocessor.                      ;;
;;                                                                  ;;
;;;;;;;;;;;;;;;;;;;;;;;;;;;;;;;;;;;;;;;;;;;;;;;;;;;;;;;;;;;;;;;;;;;;;;

(defn standard-hyps (mar read write dtack reset no-store data-out
                         reg-file addr-out c-flag v-flag z-flag n-flag
                         a-reg b-reg i-reg visual-mem real-mem)
  (and (romp (micro-store) 20 (exp 2 (nxsz)))
       (sizep mar (nxsz))
       (boolp read)
       (boolp write)
       (boolp dtack)
       (boolp reset)
       (boolp no-store)
       (sizep data-out (machine-size))
       (ramp reg-file (machine-size) 8)
       (sizep addr-out (machine-size))
       (boolp c-flag)
       (boolp v-flag)
       (boolp z-flag)
       (boolp n-flag)
       (sizep a-reg (machine-size))
       (sizep b-reg (machine-size))
       (sizep i-reg (machine-size))
       (sizep visual-mem (machine-size))
       (ramp real-mem (machine-size) (exp 2 16))))
```

```
;;;;;;;;;;;;;;;;;;;;;;;;;;;;;;;;;;;;;;;;;;;;;;;;;;;;;;;;;;;;;;;;;;;;;;;;;
;;                                                                     ;;
;;                      Miscellanous Lemmas                            ;;
;;                                                                     ;;
;;;;;;;;;;;;;;;;;;;;;;;;;;;;;;;;;;;;;;;;;;;;;;;;;;;;;;;;;;;;;;;;;;;;;;;;;

(prove-lemma every-member-sizep-implies-bitvp (rewrite)
  (implies (and (every-member-sizep lst width)
                (lessp n (length lst))
                (not (zerop width)))
           (bitvp (nth n lst))))

(prove-lemma every-member-sizep-implies-bitvp-machine-size (rewrite)
  (implies (and (every-member-sizep lst (machine-size))
                (lessp n (length lst)))
           (bitvp (nth n lst))))

(prove-lemma sizep-implies-bitvp (rewrite)
  (implies (equal (size a) (add1 n))
           (bitvp a)))

;  The following lemma subsumes trunc-size.

(prove-lemma trunc-size-bridge (rewrite)
  (implies (and (bitvp a)
                (equal n (size a)))
           (equal (trunc a n) a)))

(prove-lemma b-if-works (rewrite)
  (implies (and (boolp c)
                (boolp a)
                (boolp b))
           (equal (b-if c a b) (if c a b)))
  ((enable boolp)))
```

```
;;;;;;;;;;;;;;;;;;;;;;;;;;;;;;;;;;;;;;;;;;;;;;;;;;;;;;;;;;;;;;;;;;;;;;;;;;;
;;                                                                       ;;
;;          Functions for Composing the Microprocessor                  ;;
;;                                                                       ;;
;;;;;;;;;;;;;;;;;;;;;;;;;;;;;;;;;;;;;;;;;;;;;;;;;;;;;;;;;;;;;;;;;;;;;;;;;;;

(defn bv-reg-select (i-reg mar reset)
  (bv-if (b-or reset
               (b-pc-regnum (micro-rom mar)))
         (nat-to-bv 0 3)                                ; PC is register 0
         (bv-if (b-oprda-oprdb (micro-rom mar))
                (bv-oprd-a i-reg)
                (bv-oprd-b i-reg))))

(defn bv-reg-select-with-ifs (i-reg mar reset)
  (if (b-or reset
            (b-pc-regnum (micro-rom mar)))
      (nat-to-bv 0 3)                                   ; PC is register 0
      (if (b-oprda-oprdb (micro-rom mar))
          (bv-oprd-a i-reg)
          (bv-oprd-b i-reg))))

(prove-lemma bv-reg-select-ifs (rewrite)
  (equal (bv-reg-select i-reg mar reset)
         (bv-reg-select-with-ifs i-reg mar reset)))

(defn b-oprd-mem-ref (mar i-reg)
  (b-if (b-oprda-oprdb (micro-rom mar))
        (b-not (b-direct-reg-a i-reg))
        (b-not (b-direct-reg-b i-reg))))

(defn b-oprd-mem-ref-with-ifs (mar i-reg)
  (if (b-oprda-oprdb (micro-rom mar))
      (b-not (b-direct-reg-a i-reg))
      (b-not (b-direct-reg-b i-reg))))

(prove-lemma b-oprd-mem-ref-ifs (rewrite)
  (equal (b-oprd-mem-ref mar i-reg)
         (b-oprd-mem-ref-with-ifs mar i-reg)))

(disable b-oprd-mem-ref)

; Next micro-address

(defn mar (mar i-reg dtack reset no-store)
  (update-v (b-or (b-or reset
                        (b-or dtack
                              (b-seq (micro-rom mar))))
                  (b-or (b-and (b-en-no-store (micro-rom mar))
```

```
                                 no-store)
                       (b-and (b-not (b-oprd-mem-ref mar i-reg))
                              (b-not (b-ir-mem-ref (micro-rom mar))))))))
             mar
             (bv-if reset
                    (nat-to-bv 0 (nxsz))
                    (bv-next (micro-rom mar)))))))

; Read register

(defn read (mar i-reg)
  (b-and (b-or (b-oprd-mem-ref mar i-reg)
               (b-ir-mem-ref (micro-rom mar)))
         (b-rd (micro-rom mar))))

; Write register

(defn write (mar i-reg no-store)
  (b-and (b-wr (micro-rom mar))
         (b-and (b-oprd-mem-ref mar i-reg)
                (b-not no-store))))

; Data acknowledgement

(defn dtack (current-oracle-entry)
  (fix-bool (car current-oracle-entry)))

; Reset function

(defn reset (current-oracle-entry)
  (fix-bool (cadr current-oracle-entry)))

; No-store -- defines the flag which allows FM8501 to do conditional
; stores.

(defn no-store (no-store c-flag v-flag z-flag n-flag i-reg mar)
  (update-v (b-we-alu-result (micro-rom mar))
            no-store
            (b-not (b-store-alu-result
                    c-flag v-flag z-flag n-flag i-reg))))

(defn no-store-with-ifs (no-store c-flag v-flag z-flag n-flag i-reg mar)
  (if (b-we-alu-result (micro-rom mar))
      (not (b-store-alu-result-with-ifs
            c-flag v-flag z-flag n-flag i-reg))
      no-store))

(prove-lemma no-store-ifs (rewrite)
  (equal (no-store no-store c-flag v-flag z-flag n-flag i-reg mar)
```

```
          (no-store-with-ifs no-store
                             c-flag v-flag z-flag n-flag i-reg mar))
  ((disable b-store-alu-result-with-ifs)))

(disable no-store)

;  Bit-vector result of the ALU

(defn data-out (data-out a-reg b-reg c-flag i-reg mar)
  (update-v (b-we-alu-result (micro-rom mar))
            data-out
            (bv (bv-alu-cv a-reg b-reg c-flag (bv-alu-op-code i-reg)))))

(defn data-out-with-ifs (data-out a-reg b-reg c-flag i-reg mar)
  (if (b-we-alu-result (micro-rom mar))
      (bv (bv-alu-cv a-reg b-reg c-flag (bv-alu-op-code i-reg)))
      data-out))

(prove-lemma data-out-ifs (rewrite)
  (equal (data-out data-out a-reg b-reg c-flag i-reg mar)
         (data-out-with-ifs data-out a-reg b-reg c-flag i-reg mar)))

(disable data-out)

;  Calculates the next value of the register file.

(defn reg-file (reg-file data-out i-reg mar no-store reset)
  (update-v-nth
   (b-or (b-or reset
               (b-force-inc (micro-rom mar)))
         (b-or (b-or (b-pc-regnum (micro-rom mar))
                     (b-and (b-wr (micro-rom mar))
                            (b-and (b-not no-store)
                                   (b-direct-reg-b i-reg))))
               (b-or (b-and (b-predec (micro-rom mar))
                            (b-if (b-oprda-oprdb (micro-rom mar))
                                  (b-indirect-reg-a-dec i-reg)
                                  (b-indirect-reg-b-dec i-reg)))
                     (b-and (b-postinc (micro-rom mar))
                            (b-if (b-oprda-oprdb (micro-rom mar))
                                  (b-indirect-reg-a-inc i-reg)
                                  (b-indirect-reg-b-inc i-reg))))))
   (bv-reg-select i-reg mar reset)
   reg-file
   (bv-if (b-or (b-dout-incdec (micro-rom mar))
                reset)
          (bv-if reset
                 (nat-to-bv 0 (machine-size))
                 data-out)
```

```
                  (bv-if (b-or (b-force-inc (micro-rom mar))
                               (b-if (b-oprda-oprdb (micro-rom mar))
                                     (b-indirect-reg-a-inc i-reg)
                                     (b-indirect-reg-b-inc i-reg)))
                     (bv-adder-output
                      t
                      (nat-to-bv 0 (machine-size))
                      (v-nth (bv-reg-select i-reg mar reset) reg-file))
                     (bv-subtracter-output
                      t
                      (nat-to-bv 0 (machine-size))
                      (v-nth (bv-reg-select i-reg mar reset)
                             reg-file))))))

; Defines the output address presented by FM8501.

(defn addr-out (addr-out reg-file i-reg mar reset)
  (update-v (b-we-addr-out (micro-rom mar))
            addr-out
            (bv-if (b-and (b-predec (micro-rom mar))
                          (b-if (b-oprda-oprdb (micro-rom mar))
                                (b-indirect-reg-a-dec i-reg)
                                (b-indirect-reg-b-dec i-reg)))
               (bv-subtracter-output
                t
                (nat-to-bv 0 (machine-size))
                (v-nth (bv-reg-select i-reg mar reset) reg-file))
               (v-nth (bv-reg-select i-reg mar reset) reg-file))))

; Carry flag

(defn c-flag (c-flag a-reg b-reg i-reg mar)
  (update-v (b-and (b-we-alu-result (micro-rom mar))
                   (b-cc-set i-reg))
            c-flag
            (c (bv-alu-cv a-reg b-reg c-flag (bv-alu-op-code i-reg)))))

(defn c-flag-with-ifs (c-flag a-reg b-reg i-reg mar)
  (if (b-and (b-we-alu-result (micro-rom mar))
             (b-cc-set i-reg))
      (c (bv-alu-cv a-reg b-reg c-flag (bv-alu-op-code i-reg)))
      c-flag))

(prove-lemma c-flag-ifs (rewrite)
  (equal (c-flag c-flag a-reg b-reg i-reg mar)
         (c-flag-with-ifs c-flag a-reg b-reg i-reg mar)))

(disable c-flag)
```

```
;  The overflow flag

(defn v-flag (v-flag a-reg b-reg c-flag i-reg mar)
  (update-v (b-and (b-we-alu-result (micro-rom mar))
                   (b-cc-set i-reg))
            v-flag
            (v (bv-alu-cv a-reg b-reg c-flag (bv-alu-op-code i-reg)))))))

(defn v-flag-with-ifs (v-flag a-reg b-reg c-flag i-reg mar)
  (if (b-and (b-we-alu-result (micro-rom mar))
             (b-cc-set i-reg))
      (v (bv-alu-cv a-reg b-reg c-flag (bv-alu-op-code i-reg)))
      v-flag))

(prove-lemma v-flag-ifs (rewrite)
  (equal (v-flag v-flag a-reg b-reg c-flag i-reg mar)
         (v-flag-with-ifs v-flag a-reg b-reg c-flag i-reg mar)))

(disable v-flag)

;  The zero flag

(defn z-flag (z-flag a-reg b-reg c-flag i-reg mar)
  (update-v (b-and (b-we-alu-result (micro-rom mar))
                   (b-cc-set i-reg))
            z-flag
            (b-bv-zerop (bv (bv-alu-cv a-reg b-reg c-flag
                                       (bv-alu-op-code i-reg))))))))

(defn z-flag-with-ifs (z-flag a-reg b-reg c-flag i-reg mar)
  (if (b-and (b-we-alu-result (micro-rom mar))
             (b-cc-set i-reg))
      (b-bv-zerop (bv (bv-alu-cv a-reg b-reg c-flag
                                 (bv-alu-op-code i-reg))))
      z-flag))

(prove-lemma z-flag-ifs (rewrite)
  (equal (z-flag z-flag a-reg b-reg c-flag i-reg mar)
         (z-flag-with-ifs z-flag a-reg b-reg c-flag i-reg mar)))

(disable z-flag)

;  Two's complement negative flag

(defn n-flag (n-flag a-reg b-reg c-flag i-reg mar)
  (update-v (b-and (b-we-alu-result (micro-rom mar))
                   (b-cc-set i-reg))
            n-flag
            (bitn (bv (bv-alu-cv a-reg b-reg c-flag
                                 (bv-alu-op-code i-reg)))
                  (machine-size))))
```

```
(defn n-flag-with-ifs (n-flag a-reg b-reg c-flag i-reg mar)
  (if (b-and (b-we-alu-result (micro-rom mar))
             (b-cc-set i-reg))
      (bitn (bv (bv-alu-cv a-reg b-reg c-flag (bv-alu-op-code i-reg)))
            (machine-size))
      n-flag))

(prove-lemma n-flag-ifs (rewrite)
  (equal (n-flag n-flag a-reg b-reg c-flag i-reg mar)
         (n-flag-with-ifs n-flag a-reg b-reg c-flag i-reg mar)))

(disable n-flag)

;  Operand A for the ALU

(defn a-reg (a-reg visual-mem reg-file i-reg mar reset)
  (update-v (b-we-a-reg (micro-rom mar))
            a-reg
            (bv-if (b-direct-reg-a i-reg)
                   (v-nth (bv-reg-select i-reg mar reset)
                          reg-file)
                   visual-mem)))

;  Operand B for the ALU

(defn b-reg (b-reg visual-mem reg-file i-reg mar reset)
  (update-v (b-we-b-reg (micro-rom mar))
            b-reg
            (bv-if (b-direct-reg-b i-reg)
                   (v-nth (bv-reg-select i-reg mar reset)
                          reg-file)
                   visual-mem)))

;  Fills the instruction register

(defn i-reg (i-reg visual-mem mar)
  (update-v (b-we-ir (micro-rom mar))
            i-reg
            visual-mem))

(defn i-reg-with-ifs (i-reg visual-mem mar)
  (if (b-we-ir (micro-rom mar))
      visual-mem
      i-reg))

(prove-lemma i-reg-ifs (rewrite)
  (equal (i-reg i-reg visual-mem mar)
         (i-reg-with-ifs i-reg visual-mem mar)))

(disable i-reg)
```

```
;;;;;;;;;;;;;;;;;;;;;;;;;;;;;;;;;;;;;;;;;;;;;;;;;;;;;;;;;;;;;;;;;;;;;;;;;;;;;
;;                                                                       ;;
;;                       Memory Process                                  ;;
;;                                                                       ;;
;; The memory process is interesting as it requires history to          ;;
;; operate.  VISUAL-MEM is the description of how a memory that          ;;
;; FM8501 reads is expected to act.  A "correct" memory value is        ;;
;; only returned after the READ line has been on for two clock "ticks",;;
;; the WRITE line is off, DTACK is on, RESET is off, and DATA-OUT       ;;
;; and ADDR-OUT have been stable for two clock "ticks".  VISUAL-MEM     ;;
;; embodies the assumptions made about reading memory.  REAL-MEM        ;;
;; is a function that actually updates the memory.  Its assumptions     ;;
;; are expressed similarily as VISUAL-MEM.  The WATCH-DOG allows        ;;
;; one tick's worth of state to be kept concerning READ, WRITE,         ;;
;; DTACK, DATA-OUT, and ADDR-OUT.                                       ;;
;;                                                                       ;;
;;;;;;;;;;;;;;;;;;;;;;;;;;;;;;;;;;;;;;;;;;;;;;;;;;;;;;;;;;;;;;;;;;;;;;;;;;;;;

(add-shell watch-dog nil watch-dogp
           ((read-1          (none-of) false)
            (write-1         (none-of) false)
            (dtack-1-oracle  (none-of) false)
            (data-out-1      (one-of bitvp) btm)
            (addr-out-1      (one-of bitvp) btm)))

; Default value from memory when memory has not been selected to return a
; value.

(dcl default-visual-mem-value ())


(defn visual-mem (real-mem read write addr-out
                  memory-watch-dog-history dtack-oracle reset-oracle)
  (trunc (if (and (and read (read-1 memory-watch-dog-history))
                  (and (not write)
                       (not (write-1 memory-watch-dog-history)))
                  (equal addr-out (addr-out-1 memory-watch-dog-history))
                  (and dtack-oracle
                       (dtack-1-oracle memory-watch-dog-history))
                  (not reset-oracle))
             (v-nth addr-out real-mem)
             (default-visual-mem-value))
         (machine-size)))

(defn real-mem (real-mem read write addr-out data-out
                  memory-watch-dog-history dtack-oracle reset-oracle)
  (update-v-nth
   (and (and write (write-1 memory-watch-dog-history))
        (and (not read)
```

```
                   (not (read-1 memory-watch-dog-history)))
        (equal addr-out (addr-out-1 memory-watch-dog-history))
        (and dtack-oracle
             (not (dtack-1-oracle memory-watch-dog-history)))
        (not reset-oracle))
   addr-out
   real-mem
   data-out))
```

```
;;;;;;;;;;;;;;;;;;;;;;;;;;;;;;;;;;;;;;;;;;;;;;;;;;;;;;;;;;;;;;;;;;;;;;;;
;;                                                                    ;;
;;   "BIG-MACHINE" -- the definition of the microprocessor            ;;
;;                                                                    ;;
;;   This function is the definition of the FM8501 microprocessor.    ;;
;;   BIG-MACHINE executes as along as there are clock "ticks".  Clock ;;
;;   "ticks" are characterized by there being elements left in the    ;;
;;   ORACLE.  Otherwise, this function just stops, effectively        ;;
;;   freezing the value of its variables (registers).                 ;;
;;                                                                    ;;
;;;;;;;;;;;;;;;;;;;;;;;;;;;;;;;;;;;;;;;;;;;;;;;;;;;;;;;;;;;;;;;;;;;;;;;;

(defn big-machine (mar read write dtack reset no-store data-out
                       reg-file addr-out c-flag v-flag z-flag n-flag
                       a-reg b-reg i-reg
                       visual-mem real-mem
                       memory-watch-dog-history oracle)
  (if (nlistp oracle)
      (list mar read write dtack reset no-store data-out
            reg-file addr-out c-flag v-flag z-flag n-flag
            a-reg b-reg i-reg visual-mem real-mem
            memory-watch-dog-history)
      (big-machine
       (mar mar i-reg dtack reset no-store)
       (read mar i-reg)
       (write mar i-reg no-store)
       (dtack (car oracle))
       (reset (car oracle))
       (no-store no-store c-flag v-flag z-flag n-flag i-reg mar)
       (data-out data-out a-reg b-reg c-flag i-reg mar)
       (reg-file reg-file data-out i-reg mar no-store reset)
       (addr-out addr-out reg-file i-reg mar reset)
       (c-flag c-flag a-reg b-reg i-reg mar)
       (v-flag v-flag a-reg b-reg c-flag i-reg mar)
       (z-flag z-flag a-reg b-reg c-flag i-reg mar)
       (n-flag n-flag a-reg b-reg c-flag i-reg mar)
       (a-reg a-reg visual-mem reg-file i-reg mar reset)
       (b-reg b-reg visual-mem reg-file i-reg mar reset)
       (i-reg i-reg visual-mem mar)
       (visual-mem real-mem read write addr-out
                   memory-watch-dog-history
                   (dtack (car oracle)) (reset (car oracle)))
       (real-mem real-mem read write addr-out data-out
                 memory-watch-dog-history
                 (dtack (car oracle)) (reset (car oracle)))
       (watch-dog read write (dtack (car oracle)) data-out addr-out)
       (cdr oracle)
       )))
```

```
;;;;;;;;;;;;;;;;;;;;;;;;;;;;;;;;;;;;;;;;;;;;;;;;;;;;;;;;;;;;;;;;;;;;;;;
;;                                                                  ;;
;;        "BIG-MACHINE" Operation on Lists and Empty Lists          ;;
;;                                                                  ;;
;;   The following two lemmas describe what BIG-MACHINE does when    ;;
;;   clock "ticks" are available or the clock has been exhausted.    ;;
;;   This information is easily available by looking at the definition ;;
;;   of BIG-MACHINE; however, these formulations make it easier for the ;;
;;   theorem-prover to reason about BIG-MACHINE.                     ;;
;;                                                                  ;;
;;;;;;;;;;;;;;;;;;;;;;;;;;;;;;;;;;;;;;;;;;;;;;;;;;;;;;;;;;;;;;;;;;;;;;;

(prove-lemma open-big-machine-on-nlistp (rewrite)
  (implies (not (listp oracle))
           (equal (big-machine mar read write dtack reset
                               no-store data-out
                               reg-file addr-out
                               c-flag v-flag z-flag n-flag
                               a-reg b-reg i-reg
                               visual-mem real-mem
                               memory-watch-dog-history oracle)
                  (list mar read write dtack reset
                        no-store data-out
                        reg-file addr-out c-flag v-flag z-flag n-flag
                        a-reg b-reg i-reg visual-mem real-mem
                        memory-watch-dog-history))))

(prove-lemma open-big-machine-on-listp (rewrite)
  (implies
   (listp oracle)
   (equal (big-machine mar read write dtack reset
                       no-store data-out
                       reg-file addr-out
                       c-flag v-flag z-flag n-flag
                       a-reg b-reg i-reg
                       visual-mem real-mem
                       memory-watch-dog-history oracle)
          (big-machine
           (mar mar i-reg dtack reset no-store)
           (read mar i-reg)
           (write mar i-reg no-store)
           (dtack (car oracle))
           (reset (car oracle))
           (no-store-with-ifs no-store c-flag v-flag
                              z-flag n-flag i-reg mar)
           (data-out-with-ifs data-out a-reg b-reg c-flag i-reg bmar)
           (reg-file reg-file data-out i-reg mar no-store reset)
           (addr-out addr-out reg-file i-reg mar reset)
```

```
          (c-flag-with-ifs c-flag a-reg b-reg i-reg mar)
          (v-flag-with-ifs v-flag a-reg b-reg c-flag i-reg mar)
          (z-flag-with-ifs z-flag a-reg b-reg c-flag i-reg mar)
          (n-flag-with-ifs n-flag a-reg b-reg c-flag i-reg mar)
          (a-reg a-reg visual-mem reg-file i-reg mar reset)
          (b-reg b-reg visual-mem reg-file i-reg mar reset)
          (i-reg-with-ifs i-reg visual-mem mar)
          (visual-mem real-mem read write addr-out
                      memory-watch-dog-history
                      (dtack (car oracle)) (reset (car oracle)))
          (real-mem real-mem read write addr-out data-out
                    memory-watch-dog-history
                    (dtack (car oracle)) (reset (car oracle)))
          (watch-dog read write (dtack (car oracle)) data-out addr-out)
          (cdr oracle))))
  ((disable mar read write dtack reset no-store-with-ifs
            data-out-with-ifs reg-file addr-out c-flag-with-ifs
            v-flag-with-ifs z-flag-with-ifs n-flag-with-ifs
            a-reg b-reg
            i-reg-with-ifs visual-mem real-mem)))

(disable big-machine)
```

```
;;;;;;;;;;;;;;;;;;;;;;;;;;;;;;;;;;;;;;;;;;;;;;;;;;;;;;;;;;;;;;;;;;;;;;;;;;;;;;;;;
;;                                                                            ;;
;;  The following contains definitions and lemmas concerning the              ;;
;;  sequencing of big-machine. The proofs for the correctness of              ;;
;;  the micro-code are given here.                                            ;;
;;                                                                            ;;
;;;;;;;;;;;;;;;;;;;;;;;;;;;;;;;;;;;;;;;;;;;;;;;;;;;;;;;;;;;;;;;;;;;;;;;;;;;;;;;;;


;;;;;;;;;;;;;;;;;;;;;;;;;;;;;;;;;;;;;;;;;;;;;;;;;;;;;;;;;;;;;;;;;;;;;;;;;;;;;;;;;
;;                                                                            ;;
;;          Lemma Used to Tear Apart "APPEND"ed Oracles                       ;;
;;  This is the fundamental lemma for sequencing big-machine.                 ;;
;;  It permits us to express computations on an (APPEND a b) in terms         ;;
;;  of a computation on b applied to the state produced by a.  We can         ;;
;;  then get results about long computations by composing them from           ;;
;;  simple ones.                                                              ;;
;;                                                                            ;;
;;;;;;;;;;;;;;;;;;;;;;;;;;;;;;;;;;;;;;;;;;;;;;;;;;;;;;;;;;;;;;;;;;;;;;;;;;;;;;;;;

(prove-lemma big-machine-append (rewrite)
  (implies
    (equal m (big-machine mar read write dtack reset
                          no-store data-out reg-file addr-out
                          c-flag v-flag z-flag n-flag
                          a-reg b-reg i-reg
                          visual-mem real-mem
                          memory-watch-dog-history oracle1))
    (equal (big-machine mar read write dtack reset
                        no-store data-out
                        reg-file addr-out c-flag v-flag z-flag n-flag
                        a-reg b-reg i-reg
                        visual-mem real-mem
                        memory-watch-dog-history (append oracle1 oracle2))
           (big-machine (car m)
                        (cadr m)
                        (caddr m)
                        (cadddr m)
                        (caddddr m)
                        (cadddddr m)
                        (caddddddr m)
                        (cadddddddr m)
                        (caddddddddr m)
                        (cadddddddddr m)
                        (caddddddddddr m)
                        (cadddddddddddr m)
                        (caddddddddddddr m)
                        (cadddddddddddddr m)
                        (caddddddddddddddr m)
```

```
                   (caddddddddddddddddr m)
                   (cadddddddddddddddddr m)
                   (caddddddddddddddddddr m)
                   (cadddddddddddddddddddr m)
                   oracle2)))
      ((disable mar read write dtack reset no-store-with-ifs
              data-out-with-ifs reg-file addr-out c-flag-with-ifs
              v-flag-with-ifs z-flag-with-ifs n-flag-with-ifs
              a-reg b-reg i-reg-with-ifs visual-mem real-mem)
       (induct (big-machine mar read write dtack reset
                           no-store data-out
                           reg-file addr-out c-flag v-flag z-flag n-flag
                           a-reg b-reg i-reg
                           visual-mem real-mem
                           memory-watch-dog-history oracle1))))
```

```
;;;;;;;;;;;;;;;;;;;;;;;;;;;;;;;;;;;;;;;;;;;;;;;;;;;;;;;;;;;;;;;;;;;;;;;;;;;;;;
;;                                                                          ;;
;;         Miscellaneous Lemmas about INC/DEC and Updating                  ;;
;;                                                                          ;;
;;;;;;;;;;;;;;;;;;;;;;;;;;;;;;;;;;;;;;;;;;;;;;;;;;;;;;;;;;;;;;;;;;;;;;;;;;;;;;

(prove-lemma bv-incrementer-truncates-to-machine-size (rewrite)
  (implies (and (equal zero (nat-to-bv 0 (machine-size)))
                (bitvp bit-vec)
                (equal (size bit-vec) (machine-size)))
           (equal (bv-adder-output t zero bit-vec)
                  (v-nat-inc bit-vec)))
  ((hands-off bv-adder-output)
   (enable nat-to-bv-ignores-remainder)
   (use (nat-bv-adder-output-seen-as-bit-vector
         (a (nat-to-bv 0 (machine-size)))
         (b bit-vec)
         (c t)))))

(disable bv-incrementer-truncates-to-machine-size)

(prove-lemma bv-decrementer-truncates-to-machine-size-help (rewrite)
  (implies
    (and (not (lessp (bv-to-nat bit-vec) 1))
         (bitvp bit-vec)
         (equal (size bit-vec) 16)
         (not (equal (bv-to-nat bit-vec) 0)))
    (equal (nat-to-bv (difference (bv-to-nat bit-vec) 1)
                      16)
           (nat-to-bv (sub1 (bv-to-nat bit-vec))
                      16))))

(prove-lemma bv-decrementer-truncates-to-machine-size (rewrite)
  (implies (and (equal zero (nat-to-bv 0 (machine-size)))
                (bitvp bit-vec)
                (equal (size bit-vec) (machine-size)))
           (equal (bv-subtracter-output t zero bit-vec)
                  (v-nat-dec bit-vec)))
  ((hands-off bv-subtracter-output)
   (disable nat-to-bv bv-to-nat)
   (use (nat-bv-subtracter-output-seen-as-bit-vector
         (a (nat-to-bv 0 (machine-size)))
         (b bit-vec)
         (c t)))))

(disable bv-decrementer-truncates-to-machine-size-help)

(disable bv-decrementer-truncates-to-machine-size)
```

```
(prove-lemma trunc-size-1 (rewrite)
  (implies (equal n (size a))
           (equal (trunc a n)
                  (if (bitvp a) a (btm)))))

(prove-lemma size-v-nth (rewrite)
  (implies (and (equal (size a) 3)
                (equal (length reg-file) 8)
                (every-member-sizep reg-file (machine-size)))
           (equal (size (v-nth a reg-file))
                  (machine-size)))
  ((use (upper-bound-on-bv-to-nat (a a)))))

(prove-lemma update-update-nth (rewrite)
  (equal (update-nth c n (update-nth c n lst value2) value1)
         (update-nth c n lst value1)))
```

```
;;;;;;;;;;;;;;;;;;;;;;;;;;;;;;;;;;;;;;;;;;;;;;;;;;;;;;;;;;;;;;;;;;;;;;;;;;;;;;
;;                                                                          ;;
;;                     Resetting "BIG-MACHINE"                             ;;
;;                                                                          ;;
;;;;;;;;;;;;;;;;;;;;;;;;;;;;;;;;;;;;;;;;;;;;;;;;;;;;;;;;;;;;;;;;;;;;;;;;;;;;;;

(prove-lemma mar-on-reset (rewrite)
  (equal (mar mar i-reg dtack t no-store)
         (nat-to-bv 0 (nxsz))))

(prove-lemma reg-file-on-reset (rewrite)
  (equal (reg-file reg-file data-out i-reg mar no-store t)
         (update-nth t 0 reg-file (nat-to-bv 0 (machine-size)))))

(prove-lemma listp-reg-file (rewrite)
  (equal (listp (reg-file reg-file data-out i-reg mar no-store reset))
         (listp reg-file)))


; The following lemma describes the first three clock "ticks" after a
; reset occurs.  The memory-address register (MAR) is set to zero, the
; read and write outputs are set to "false", and the reset latch is set
; to "true".  Since nothing is known about the WATCH-DOG-HISTORY, it is
; not possible to characterize what the memory state is.  However, after
; these three clock "ticks" everything is stable (unchanging) until
; reset is turned off.

(prove-lemma reset-to-state-0 (rewrite)
  (implies
   (and (standard-hyps mar read write dtack reset no-store data-out
                       reg-file addr-out c-flag v-flag z-flag n-flag
                       a-reg b-reg i-reg visual-mem real-mem)
        (equal m (big-machine mar read write dtack reset
                              no-store data-out
                              reg-file addr-out
                              c-flag v-flag z-flag n-flag
                              a-reg b-reg i-reg
                              visual-mem real-mem
                              memory-watch-dog-history
                              (list (list dt1 t)
                                    (list dt2 t)
                                    (list dt3 t)))))
   (and (equal (car m) (nat-to-bv 0 (nxsz)))
        (equal (cadr m) f)
        (equal (caddr m) f)
        (equal (caddddr m) t)
        (equal (nth 0 (caddddddr m))
               (nat-to-bv 0 (machine-size)))))
   ((disable mar no-store-with-ifs
```

```
                    data-out-with-ifs reg-file addr-out c-flag-with-ifs
                    v-flag-with-ifs z-flag-with-ifs n-flag-with-ifs a-reg
                    b-reg i-reg-with-ifs visual-mem real-mem length-update-nth)))

(disable reset-to-state-0)

(defn list-of-n-plus-1-dtack-off-reset-on (count)
  (if (zerop count)
      (list (list f t))
      (cons (list f t)
            (list-of-n-plus-1-dtack-off-reset-on (sub1 count)))))

(prove-lemma state-0-to-0-wait-help (rewrite)
  (implies
   (equal mar0 (nat-to-bv 0 (nxsz)))
   (equal (big-machine mar0 f f dtack t
                       no-store data-out
                       reg-file addr-out
                       c-flag v-flag z-flag n-flag
                       a-reg b-reg i-reg
                       visual-mem real-mem
                       watch-dog-history
                       (cons (list dt-any t) oracle))
          (big-machine mar0 f f (fix-bool dt-any) t
                       no-store data-out
                       (update-nth t 0 reg-file
                                   (nat-to-bv 0 (machine-size)))
                       addr-out c-flag v-flag z-flag n-flag
                       a-reg b-reg i-reg
                       (trunc (default-visual-mem-value) (machine-size))
                       real-mem
                       (watch-dog f f (fix-bool dt-any)
                                  data-out addr-out)
                       oracle))))

(disable state-0-to-0-wait-help)

(defn state-0-to-0-induction (dtack data-out reg-file addr-out visual-mem
                                    watch-dog n)
  (if (zerop n)
      t
      (state-0-to-0-induction
        f
        data-out
        (update-nth t 0 reg-file (nat-to-bv 0 (machine-size)))
        addr-out
        (trunc (default-visual-mem-value) (machine-size))
        (watch-dog f f f data-out addr-out)
        (sub1 n))))
```

```
(prove-lemma state-0-to-0-wait (rewrite)
  (implies
   (equal mar0 (nat-to-bv 0 (nxsz)))
   (equal (big-machine mar0 f f dtack t
                       no-store data-out
                       reg-file addr-out
                       c-flag v-flag z-flag n-flag
                       a-reg b-reg i-reg
                       visual-mem real-mem
                       watch-dog-history
                       (list-of-n-plus-1-dtack-off-reset-on n))
          (list (nat-to-bv 0 (nxsz)) f f f t
                no-store data-out
                (update-nth t 0 reg-file (nat-to-bv 0 (machine-size)))
                addr-out c-flag v-flag z-flag n-flag
                a-reg b-reg i-reg
                (trunc (default-visual-mem-value) (machine-size))
                real-mem
                (watch-dog f f f data-out addr-out)))))
  ((disable mar read write no-store-with-ifs
           data-out-with-ifs addr-out c-flag-with-ifs
           v-flag-with-ifs z-flag-with-ifs n-flag-with-ifs a-reg b-reg
           i-reg-with-ifs visual-mem real-mem bv-adder-output
           bv-subtracter-output b-store-alu-result
           append open-big-machine-on-listp
           update-nth nth v-nth v-nat-inc v-nat-dec nat-to-bv bv-to-nat)
   (hands-off bv-alu-cv)
   (enable state-0-to-0-wait-help)
   (induct (state-0-to-0-induction dtack data-out reg-file
                                   addr-out visual-mem
                                   watch-dog-history n))))

(disable state-0-to-0-wait)

(prove-lemma state-0-to-1 (rewrite)
  (implies
   (equal mar0 (nat-to-bv 0 (nxsz)))
   (equal (big-machine mar0 f f dtack t
                       no-store data-out
                       reg-file
                       addr-out c-flag v-flag z-flag n-flag
                       a-reg b-reg i-reg
                       visual-mem real-mem
                       memory-watch-dog-history
                       (list (list dt-any1 f) (list dt-any2 f)))
          (list (nat-to-bv 1 (nxsz))
                f f (fix-bool dt-any2) f no-store data-out
                (update-nth t 0 reg-file (nat-to-bv 0 (machine-size)))
                addr-out c-flag v-flag z-flag n-flag
```

```
                    a-reg b-reg i-reg
                    (trunc (default-visual-mem-value) 16)
                    real-mem
                    (watch-dog f f (fix-bool dt-any2) data-out addr-out))))
      ((disable bv-adder-output bv-subtracter-output b-store-alu-result)
       (hands-off bv-alu-cv)))

(disable state-0-to-1)

(defn state-0-to-0-wait-to-1-oracle (n)
  (append (list-of-n-plus-1-dtack-off-reset-on n)
          (list (list f f) (list f f))))


;  After the MAR has been set to zero, this lemma describes the steps
;  taken by FM8501 to prepare itself for executing instructions.

(prove-lemma state-0-to-0-wait-to-1 (rewrite)
  (implies
    (and (standard-hyps mar0 f f dtack t no-store data-out
                        reg-file addr-out c-flag v-flag z-flag n-flag
                        a-reg b-reg i-reg visual-mem real-mem)
        (equal mar0 (nat-to-bv 0 (nxsz))))
    (equal (big-machine mar0 f f dtack t
                        no-store data-out
                        reg-file
                        addr-out c-flag v-flag z-flag n-flag
                        a-reg b-reg i-reg
                        visual-mem real-mem
                        watch-dog-history
                        (state-0-to-0-wait-to-1-oracle n))
           (list (nat-to-bv 1 (nxsz))
                 f f f f no-store data-out
                 (update-nth t 0 reg-file (nat-to-bv 0 (machine-size)))
                 addr-out c-flag v-flag z-flag n-flag
                 a-reg b-reg i-reg
                 (trunc (default-visual-mem-value) 16) real-mem
                 (watch-dog f f f data-out addr-out))))
    ((disable no-store-with-ifs data-out-with-ifs addr-out c-flag-with-ifs
              v-flag-with-ifs z-flag-with-ifs n-flag-with-ifs a-reg b-reg
              i-reg-with-ifs visual-mem real-mem
              bv-adder-output bv-subtracter-output
              b-store-alu-result append open-big-machine-on-listp
              update-nth nth v-nth v-nat-inc v-nat-dec nat-to-bv bv-to-nat)
     (hands-off bv-alu-cv)
     (enable state-0-to-0-wait state-0-to-1)))

(disable state-0-to-0-wait-to-1)
```

```
;;;;;;;;;;;;;;;;;;;;;;;;;;;;;;;;;;;;;;;;;;;;;;;;;;;;;;;;;;;;;;;;;;;;;;;;;
;;                                                                     ;;
;;     "BIG-MACHINE" Instruction Loop -- Micro-State by Micro-State    ;;
;;                                                                     ;;
;;;;;;;;;;;;;;;;;;;;;;;;;;;;;;;;;;;;;;;;;;;;;;;;;;;;;;;;;;;;;;;;;;;;;;;;;

;;;;;;;;;;;;;;;;;;;;;;;;;;;;;;;;;;;;;;;;;;;;;;;;;;;;;;;;;;;;;;;;;;;;;;;;;
;;                                                                     ;;
;;          Fetch the Instruction, and Increment the PC               ;;
;;                                                                     ;;
;;;;;;;;;;;;;;;;;;;;;;;;;;;;;;;;;;;;;;;;;;;;;;;;;;;;;;;;;;;;;;;;;;;;;;;;;

; We are about to embark on a litany of lemmas that move us from one
; microcode state to another.  By inspection of the oracles used below
; one can deduce the timing diagrams.  For example, the lemma below moves
; us from microcode state 1, where mar=1, and read, write, and reset are
; f, to microcode state 2, where mar=2, read, write, dtack and reset are
; f, the pc has been incremented, and addr-out contains the old pc.  To
; move from state 1 to 2, we need one clock tick with both dtack and
; reset f.

; We will similarly move through every state, some of which have several
; substates as we set lines, wait for acknowledgment, and then move.
; Once we get all the way through the microcode, we will append together
; the oracles to get an oracle that moves us all the way around from
; state 1 to state 1.

; These lemmas make it perfectly clear what each state in the microcode
; does and how long each takes.

(prove-lemma state-1-to-2 (rewrite)
  (implies
    (and (ramp reg-file (machine-size) 8)
         (equal mar1 (nat-to-bv 1 (nxsz))))
    (equal (big-machine mar1 f f dtack f
                        no-store data-out
                        reg-file
                        addr-out c-flag v-flag z-flag n-flag
                        a-reg b-reg i-reg
                        visual-mem real-mem
                        memory-watch-dog-history
                        (list (list f f)))
           (list (nat-to-bv 2 (nxsz))
                 f f f f no-store data-out
                 (update-nth t 0 reg-file (v-nat-inc (nth 0 reg-file)))
                 (nth 0 reg-file) c-flag v-flag z-flag n-flag
                 a-reg b-reg i-reg
                 (trunc (default-visual-mem-value) 16)
```

```
                real-mem
                (watch-dog f f f data-out addr-out))))
     ((disable bv-adder-output bv-subtracter-output b-store-alu-result)
     (hands-off bv-alu-cv)
     (enable bv-incrementer-truncates-to-machine-size)))

(disable state-1-to-2)

(prove-lemma state-2-to-3-init (rewrite)
  (implies (equal mar2 (nat-to-bv 2 (nxsz)))
          (equal (big-machine mar2 f f f
                              no-store data-out
                              reg-file addr-out
                              c-flag v-flag z-flag n-flag
                              a-reg b-reg i-reg
                              visual-mem real-mem
                              watch-dog-history
                              (list (list f f)))
                 (list (nat-to-bv 2 (nxsz))
                       t f f f no-store data-out
                       reg-file addr-out
                       c-flag v-flag z-flag n-flag
                       a-reg b-reg i-reg
                       (trunc (default-visual-mem-value) 16) real-mem
                       (watch-dog f f f data-out addr-out))))
    ((disable bv-adder-output bv-subtracter-output b-store-alu-result)
    (hands-off bv-alu-cv)))

(defn list-of-n-plus-1-dtack-reset-off (count)
  (if (zerop count)
      (list (list f f))
      (cons (list f f)
            (list-of-n-plus-1-dtack-reset-off (sub1 count)))))

(prove-lemma state-2-to-2-wait-help (rewrite)
  (implies
   (equal mar2 (nat-to-bv 2 (nxsz)))
   (equal (big-machine mar2 t f f f
                       no-store data-out
                       reg-file addr-out
                       c-flag v-flag z-flag n-flag
                       a-reg b-reg i-reg
                       visual-mem real-mem
                       watch-dog-history
                       (cons (list f f) oracle))
          (big-machine mar2 t f f f
                       no-store data-out
                       reg-file addr-out
                       c-flag v-flag z-flag n-flag
```

```
                              a-reg b-reg i-reg
                              (trunc (default-visual-mem-value) (machine-size))
                              real-mem
                              (watch-dog t f f data-out addr-out)
                              oracle))))

(defn state-2-to-2-induction (dtack data-out addr-out visual-mem
                                     watch-dog-history n)
  (if (zerop n)
      t
      (state-2-to-2-induction
        f
        data-out
        addr-out
        (trunc (default-visual-mem-value) (machine-size))
        (watch-dog t f f data-out addr-out)
        (sub1 n))))

(prove-lemma state-2-to-3-wait (rewrite)
  (implies (equal mar2 (nat-to-bv 2 (nxsz)))
           (equal (big-machine mar2 t f f f
                               no-store data-out
                               reg-file addr-out
                               c-flag v-flag z-flag n-flag
                               a-reg b-reg i-reg
                               visual-mem real-mem
                               watch-dog-history
                               (list-of-n-plus-1-dtack-reset-off n))
                  (list (nat-to-bv 2 (nxsz))
                        t f f f no-store data-out
                        reg-file addr-out
                        c-flag v-flag z-flag n-flag
                        a-reg b-reg i-reg
                        (trunc (default-visual-mem-value) 16) real-mem
                        (watch-dog t f f data-out addr-out)))))
  ((disable no-store-with-ifs data-out-with-ifs addr-out c-flag-with-ifs
            v-flag-with-ifs z-flag-with-ifs n-flag-with-ifs a-reg b-reg
            i-reg-with-ifs visual-mem real-mem
            bv-adder-output bv-subtracter-output
            b-store-alu-result append
            open-big-machine-on-listp update-nth
            nth v-nth v-nat-inc v-nat-dec nat-to-bv bv-to-nat)
   (hands-off bv-alu-cv)
   (induct (state-2-to-2-induction dtack data-out addr-out visual-mem
                                   watch-dog-history
                                   n))))

(disable state-2-to-3-wait)
```

```
(prove-lemma upper-bound-bridge (rewrite)
  (implies (equal n (exp 2 (size a)))
           (lessp (bv-to-nat a) n)))

(prove-lemma state-2-to-3-step3 (rewrite)
  (implies (and (ramp real-mem (machine-size) (exp 2 (machine-size)))
                (sizep addr-out (machine-size))
                (equal mar2 (nat-to-bv 2 (nxsz)))
                (equal visual-mem (v-nth addr-out real-mem)))
           (equal (big-machine mar2 t f f f
                               no-store data-out
                               reg-file addr-out
                               c-flag v-flag z-flag n-flag
                               a-reg b-reg i-reg
                               visual-mem real-mem
                               (watch-dog t f f data-out addr-out)
                               (list (list t f) (list t f)))
                  (list (nat-to-bv 3 (nxsz))
                        t f t f no-store data-out
                        reg-file addr-out
                        c-flag v-flag z-flag n-flag
                        a-reg b-reg i-reg
                        (v-nth addr-out real-mem) real-mem
                        (watch-dog t f t data-out addr-out))))
  ((disable bv-adder-output bv-subtracter-output b-store-alu-result)
   (hands-off bv-alu-cv)))

(disable state-2-to-3-step3)

(prove-lemma state-3-to-4 (rewrite)
  (implies (and (ramp real-mem (machine-size) (exp 2 (machine-size)))
                (sizep addr-out (machine-size))
                (equal mar3 (nat-to-bv 3 (nxsz)))
                (equal visual-mem (v-nth addr-out real-mem)))
           (equal (big-machine mar3 t f t f
                               no-store data-out
                               reg-file addr-out
                               c-flag v-flag z-flag n-flag
                               a-reg b-reg i-reg
                               visual-mem real-mem
                               (watch-dog t f t data-out addr-out)
                               (list (list t f)))
                  (list (nat-to-bv 4 (nxsz))
                        f f t f no-store data-out
                        reg-file addr-out
                        c-flag v-flag z-flag n-flag
                        a-reg b-reg (v-nth addr-out real-mem)
                        (v-nth addr-out real-mem) real-mem
                        (watch-dog t f t data-out addr-out))))
```

```
   ((disable bv-adder-output bv-subtracter-output b-store-alu-result)
    (hands-off bv-alu-cv)))

(disable state-3-to-4)

;  This proof is required because it is impossible to keep "APPEND"
;  from opening up on constants.  The opening does not allow
;  "BIG-MACHINE-APPEND" to apply because the 'append' will have
;  disappeared before it get a chance to apply.

(prove-lemma state-2-to-3-step3-to-4 (rewrite)
  (implies (and (ramp real-mem (machine-size) (exp 2 (machine-size)))
                (sizep addr-out (machine-size))
                (equal mar2 (nat-to-bv 2 (nxsz))))
           (equal (big-machine mar2 t f f f
                                 no-store data-out
                                 reg-file addr-out
                                 c-flag v-flag z-flag n-flag
                                 a-reg b-reg i-reg
                                 visual-mem real-mem
                                 (watch-dog t f f data-out addr-out)
                                 (list (list t f) (list t f) (list t f)))
                  (list (nat-to-bv 4 (nxsz))
                        f f t f no-store data-out
                        reg-file addr-out
                        c-flag v-flag z-flag n-flag
                        a-reg b-reg (v-nth addr-out real-mem)
                        (v-nth addr-out real-mem) real-mem
                        (watch-dog t f t data-out addr-out))))
  ((disable bv-adder-output bv-subtracter-output b-store-alu-result
            big-machine-append)
   (hands-off bv-alu-cv)))

(disable state-2-to-3-step3-to-4)

(defn fetch-ir-oracle (n)
  (append (list (list f f))
          (append (list (list f f))
                  (append (list-of-n-plus-1-dtack-reset-off n)
                          (list (list t f) (list t f) (list t f)))))))

(prove-lemma state-1-to-4 (rewrite)
  (implies
   (and (ramp reg-file (machine-size) 8)
        (sizep addr-out (machine-size))
        (ramp real-mem (machine-size) (exp 2 (machine-size)))
        (equal mar1 (nat-to-bv 1 (nxsz))))
   (equal (big-machine mar1 f f f f
                        no-store data-out
```

```
                    reg-file
                    addr-out c-flag v-flag z-flag n-flag
                    a-reg b-reg i-reg
                    visual-mem real-mem
                    memory-watch-dog-history
                    (fetch-ir-oracle n))
          (list (nat-to-bv 4 (nxsz))
                f f t f no-store data-out
                (update-nth t 0 reg-file (v-nat-inc (nth 0 reg-file)))
                (nth 0 reg-file) c-flag v-flag z-flag n-flag
                a-reg b-reg (v-nth (nth 0 reg-file) real-mem)
                (v-nth (nth 0 reg-file) real-mem) real-mem
                (watch-dog t f t data-out (nth 0 reg-file)))))
    ((disable mar read write no-store-with-ifs
              data-out-with-ifs addr-out c-flag-with-ifs
              v-flag-with-ifs z-flag-with-ifs n-flag-with-ifs a-reg b-reg
              i-reg-with-ifs visual-mem real-mem bv-adder-output
              bv-subtracter-output b-store-alu-result
              append open-big-machine-on-listp
              update-nth nth v-nth v-nat-inc
              v-nat-dec nat-to-bv bv-to-nat)
     (hands-off bv-alu-cv)
     (enable state-1-to-2
             state-2-to-3-init
             state-2-to-3-wait
             state-2-to-3-step3-to-4
             )))

(disable state-1-to-4)
```

```
;;;;;;;;;;;;;;;;;;;;;;;;;;;;;;;;;;;;;;;;;;;;;;;;;;;;;;;;;;;;;;;;;;;;;;;;;
;;                                                                     ;;
;;                      Some SIZE Lemmas                               ;;
;;                                                                     ;;
;;;;;;;;;;;;;;;;;;;;;;;;;;;;;;;;;;;;;;;;;;;;;;;;;;;;;;;;;;;;;;;;;;;;;;;;;

(prove-lemma size-bv-reg-select (rewrite)
  (equal (size (bv-reg-select i-reg mar reset)) 3))

(prove-lemma size-bv-oprd-a (rewrite)
  (equal (size (bv-oprd-a i-reg)) 3))

(prove-lemma size-bv-oprd-b (rewrite)
  (equal (size (bv-oprd-b i-reg)) 3))
```

```
;;;;;;;;;;;;;;;;;;;;;;;;;;;;;;;;;;;;;;;;;;;;;;;;;;;;;;;;;;;;;;;;;;;;;;;;;;;;
;;                                                                        ;;
;;      Fetch Operand A, doing Pre-decrement if necessary                 ;;
;;                                                                        ;;
;;;;;;;;;;;;;;;;;;;;;;;;;;;;;;;;;;;;;;;;;;;;;;;;;;;;;;;;;;;;;;;;;;;;;;;;;;;;

(defn fetch-oprd-a-reg-file (i-reg reg-file)
  (update-v-nth (b-indirect-reg-a-dec i-reg)
                (bv-oprd-a i-reg)
                reg-file
                (v-nat-dec (v-nth (bv-oprd-a i-reg)
                                  reg-file))))

(prove-lemma every-member-sizep-update-nth (rewrite)
  (implies (and (equal (size x) width)
                (every-member-sizep lst width))
           (every-member-sizep (update-nth bool n lst x) width)))


; Both of the following two lemmas are needed, as we sometimes have RAMP
; enabled.

(prove-lemma ramp-fetch-oprd-a-reg-file (rewrite)
  (implies
   (and (equal m (machine-size))
        (ramp reg-file (machine-size) 8))
   (and (equal (length (fetch-oprd-a-reg-file i-reg reg-file)) 8)
        (every-member-sizep (fetch-oprd-a-reg-file i-reg reg-file) m)))
  ((disable update-nth bv-oprd-a)))

(prove-lemma ramp-fetch-oprd-a-reg-file-2 (rewrite)
  (implies (and (equal m (machine-size))
                (ramp reg-file (machine-size) 8))
           (ramp (fetch-oprd-a-reg-file i-reg reg-file) m 8))
  ((disable update-nth bv-oprd-a)))

(defn fetch-oprd-a-addr-out (i-reg reg-file)
  (if (b-indirect-reg-a-dec i-reg)
      (v-nat-dec (v-nth (bv-oprd-a i-reg) reg-file))
      (v-nth (bv-oprd-a i-reg) reg-file)))

(prove-lemma sizep-fetch-oprd-a-addr-out (rewrite)
  (implies (and (equal m (machine-size))
                (ramp reg-file (machine-size) 8))
           (equal (size (fetch-oprd-a-addr-out i-reg reg-file)) m))
  ((disable bv-oprd-a)))

(prove-lemma state-4-to-5 (rewrite)
  (implies (and (ramp reg-file (machine-size) 8)
```

```
                   (equal mar4 (nat-to-bv 4 (nxsz))))
          (equal (big-machine mar4 f f t f
                               no-store data-out
                               reg-file addr-out
                               c-flag v-flag z-flag n-flag
                               a-reg b-reg i-reg
                               visual-mem real-mem
                               watch-dog
                               (list (list f f)))
                 (list (nat-to-bv 5 (nxsz))
                       f f f f no-store data-out
                       (fetch-oprd-a-reg-file i-reg reg-file)
                       (fetch-oprd-a-addr-out i-reg reg-file)
                       c-flag v-flag z-flag n-flag
                       a-reg b-reg i-reg
                       (trunc (default-visual-mem-value) 16) real-mem
                       (watch-dog f f f data-out addr-out)))))
   ((disable bv-adder-output bv-subtracter-output b-store-alu-result
             v-nat-dec v-nat-inc fix-bool bv-oprd-a)
    (hands-off bv-alu-cv)
    (enable bv-decrementer-truncates-to-machine-size
            bv-incrementer-truncates-to-machine-size)))

(disable state-4-to-5)


; The next two prove-lemmas are of type nil -- we never use them as
; rewrite rules.  Ideally we would like to append together the two
; clocks for state-5-to-6-reg and state-6-to-7-reg.  But the two clocks
; are both constant so the append computes and big-machine-append will
; not apply.  So we will actually prove state-4-to-5-to-6-to-7-reg as
; one rewrite rule.  But for the sake of exposition, we prove individual
; lemmas about each state transition.

(prove-lemma state-5-to-6-reg nil
  (implies (and (ramp reg-file (machine-size) 8)
                (equal mar5 (nat-to-bv 5 (nxsz)))
                (b-direct-reg-a i-reg))
           (equal (big-machine mar5 f f dt-any f
                               no-store data-out
                               reg-file addr-out
                               c-flag v-flag z-flag n-flag
                               a-reg b-reg i-reg
                               visual-mem real-mem
                               watch-dog-history
                               (list (list f f)))
                  (list (nat-to-bv 6 (nxsz))
                        f f f f no-store data-out
                        reg-file addr-out
```

```
                    c-flag v-flag z-flag n-flag
                    a-reg b-reg i-reg
                    (trunc (default-visual-mem-value) 16) real-mem
                    (watch-dog f f f data-out addr-out))))
      ((disable bv-adder-output bv-subtracter-output b-store-alu-result
              b-indirect-reg-a-dec v-nat-dec v-nat-inc)
       (hands-off bv-alu-cv)))

(prove-lemma state-6-to-7-reg nil
  (implies (and (ramp reg-file (machine-size) 8)
                (equal mar6 (nat-to-bv 6 (nxsz)))
                (b-direct-reg-a i-reg))
           (equal (big-machine mar6 f f f
                               no-store data-out
                               reg-file addr-out
                               c-flag v-flag z-flag n-flag
                               a-reg b-reg i-reg
                               visual-mem real-mem
                               watch-dog-history
                               (list (list f f)))
                  (list (nat-to-bv 7 (nxsz))
                        f f f f no-store data-out
                        reg-file addr-out
                        c-flag v-flag z-flag n-flag
                        (v-nth (bv-oprd-a i-reg) reg-file) b-reg i-reg
                        (trunc (default-visual-mem-value) 16) real-mem
                        (watch-dog f f f data-out addr-out))))
      ((disable bv-adder-output bv-subtracter-output b-store-alu-result
              bv-oprd-a b-indirect-reg-a-dec v-nat-dec v-nat-inc)
       (hands-off bv-alu-cv)))

(prove-lemma state-5-to-6-mem-init (rewrite)
  (implies (and (equal mar5 (nat-to-bv 5 (nxsz)))
                (not (b-direct-reg-a i-reg)))
           (equal (big-machine mar5 f f f
                                no-store data-out
                                reg-file addr-out
                                c-flag v-flag z-flag n-flag
                                a-reg b-reg i-reg
                                visual-mem real-mem
                                memory-watch-dog-history
                                (list (list f f)))
                  (list (nat-to-bv 5 (nxsz))
                        t f f f no-store data-out
                        reg-file addr-out
                        c-flag v-flag z-flag n-flag
                        a-reg b-reg i-reg
                        (trunc (default-visual-mem-value) 16) real-mem
                        (watch-dog f f f data-out addr-out))))
```

```
     ((disable bv-adder-output bv-subtracter-output b-store-alu-result
             b-indirect-reg-a-dec v-nat-dec v-nat-inc)
      (hands-off bv-alu-cv)))

(disable state-5-to-6-mem-init)

(prove-lemma state-5-to-6-mem-help (rewrite)
  (implies (and (equal mar5 (nat-to-bv 5 (nxsz)))
                (not (b-direct-reg-a i-reg)))
           (equal (big-machine mar5 t f f f
                               no-store data-out
                               reg-file addr-out
                               c-flag v-flag z-flag n-flag
                               a-reg b-reg i-reg
                               visual-mem real-mem
                               watch-dog-history
                               (cons (list f f) oracle))
                  (big-machine mar5 t f f f
                               no-store data-out
                               reg-file addr-out
                               c-flag v-flag z-flag n-flag
                               a-reg b-reg i-reg
                               (trunc (default-visual-mem-value)
                                      (machine-size))
                               real-mem
                               (watch-dog t f f data-out addr-out)
                               oracle))))

(disable state-5-to-6-mem-help)

(prove-lemma state-5-to-6-mem-wait (rewrite)
  (implies (and (equal mar5 (nat-to-bv 5 (nxsz)))
                (not (b-direct-reg-a i-reg)))
           (equal (big-machine mar5 t f f f
                               no-store data-out
                               reg-file addr-out
                               c-flag v-flag z-flag n-flag
                               a-reg b-reg i-reg
                               visual-mem real-mem
                               watch-dog-history
                               (list-of-n-plus-1-dtack-reset-off n))
                  (list (nat-to-bv 5 (nxsz))
                        t f f f no-store data-out
                        reg-file addr-out
                        c-flag v-flag z-flag n-flag
                        a-reg b-reg i-reg
                        (trunc (default-visual-mem-value) 16) real-mem
                        (watch-dog t f f data-out addr-out))))
  ((disable no-store-with-ifs data-out-with-ifs addr-out c-flag-with-ifs
```

```
                      v-flag-with-ifs z-flag-with-ifs n-flag-with-ifs a-reg b-reg
                      i-reg-with-ifs visual-mem real-mem
                      bv-adder-output bv-subtracter-output
                      b-store-alu-result append
                      open-big-machine-on-listp update-nth
                      nth v-nth v-nat-inc v-nat-dec nat-to-bv bv-to-nat)
          (hands-off bv-alu-cv)
          (enable state-5-to-6-mem-help)
          (induct (state-2-to-2-induction dtack data-out addr-out visual-mem
                                          watch-dog-history
                                          n))))

(disable state-5-to-6-mem-wait)

; The next two lemmas we never use as rewrite rules, for the same reasons
; as explained above.

(prove-lemma state-5-to-6-mem-dtack nil
  (implies (and (equal mar5 (nat-to-bv 5 (nxsz)))
                (ramp reg-file (machine-size) 8)
                (sizep addr-out (machine-size))
                (not (b-direct-reg-a i-reg)))
           (equal (big-machine mar5 t f f f
                               no-store data-out
                               reg-file addr-out
                               c-flag v-flag z-flag n-flag
                               a-reg b-reg i-reg
                               visual-mem real-mem
                               (watch-dog t f f data-out addr-out)
                               (list (list t f) (list t f)))
                  (list (nat-to-bv 6 (nxsz))
                        t f t f no-store data-out
                        reg-file addr-out
                        c-flag v-flag z-flag n-flag
                        a-reg b-reg i-reg
                        (trunc (v-nth addr-out real-mem) (machine-size))
                        real-mem
                        (watch-dog t f t data-out addr-out))))
  ((disable bv-adder-output bv-subtracter-output b-store-alu-result
            b-indirect-reg-a-dec v-nat-dec v-nat-inc)
   (hands-off bv-alu-cv)))

(prove-lemma state-6-to-7-mem nil
  (implies (and (equal mar6 (nat-to-bv 6 (nxsz)))
                (ramp reg-file (machine-size) 8)
                (sizep visual-mem (machine-size))
                (sizep addr-out (machine-size))
                (not (b-direct-reg-a i-reg)))
           (equal (big-machine mar6 t f t f
```

```
                                    no-store data-out
                                    reg-file addr-out
                                    c-flag v-flag z-flag n-flag
                                    a-reg b-reg i-reg
                                    visual-mem real-mem
                                    (watch-dog t f t data-out addr-out)
                                    (list (list t f)))
                      (list (nat-to-bv 7 (nxsz))
                            f f t f no-store data-out
                            reg-file addr-out
                            c-flag v-flag z-flag n-flag
                            visual-mem b-reg i-reg
                            (trunc (v-nth addr-out real-mem) (machine-size))
                            real-mem
                            (watch-dog t f t data-out addr-out))))
    ((disable bv-adder-output bv-subtracter-output b-store-alu-result
              b-indirect-reg-a-dec v-nat-dec v-nat-inc)
     (hands-off bv-alu-cv)))


; We now piece together states 4, 5, 6, and 7 for the reg case:

(prove-lemma state-4-to-5-to-6-to-7-reg (rewrite)
  (implies
    (and (ramp reg-file (machine-size) 8)
         (equal mar4 (nat-to-bv 4 (nxsz)))
         (b-direct-reg-a i-reg))
    (equal (big-machine mar4 f f t f
                        no-store data-out
                        reg-file addr-out
                        c-flag v-flag z-flag n-flag
                        a-reg b-reg i-reg
                        visual-mem real-mem
                        watch-dog
                        (list (list f f) (list f f) (list f f)))
           (list (nat-to-bv 7 (nxsz))
                 f f f f no-store data-out
                 (fetch-oprd-a-reg-file i-reg reg-file)
                 (fetch-oprd-a-addr-out i-reg reg-file)
                 c-flag v-flag z-flag n-flag
                 (v-nth (bv-oprd-a i-reg)
                        (fetch-oprd-a-reg-file i-reg reg-file))
                 b-reg i-reg
                 (trunc (default-visual-mem-value) 16) real-mem
                 (watch-dog f f f data-out
                            (fetch-oprd-a-addr-out i-reg reg-file)))))
    ((disable bv-adder-output bv-subtracter-output b-store-alu-result
              v-nat-dec v-nat-inc fix-bool bv-oprd-a)
     (hands-off bv-alu-cv))
```

```
      (enable bv-decrementer-truncates-to-machine-size
              bv-incrementer-truncates-to-machine-size)))

(disable state-4-to-5-to-6-to-7-reg)

; and now we do the same thing for 5, 6, and 7 in the mem case:

(prove-lemma state-5-to-6-to-7-mem-dtack (rewrite)
  (implies (and (equal mar5 (nat-to-bv 5 (nxsz)))
                (ramp reg-file (machine-size) 8)
                (sizep addr-out (machine-size))
                (not (b-direct-reg-a i-reg)))
           (equal (big-machine mar5 t f f f
                               no-store data-out
                               reg-file addr-out
                               c-flag v-flag z-flag n-flag
                               a-reg b-reg i-reg
                               visual-mem real-mem
                               (watch-dog t f f data-out addr-out)
                               (list (list t f) (list t f) (list t f)))
                  (list (nat-to-bv 7 (nxsz))
                        f f t f no-store data-out
                        reg-file addr-out
                        c-flag v-flag z-flag n-flag
                        (trunc (v-nth addr-out real-mem) (machine-size))
                        b-reg i-reg
                        (trunc (v-nth addr-out real-mem) (machine-size))
                        real-mem
                        (watch-dog t f t data-out addr-out))))
  ((disable bv-adder-output bv-subtracter-output b-store-alu-result
            b-indirect-reg-a-dec v-nat-dec v-nat-inc)
   (hands-off bv-alu-cv)))

(disable state-5-to-6-to-7-mem-dtack)

; Finally, we do the entire transition from state 4 to state 7.  We first
; define the oracle necessary to drive the machine through the sequence.

(defn fetch-oprd-a-oracle (i-reg n)
  (if (b-direct-reg-a i-reg)
      (list (list f f) (list f f) (list f f))
      (append (list (list f f))
              (append (list (list f f))
                      (append (list-of-n-plus-1-dtack-reset-off n)
                              (list (list t f)
                                    (list t f)
                                    (list t f)))))))

(prove-lemma every-member-sizep-update-nth-machine-size (rewrite)
```

```
   (implies (and (equal (size x) 16)
                 (every-member-sizep lst 16))
            (every-member-sizep (update-nth bool n lst x) 16)))

(disable every-member-sizep-update-nth)

(prove-lemma state-4-to-7 (rewrite)
  (implies
    (and (ramp reg-file (machine-size) 8)
         (sizep addr-out (machine-size))
         (ramp real-mem (machine-size) (exp 2 (machine-size)))
         (equal mar4 (nat-to-bv 4 (nxsz))))
    (equal (big-machine mar4 f f t f
                        no-store data-out
                        reg-file addr-out
                        c-flag v-flag z-flag n-flag
                        a-reg b-reg i-reg
                        visual-mem real-mem
                        watch-dog
                        (fetch-oprd-a-oracle i-reg n))
           (list (nat-to-bv 7 (nxsz))
                 f f (not (b-direct-reg-a i-reg)) f
                 no-store data-out
                 (fetch-oprd-a-reg-file i-reg reg-file)
                 (fetch-oprd-a-addr-out i-reg reg-file)
                 c-flag v-flag z-flag n-flag
                 (if (b-direct-reg-a i-reg)
                     (v-nth (bv-oprd-a i-reg)
                            (fetch-oprd-a-reg-file i-reg reg-file))
                   (v-nth (fetch-oprd-a-addr-out i-reg reg-file)
                          real-mem))
                 b-reg i-reg
                 (if (b-direct-reg-a i-reg)
                     (trunc (default-visual-mem-value) 16)
                   (v-nth (fetch-oprd-a-addr-out i-reg reg-file)
                          real-mem))
                 real-mem
                 (watch-dog (not (b-direct-reg-a i-reg))
                            f
                            (not (b-direct-reg-a i-reg))
                            data-out
                            (fetch-oprd-a-addr-out i-reg reg-file)))))

  ((disable fetch-oprd-a-reg-file fetch-oprd-a-addr-out
            mar read write no-store-with-ifs
            data-out-with-ifs addr-out c-flag-with-ifs
            v-flag-with-ifs z-flag-with-ifs n-flag-with-ifs a-reg b-reg
            i-reg-with-ifs visual-mem real-mem bv-adder-output
            bv-subtracter-output b-store-alu-result
```

```
          append open-big-machine-on-listp
          update-nth nth v-nat-inc v-nat-dec nat-to-bv bv-to-nat)
(hands-off bv-alu-cv)
(enable state-4-to-5
          state-4-to-5-to-6-to-7-reg
          state-5-to-6-mem-init
          state-5-to-6-mem-wait
          state-5-to-6-to-7-mem-dtack)))

(disable state-4-to-7)
```

```
;;;;;;;;;;;;;;;;;;;;;;;;;;;;;;;;;;;;;;;;;;;;;;;;;;;;;;;;;;;;;;;;;;;;;;;;
;;                                                                  ;;
;;      Fetch Operand B, doing Pre-decrement if necessary           ;;
;;                                                                  ;;
;;;;;;;;;;;;;;;;;;;;;;;;;;;;;;;;;;;;;;;;;;;;;;;;;;;;;;;;;;;;;;;;;;;;;;;;

(defn fetch-oprd-b-reg-file (i-reg reg-file)
  (update-v-nth (b-indirect-reg-b-dec i-reg)
                (bv-oprd-b i-reg)
                reg-file
                (v-nat-dec (v-nth (bv-oprd-b i-reg)
                                  reg-file))))

; Both of the following lemmas are needed, as RAMP is enabled sometimes

(prove-lemma ramp-fetch-oprd-b-reg-file (rewrite)
  (implies
    (and (equal m (machine-size))
         (ramp reg-file (machine-size) 8))
    (and (equal (length (fetch-oprd-b-reg-file i-reg reg-file)) 8)
         (every-member-sizep (fetch-oprd-b-reg-file i-reg reg-file) m)))
  ((disable update-nth bv-oprd-b)))

(prove-lemma ramp-fetch-oprd-b-reg-file-2 (rewrite)
  (implies (and (equal m (machine-size))
                (ramp reg-file (machine-size) 8))
           (ramp (fetch-oprd-b-reg-file i-reg reg-file) m 8))
  ((disable update-nth bv-oprd-b)))

(defn fetch-oprd-b-addr-out (i-reg reg-file)
  (if (b-indirect-reg-b-dec i-reg)
      (v-nat-dec (v-nth (bv-oprd-b i-reg) reg-file))
      (v-nth (bv-oprd-b i-reg) reg-file)))

(prove-lemma sizep-fetch-oprd-b-addr-out (rewrite)
  (implies (and (equal m (machine-size))
                (ramp reg-file (machine-size) 8))
           (equal (size (fetch-oprd-b-addr-out i-reg reg-file)) m))
  ((disable bv-oprd-b)))

(prove-lemma state-7-to-8 (rewrite)
  (implies (and (ramp reg-file (machine-size) 8)
                (equal mar7 (nat-to-bv 7 (nxsz))))
           (equal (big-machine mar7 f f dtack f
                               no-store data-out
                                    reg-file addr-out
                                    c-flag v-flag z-flag n-flag
                                    a-reg b-reg i-reg
                                    visual-mem real-mem
```

```
                              watch-dog
                              (list (list f f)))
                 (list (nat-to-bv 8 (nxsz))
                       f f f f no-store data-out
                       (fetch-oprd-b-reg-file i-reg reg-file)
                       (fetch-oprd-b-addr-out i-reg reg-file)
                       c-flag v-flag z-flag n-flag
                       a-reg b-reg i-reg
                       (trunc (default-visual-mem-value) 16) real-mem
                       (watch-dog f f f data-out addr-out)))))
  ((disable bv-adder-output bv-subtracter-output b-store-alu-result
            v-nat-dec v-nat-inc fix-bool bv-oprd-b)
   (hands-off bv-alu-cv)
   (enable bv-decrementer-truncates-to-machine-size
           bv-incrementer-truncates-to-machine-size)))

(disable state-7-to-8)

; The next two lemmas are never used as rewrite rules.

(prove-lemma state-8-to-9-reg nil
  (implies (and (ramp reg-file (machine-size) 8)
                (equal mar8 (nat-to-bv 8 (nxsz)))
                (b-direct-reg-b i-reg))
           (equal (big-machine mar8 f f dt-any f
                               no-store data-out
                               reg-file addr-out
                               c-flag v-flag z-flag n-flag
                               a-reg b-reg i-reg
                               visual-mem real-mem
                               watch-dog-history
                               (list (list f f)))
                  (list (nat-to-bv 9 (nxsz))
                        f f f f no-store data-out
                        reg-file addr-out
                        c-flag v-flag z-flag n-flag
                        a-reg b-reg i-reg
                        (trunc (default-visual-mem-value) 16) real-mem
                        (watch-dog f f f data-out addr-out)))))
    ((disable bv-adder-output bv-subtracter-output b-store-alu-result
              b-indirect-reg-b-dec v-nat-dec v-nat-inc)
     (hands-off bv-alu-cv)))

(prove-lemma state-9-to-10-reg nil
  (implies (and (ramp reg-file (machine-size) 8)
                (equal mar9 (nat-to-bv 9 (nxsz)))
                (b-direct-reg-b i-reg))
           (equal (big-machine mar9 f f f f
                               no-store data-out
```

```
                              reg-file addr-out
                              c-flag v-flag z-flag n-flag
                              a-reg b-reg i-reg
                              visual-mem real-mem
                              watch-dog-history
                              (list (list f f)))
                  (list (nat-to-bv 10 (nxsz))
                        f f f f no-store data-out
                        reg-file addr-out
                        c-flag v-flag z-flag n-flag
                        a-reg (v-nth (bv-oprd-b i-reg) reg-file) i-reg
                        (trunc (default-visual-mem-value) 16) real-mem
                        (watch-dog f f f data-out addr-out))))
      ((disable bv-adder-output bv-subtracter-output b-store-alu-result
               bv-oprd-b b-indirect-reg-b-dec v-nat-dec v-nat-inc)
       (hands-off bv-alu-cv)))

(prove-lemma state-8-to-9-mem-init (rewrite)
  (implies (and (equal mar8 (nat-to-bv 8 (nxsz)))
                (not (b-direct-reg-b i-reg)))
           (equal (big-machine mar8 f f f f
                               no-store data-out
                               reg-file addr-out
                               c-flag v-flag z-flag n-flag
                               a-reg b-reg i-reg
                               visual-mem real-mem
                               memory-watch-dog-history
                               (list (list f f)))
                  (list (nat-to-bv 8 (nxsz))
                        t f f f no-store data-out
                        reg-file addr-out
                        c-flag v-flag z-flag n-flag
                        a-reg b-reg i-reg
                        (trunc (default-visual-mem-value) 16) real-mem
                        (watch-dog f f f data-out addr-out))))
      ((disable bv-adder-output bv-subtracter-output b-store-alu-result
               b-indirect-reg-b-dec v-nat-dec v-nat-inc)
       (hands-off bv-alu-cv)))

(disable state-8-to-9-mem-init)

(prove-lemma state-8-to-9-mem-help (rewrite)
  (implies (and (equal mar8 (nat-to-bv 8 (nxsz)))
                (not (b-direct-reg-b i-reg)))
           (equal (big-machine mar8 t f f f
                               no-store data-out
                               reg-file addr-out
                               c-flag v-flag z-flag n-flag
                               a-reg b-reg i-reg
```

```
                              visual-mem real-mem
                              watch-dog-history
                              (cons (list f f) oracle))
                (big-machine mar8 t f f f
                              no-store data-out
                              reg-file addr-out
                              c-flag v-flag z-flag n-flag
                              a-reg b-reg i-reg
                              (trunc (default-visual-mem-value)
                                     (machine-size))
                              real-mem
                              (watch-dog t f f data-out addr-out)
                              oracle)))))


(disable state-8-to-9-mem-help)

(prove-lemma state-8-to-9-mem-wait (rewrite)
  (implies (and (equal mar8 (nat-to-bv 8 (nxsz)))
                (not (b-direct-reg-b i-reg)))
           (equal (big-machine mar8 t f f f
                                no-store data-out
                                reg-file addr-out
                                c-flag v-flag z-flag n-flag
                                a-reg b-reg i-reg
                                visual-mem real-mem
                                watch-dog-history
                                (list-of-n-plus-1-dtack-reset-off n))
                  (list (nat-to-bv 8 (nxsz))
                        t f f f no-store data-out
                        reg-file addr-out
                        c-flag v-flag z-flag n-flag
                        a-reg b-reg i-reg
                        (trunc (default-visual-mem-value) 16) real-mem
                        (watch-dog t f f data-out addr-out)))))
    ((disable no-store-with-ifs data-out-with-ifs addr-out c-flag-with-ifs
              v-flag-with-ifs z-flag-with-ifs n-flag-with-ifs a-reg b-reg
              i-reg-with-ifs visual-mem real-mem
              bv-adder-output bv-subtracter-output
              b-store-alu-result append
              open-big-machine-on-listp update-nth
              nth v-nth v-nat-inc v-nat-dec nat-to-bv bv-to-nat)
    (hands-off bv-alu-cv)
    (enable state-8-to-9-mem-help)
    (induct (state-2-to-2-induction dtack data-out addr-out visual-mem
                                    watch-dog-history
                                    n))))


(disable state-8-to-9-mem-wait)
```

```
; The next two are never used as rewrites.

(prove-lemma state-8-to-9-mem-dtack nil
  (implies (and (equal mar8 (nat-to-bv 8 (nxsz)))
                (ramp reg-file (machine-size) 8)
                (sizep addr-out (machine-size))
                (not (b-direct-reg-b i-reg)))
           (equal (big-machine mar8 t f f f
                               no-store data-out
                               reg-file addr-out
                               c-flag v-flag z-flag n-flag
                               a-reg b-reg i-reg
                               visual-mem real-mem
                               (watch-dog t f f data-out addr-out)
                               (list (list t f) (list t f)))
                  (list (nat-to-bv 9 (nxsz))
                        t f t f no-store data-out
                        reg-file addr-out
                        c-flag v-flag z-flag n-flag
                        a-reg b-reg i-reg
                        (trunc (v-nth addr-out real-mem) (machine-size))
                        real-mem
                        (watch-dog t f t data-out addr-out))))
  ((disable bv-adder-output bv-subtracter-output b-store-alu-result
            b-indirect-reg-a-dec v-nat-dec v-nat-inc)
   (hands-off bv-alu-cv)))


(prove-lemma state-9-to-10-mem nil
  (implies (and (equal mar9 (nat-to-bv 9 (nxsz)))
                (ramp reg-file (machine-size) 8)
                (sizep visual-mem (machine-size))
                (sizep addr-out (machine-size))
                (not (b-direct-reg-b i-reg)))
           (equal (big-machine mar9 t f t f
                               no-store data-out
                               reg-file addr-out
                               c-flag v-flag z-flag n-flag
                               a-reg b-reg i-reg
                               visual-mem real-mem
                               (watch-dog t f t data-out addr-out)
                               (list (list t f)))
                  (list (nat-to-bv 10 (nxsz))
                        f f t f no-store data-out
                        reg-file addr-out
                        c-flag v-flag z-flag n-flag
                        a-reg visual-mem i-reg
                        (trunc (v-nth addr-out real-mem) (machine-size))
                        real-mem
```

```
                       (watch-dog t f t data-out addr-out)))))
    ((disable bv-adder-output bv-subtracter-output b-store-alu-result
              b-indirect-reg-b-dec v-nat-dec v-nat-inc)
     (hands-off bv-alu-cv)))

; We now piece together states 7, 8, 9, and 10 for the reg case:

(prove-lemma state-7-to-8-to-9-to-10-reg (rewrite)
  (implies
    (and (ramp reg-file (machine-size) 8)
         (equal mar7 (nat-to-bv 7 (nxsz)))
         (b-direct-reg-b i-reg))
    (equal (big-machine mar7 f f dtack f
                        no-store data-out
                        reg-file addr-out
                        c-flag v-flag z-flag n-flag
                        a-reg b-reg i-reg
                        visual-mem real-mem
                        watch-dog
                        (list (list f f) (list f f) (list f f)))
           (list (nat-to-bv 10 (nxsz))
                 f f f f no-store data-out
                 (fetch-oprd-b-reg-file i-reg reg-file)
                 (fetch-oprd-b-addr-out i-reg reg-file)
                 c-flag v-flag z-flag n-flag
                 a-reg
                 (v-nth (bv-oprd-b i-reg)
                        (fetch-oprd-b-reg-file i-reg reg-file))
                 i-reg
                 (trunc (default-visual-mem-value) 16) real-mem
                 (watch-dog f f f data-out
                            (fetch-oprd-b-addr-out i-reg reg-file)))))
    ((disable bv-adder-output bv-subtracter-output b-store-alu-result
              v-nat-dec v-nat-inc fix-bool bv-oprd-a)
     (hands-off bv-alu-cv)
     (enable bv-decrementer-truncates-to-machine-size
             bv-incrementer-truncates-to-machine-size)))

(disable state-7-to-8-to-9-to-10-reg)

; and now we do the same thing for 8, 9 and 10 in the mem case.

(prove-lemma state-8-to-9-to-10-mem-dtack (rewrite)
  (implies (and (equal mar8 (nat-to-bv 8 (nxsz)))
                (ramp reg-file (machine-size) 8)
                (sizep addr-out (machine-size))
                (not (b-direct-reg-b i-reg)))
           (equal (big-machine mar8 t f f f
                               no-store data-out
```

```
                              reg-file addr-out
                              c-flag v-flag z-flag n-flag
                              a-reg b-reg i-reg
                              visual-mem real-mem
                              (watch-dog t f f data-out addr-out)
                              (list (list t f) (list t f) (list t f)))
                 (list (nat-to-bv 10 (nxsz))
                         f f t f no-store data-out
                         reg-file addr-out
                         c-flag v-flag z-flag n-flag
                         a-reg
                         (trunc (v-nth addr-out real-mem) (machine-size))
                         i-reg
                         (trunc (v-nth addr-out real-mem) (machine-size))
                         real-mem
                         (watch-dog t f t data-out addr-out)))))
   ((disable bv-adder-output bv-subtracter-output b-store-alu-result
            b-indirect-reg-a-dec v-nat-dec v-nat-inc bv-oprd-b)
    (hands-off bv-alu-cv)))

(disable state-5-to-6-to-7-mem-dtack)


; Finally, we do the entire transition from state 7 to state 10. We
; first define the oracle necessary to drive the machine through the
; sequence.

(defn fetch-oprd-b-oracle (i-reg n)
  (if (b-direct-reg-b i-reg)
      (list (list f f) (list f f) (list f f))
      (append (list (list f f))
              (append (list (list f f))
                      (append (list-of-n-plus-1-dtack-reset-off n)
                              (list (list t f)
                                    (list t f)
                                    (list t f)))))))

(prove-lemma state-7-to-10 (rewrite)
  (implies
   (and (ramp reg-file (machine-size) 8)
        (sizep addr-out (machine-size))
        (ramp real-mem (machine-size) (exp 2 (machine-size)))
        (equal mar7 (nat-to-bv 7 (nxsz))))
   (equal (big-machine mar7 f f dtack f
                       no-store data-out
                       reg-file addr-out
                       c-flag v-flag z-flag n-flag
                       a-reg b-reg i-reg
                       visual-mem real-mem
```

```
                        watch-dog
                        (fetch-oprd-b-oracle i-reg n))
          (list (nat-to-bv 10 (nxsz))
                f f
                (not (b-direct-reg-b i-reg))
                f
                no-store data-out
                (fetch-oprd-b-reg-file i-reg reg-file)
                (fetch-oprd-b-addr-out i-reg reg-file)
                c-flag v-flag z-flag n-flag
                a-reg
                (if (b-direct-reg-b i-reg)
                    (v-nth (bv-oprd-b i-reg)
                           (fetch-oprd-b-reg-file i-reg reg-file))
                  (v-nth (fetch-oprd-b-addr-out i-reg reg-file)
                         real-mem))
                i-reg
                (if (b-direct-reg-b i-reg)
                    (trunc (default-visual-mem-value) 16)
                  (v-nth (fetch-oprd-b-addr-out i-reg reg-file)
                         real-mem))
                real-mem
                (watch-dog (not (b-direct-reg-b i-reg))
                           f
                           (not (b-direct-reg-b i-reg))
                           data-out
                           (fetch-oprd-b-addr-out i-reg reg-file)))))

   ((disable fetch-oprd-b-reg-file fetch-oprd-b-addr-out
            mar read write no-store-with-ifs
            data-out-with-ifs addr-out c-flag-with-ifs
            v-flag-with-ifs z-flag-with-ifs n-flag-with-ifs a-reg b-reg
            i-reg-with-ifs visual-mem real-mem bv-adder-output
            bv-subtracter-output b-store-alu-result
            append open-big-machine-on-listp
            update-nth nth v-nat-inc v-nat-dec nat-to-bv bv-to-nat)
    (hands-off bv-alu-cv)
    (enable state-7-to-8
            state-7-to-8-to-9-to-10-reg
            state-8-to-9-mem-init
            state-8-to-9-mem-wait
            state-8-to-9-to-10-mem-dtack)))

(disable state-7-to-10)
```

```
;;;;;;;;;;;;;;;;;;;;;;;;;;;;;;;;;;;;;;;;;;;;;;;;;;;;;;;;;;;;;;;;;;;;;;;;;
;;                                                                     ;;
;;            ALU Results to Memory or Register                        ;;
;;                                                                     ;;
;;;;;;;;;;;;;;;;;;;;;;;;;;;;;;;;;;;;;;;;;;;;;;;;;;;;;;;;;;;;;;;;;;;;;;;;;

(defn alu-c-flag (i-reg a-reg b-reg c-flag)
  (if (b-cc-set i-reg)
      (c (bv-alu-cv a-reg b-reg c-flag
                    (bv-alu-op-code i-reg)))
      c-flag))

(defn alu-v-flag (i-reg a-reg b-reg c-flag v-flag)
  (if (b-cc-set i-reg)
      (v (bv-alu-cv a-reg b-reg c-flag
                    (bv-alu-op-code i-reg)))
      v-flag))

(defn alu-z-flag (i-reg a-reg b-reg c-flag z-flag)
  (if (b-cc-set i-reg)
      (b-bv-zerop (bv (bv-alu-cv a-reg b-reg c-flag
                                 (bv-alu-op-code i-reg))))
      z-flag))

(defn alu-n-flag (i-reg a-reg b-reg c-flag n-flag)
  (if (b-cc-set i-reg)
      (bitn (bv (bv-alu-cv a-reg b-reg c-flag
                           (bv-alu-op-code i-reg)))
            (machine-size))
      n-flag))

(prove-lemma boolp-alu-c-flag (rewrite)
  (implies (boolp c-flag)
           (boolp (alu-c-flag i-reg a-reg b-reg c-flag)))
  ((enable boolp)))

(prove-lemma boolp-alu-v-flag (rewrite)
  (implies (boolp v-flag)
           (boolp (alu-v-flag i-reg a-reg b-reg c-flag v-flag)))
  ((enable boolp)))

(prove-lemma boolp-alu-z-flag (rewrite)
  (implies (boolp z-flag)
           (boolp (alu-z-flag i-reg a-reg b-reg c-flag z-flag)))
  ((enable boolp)))

(prove-lemma boolp-alu-n-flag (rewrite)
  (implies (boolp n-flag)
           (boolp (alu-n-flag i-reg a-reg b-reg c-flag n-flag)))
  ((enable boolp)))
```

```
(prove-lemma state-10-to-11 (rewrite)
  (implies (and (equal mar10 (nat-to-bv 10 (nxsz)))
                (boolp no-store)
                (boolp c-flag)
                (boolp v-flag)
                (boolp n-flag)
                (boolp z-flag)
                (sizep data-out (machine-size)))
           (equal (big-machine mar10 f f dtack f
                               no-store data-out
                               reg-file addr-out
                               c-flag v-flag z-flag n-flag
                               a-reg b-reg i-reg
                               visual-mem real-mem
                               watch-dog-history
                               (list (list f f)))
                  (list (nat-to-bv 11 (nxsz))
                        f f f f
                        (not (b-store-alu-result c-flag v-flag
                                                 z-flag n-flag i-reg))
                        (bv (bv-alu-cv a-reg b-reg c-flag
                                       (bv-alu-op-code i-reg)))
                        reg-file addr-out
                        (alu-c-flag i-reg a-reg b-reg c-flag)
                        (alu-v-flag i-reg a-reg b-reg c-flag v-flag)
                        (alu-z-flag i-reg a-reg b-reg c-flag z-flag)
                        (alu-n-flag i-reg a-reg b-reg c-flag n-flag)
                        a-reg b-reg i-reg
                        (trunc (default-visual-mem-value) 16) real-mem
                        (watch-dog f f f data-out addr-out)))))
  ((disable bv-adder-output bv-subtracter-output b-store-alu-result
            bv-oprd-b b-indirect-reg-b-dec v-nat-dec
            v-nat-inc bv-alu-op-code
            b-store-alu-result-with-ifs b-bv-zerop)
   (hands-off bv-alu-cv)))

(disable state-10-to-11)

(disable alu-c-flag)

(disable alu-v-flag)

(disable alu-z-flag)

(disable alu-n-flag)

(prove-lemma state-11-to-12-reg nil
  (implies (and (ramp reg-file (machine-size) 8)
                (sizep data-out (machine-size)))
```

```
                    (equal mar11 (nat-to-bv 11 (nxsz)))
                    (b-direct-reg-b i-reg))
           (equal (big-machine mar11 f f f f
                               no-store data-out
                               reg-file addr-out
                               c-flag v-flag z-flag n-flag
                               a-reg b-reg i-reg
                               visual-mem real-mem
                               watch-dog-history
                               (list (list f f)))
                  (list (nat-to-bv 12 (nxsz))
                        f f f f no-store data-out
                        (update-v-nth (not no-store)
                                      (bv-oprd-b i-reg)
                                      reg-file
                                      data-out)
                        addr-out
                        c-flag v-flag z-flag n-flag
                        a-reg b-reg i-reg
                        (trunc (default-visual-mem-value) 16) real-mem
                        (watch-dog f f f data-out addr-out))))
    ((disable bv-adder-output bv-subtracter-output b-store-alu-result
             b-indirect-reg-b-dec v-nat-dec v-nat-inc bv-oprd-b)
     (hands-off bv-alu-cv)))


(prove-lemma state-11-to-12-mem-no-store nil
  (implies (and (equal mar11 (nat-to-bv 11 (nxsz)))
                (equal no-store t)
                (not (b-direct-reg-b i-reg)))
           (equal (big-machine mar11 f f f f
                               no-store data-out
                               reg-file addr-out
                               c-flag v-flag z-flag n-flag
                               a-reg b-reg i-reg
                               visual-mem real-mem
                               watch-dog-history
                               (list (list f f)))
                  (list (nat-to-bv 12 (nxsz))
                        f f f f no-store data-out
                        reg-file addr-out
                        c-flag v-flag z-flag n-flag
                        a-reg b-reg i-reg
                        (trunc (default-visual-mem-value) 16)
                        real-mem
                        (watch-dog f f f data-out addr-out))))
    ((disable bv-adder-output bv-subtracter-output b-store-alu-result
             b-indirect-reg-b-dec v-nat-dec v-nat-inc)
     (hands-off bv-alu-cv)))
```

```
(prove-lemma state-11-to-12-mem-init-store (rewrite)
  (implies (and (equal mar11 (nat-to-bv 11 (nxsz)))
                (equal no-store f)
                (not (b-direct-reg-b i-reg)))
           (equal (big-machine mar11 f f f f
                               no-store data-out
                               reg-file addr-out
                               c-flag v-flag z-flag n-flag
                               a-reg b-reg i-reg
                               visual-mem real-mem
                               watch-dog-history
                               (list (list f f)))
                  (list (nat-to-bv 11 (nxsz))
                        f t f f no-store data-out
                        reg-file addr-out
                        c-flag v-flag z-flag n-flag
                        a-reg b-reg i-reg
                        (trunc (default-visual-mem-value) 16)
                        real-mem
                        (watch-dog f f f data-out addr-out))))
  ((disable bv-adder-output bv-subtracter-output b-store-alu-result
            b-indirect-reg-b-dec v-nat-dec v-nat-inc)
   (hands-off bv-alu-cv)))

(disable state-11-to-12-mem-init-store)

(prove-lemma state-11-to-12-mem-help (rewrite)
  (implies (and (equal mar11 (nat-to-bv 11 (nxsz)))
                (equal no-store f)
                (not (b-direct-reg-b i-reg)))
           (equal (big-machine mar11 f t f f
                               no-store data-out
                               reg-file addr-out
                               c-flag v-flag z-flag n-flag
                               a-reg b-reg i-reg
                               visual-mem real-mem
                               watch-dog-history
                               (cons (list f f) oracle))
                  (big-machine mar11 f t f f
                               no-store data-out
                               reg-file addr-out
                               c-flag v-flag z-flag n-flag
                               a-reg b-reg i-reg
                               (trunc (default-visual-mem-value)
                                      (machine-size))
                               real-mem
                               (watch-dog f t f data-out addr-out)
                               oracle)))
```

```
(disable state-11-to-12-mem-help)

(defn state-11-to-11-induction (dtack data-out addr-out visual-mem
                                      watch-dog-history n)
  (if (zerop n)
      t
      (state-11-to-11-induction
       f
       data-out
       addr-out
       (trunc (default-visual-mem-value) (machine-size))
       (watch-dog f t f data-out addr-out)
       (sub1 n))))

(prove-lemma state-11-to-12-mem-wait-store (rewrite)
  (implies (and (equal mar11 (nat-to-bv 11 (nxsz)))
                (equal no-store f)
                (not (b-direct-reg-b i-reg)))
           (equal (big-machine mar11 f t f f
                               no-store data-out
                               reg-file addr-out
                               c-flag v-flag z-flag n-flag
                               a-reg b-reg i-reg
                               visual-mem real-mem
                               watch-dog-history
                               (list-of-n-plus-1-dtack-reset-off n))
                  (list (nat-to-bv 11 (nxsz))
                        f t f f no-store data-out
                        reg-file addr-out
                        c-flag v-flag z-flag n-flag
                        a-reg b-reg i-reg
                        (trunc (default-visual-mem-value) 16) real-mem
                        (watch-dog f t f data-out addr-out))))
  ((disable no-store-with-ifs data-out-with-ifs addr-out c-flag-with-ifs
            v-flag-with-ifs z-flag-with-ifs n-flag-with-ifs a-reg b-reg
            i-reg-with-ifs visual-mem real-mem bv-adder-output
            bv-subtracter-output
            b-store-alu-result append
            open-big-machine-on-listp update-nth
            nth v-nth v-nat-inc v-nat-dec nat-to-bv bv-to-nat)
   (hands-off bv-alu-cv)
   (enable state-11-to-12-mem-help)
   (induct (state-11-to-11-induction dtack data-out addr-out visual-mem
                                     watch-dog-history
                                     n))))

(disable state-11-to-12-mem-wait-store)

(prove-lemma state-11-to-12-mem-dtack-store (rewrite)
```

```
  (implies (and (sizep addr-out (machine-size))
                (equal mar11 (nat-to-bv 11 (nxsz)))
                (equal no-store f)
                (not (b-direct-reg-b i-reg)))
           (equal (big-machine mar11 f t f f
                               no-store data-out
                               reg-file addr-out
                               c-flag v-flag z-flag n-flag
                               a-reg b-reg i-reg
                               visual-mem real-mem
                               (watch-dog f t f data-out addr-out)
                               (list (list t f) (list t f)))
                  (list (nat-to-bv 12 (nxsz))
                        f t t f no-store data-out
                        reg-file addr-out
                        c-flag v-flag z-flag n-flag
                        a-reg b-reg i-reg
                        (trunc (default-visual-mem-value) 16)
                        (update-v-nth t addr-out real-mem data-out)
                        (watch-dog f t t data-out addr-out))))
  ((disable bv-adder-output bv-subtracter-output b-store-alu-result
            b-indirect-reg-b-dec v-nat-dec v-nat-inc)
   (hands-off bv-alu-cv)))

(disable state-11-to-12-mem-dtack-store)

(prove-lemma state-10-to-12-reg (rewrite)
  (implies
   (and (equal mar10 (nat-to-bv 10 (nxsz)))
        (boolp no-store)
        (boolp c-flag)
        (boolp v-flag)
        (boolp n-flag)
        (boolp z-flag)
        (sizep data-out (machine-size))
        (sizep a-reg (machine-size))
        (ramp reg-file (machine-size) 8)
        (b-direct-reg-b i-reg))
   (equal (big-machine mar10 f f dtack f
                       no-store data-out
                       reg-file addr-out
                       c-flag v-flag z-flag n-flag
                       a-reg b-reg i-reg
                       visual-mem real-mem
                       watch-dog-history
                       (list (list f f) (list f f)))
          (list (nat-to-bv 12 (nxsz))
                f f f f
                (not (b-store-alu-result c-flag v-flag z-flag
```

```
                                       n-flag i-reg))
                (bv (bv-alu-cv a-reg b-reg c-flag
                              (bv-alu-op-code i-reg)))
                (update-v-nth
                 (b-store-alu-result c-flag v-flag z-flag n-flag i-reg)
                 (bv-oprd-b i-reg)
                 reg-file
                 (bv (bv-alu-cv a-reg b-reg c-flag
                              (bv-alu-op-code i-reg))))
                addr-out
                (alu-c-flag i-reg a-reg b-reg c-flag)
                (alu-v-flag i-reg a-reg b-reg c-flag v-flag)
                (alu-z-flag i-reg a-reg b-reg c-flag z-flag)
                (alu-n-flag i-reg a-reg b-reg c-flag n-flag)
                a-reg b-reg i-reg
                (trunc (default-visual-mem-value) 16) real-mem
                (watch-dog f f f
                          (bv (bv-alu-cv a-reg b-reg c-flag
                                        (bv-alu-op-code i-reg)))
                addr-out))))
  ((disable bv-adder-output bv-subtracter-output b-store-alu-result
           bv-oprd-b b-indirect-reg-b-dec v-nat-dec
           v-nat-inc bv-alu-op-code
           b-store-alu-result-with-ifs b-bv-zerop)
  (enable alu-c-flag alu-v-flag alu-z-flag alu-n-flag)
  (hands-off bv-alu-cv)))

(disable state-10-to-12-reg)

(prove-lemma state-10-to-12-mem-no-store (rewrite)
  (implies
   (and (equal mar10 (nat-to-bv 10 (nxsz)))
        (boolp c-flag)
        (boolp v-flag)
        (boolp n-flag)
        (boolp z-flag)
        (sizep data-out (machine-size))
        (sizep a-reg (machine-size))
        (not (b-direct-reg-b i-reg))
        (not (b-store-alu-result c-flag v-flag z-flag n-flag i-reg)))
   (equal (big-machine mar10 f f dtack f
                       no-store data-out
                       reg-file addr-out
                       c-flag v-flag z-flag n-flag
                       a-reg b-reg i-reg
                       visual-mem real-mem
                       watch-dog-history
                       (list (list f f) (list f f)))
          (list (nat-to-bv 12 (nxsz))
```

```
                  f f f f
                  (not (b-store-alu-result c-flag v-flag z-flag
                                           n-flag i-reg))
                  (bv (bv-alu-cv a-reg b-reg c-flag
                               (bv-alu-op-code i-reg)))
                  reg-file addr-out
                  (alu-c-flag i-reg a-reg b-reg c-flag)
                  (alu-v-flag i-reg a-reg b-reg c-flag v-flag)
                  (alu-z-flag i-reg a-reg b-reg c-flag z-flag)
                  (alu-n-flag i-reg a-reg b-reg c-flag n-flag)
                  a-reg b-reg i-reg
                  (trunc (default-visual-mem-value) 16)
                  real-mem
                  (watch-dog f f f
                             (bv (bv-alu-cv a-reg b-reg c-flag
                                          (bv-alu-op-code i-reg)))
                             addr-out))))
     ((disable bv-adder-output bv-subtracter-output b-store-alu-result
               bv-oprd-b b-indirect-reg-b-dec v-nat-dec
               v-nat-inc bv-alu-op-code
               b-store-alu-result-with-ifs b-bv-zerop)
      (enable alu-c-flag alu-v-flag alu-z-flag alu-n-flag)
      (hands-off bv-alu-cv)))

(disable state-10-to-12-mem-no-store)

(prove-lemma state-10-to-12-mem-store (rewrite)
  (implies
    (and (equal mar10 (nat-to-bv 10 (nxsz)))
         (boolp no-store)
         (boolp c-flag)
         (boolp v-flag)
         (boolp n-flag)
         (boolp z-flag)
         (sizep data-out (machine-size))
         (sizep addr-out (machine-size))
         (sizep a-reg (machine-size))
         (not (b-direct-reg-b i-reg))
         (b-store-alu-result c-flag v-flag z-flag n-flag i-reg))
    (equal (big-machine
            mar10 f f dtack f
            no-store data-out
            reg-file addr-out
            c-flag v-flag z-flag n-flag
            a-reg b-reg i-reg
            visual-mem real-mem
            watch-dog-history
            (append (list (list f f))
                    (append (list (list f f))
```

```
                        (append
                        (list-of-n-plus-1-dtack-reset-off n)
                        (list (list t f) (list t f))))))
        (list (nat-to-bv 12 (nxsz))
              f t t f
              (not (b-store-alu-result
                      c-flag v-flag z-flag n-flag i-reg))
              (bv (bv-alu-cv a-reg b-reg c-flag
                              (bv-alu-op-code i-reg)))
              reg-file addr-out
              (alu-c-flag i-reg a-reg b-reg c-flag)
              (alu-v-flag i-reg a-reg b-reg c-flag v-flag)
              (alu-z-flag i-reg a-reg b-reg c-flag z-flag)
              (alu-n-flag i-reg a-reg b-reg c-flag n-flag)
              a-reg b-reg i-reg
              (trunc (default-visual-mem-value) 16)
              (update-v-nth t addr-out real-mem
                            (bv (bv-alu-cv a-reg b-reg c-flag
                                            (bv-alu-op-code i-reg))))
              (watch-dog
               f t t
               (bv (bv-alu-cv a-reg b-reg c-flag
                               (bv-alu-op-code i-reg)))
               addr-out))))

  ((disable ramp
            b-direct-reg-b bv-alu-op-code
            mar read write no-store-with-ifs
            data-out-with-ifs addr-out c-flag-with-ifs
            v-flag-with-ifs z-flag-with-ifs n-flag-with-ifs a-reg b-reg
            i-reg-with-ifs visual-mem real-mem bv-adder-output
            bv-subtracter-output b-store-alu-result
            b-store-alu-result-with-ifs
            append open-big-machine-on-listp
            update-nth nth v-nth v-nat-inc v-nat-dec nat-to-bv bv-to-nat)
   (hands-off bv-alu-cv)
   (enable state-10-to-11
           state-11-to-12-mem-init-store
           state-11-to-12-mem-wait-store
           state-11-to-12-mem-dtack-store)))

(disable state-10-to-12-mem-store)

(defn alu-oracle (i-reg c-flag v-flag z-flag n-flag n)
   (if (b-direct-reg-b i-reg)
       (list (list f f) (list f f))
       (if (b-store-alu-result c-flag v-flag z-flag n-flag i-reg)
           (append (list (list f f))
                   (append (list (list f f))
```

```
                              (append (list-of-n-plus-1-dtack-reset-off n)
                                      (list (list t f) (list t f)))))
               (list (list f f) (list f f)))))

(prove-lemma update-nth-f (rewrite)
  (equal (update-nth f n lst val) lst))

(defn mem-store-flag (i-reg c-flag v-flag z-flag n-flag)
  (if (b-direct-reg-b i-reg)
      f
      (b-store-alu-result c-flag v-flag z-flag n-flag i-reg)))

(prove-lemma state-10-to-12 (rewrite)
  (implies
    (and (boolp no-store)
         (boolp c-flag)
         (boolp v-flag)
         (boolp n-flag)
         (boolp z-flag)
         (sizep data-out (machine-size))
         (sizep a-reg (machine-size))
         (sizep addr-out (machine-size))
         (ramp reg-file (machine-size) 8)
         (equal mar10 (nat-to-bv 10 (nxsz))))
    (equal (big-machine mar10 f f dtack f
                        no-store data-out
                        reg-file addr-out
                        c-flag v-flag z-flag n-flag
                        a-reg b-reg i-reg
                        visual-mem real-mem
                        watch-dog-history
                        (alu-oracle i-reg c-flag v-flag z-flag n-flag n))
           (list (nat-to-bv 12 (nxsz))
                 f
                 (mem-store-flag i-reg c-flag v-flag z-flag n-flag)
                 (mem-store-flag i-reg c-flag v-flag z-flag n-flag)
                 f
                 (not (b-store-alu-result c-flag v-flag z-flag
                                          n-flag i-reg))
                 (bv (bv-alu-cv a-reg b-reg c-flag
                                (bv-alu-op-code i-reg)))
                 (update-v-nth
                  (and (b-direct-reg-b i-reg)
                       (b-store-alu-result
                        c-flag v-flag z-flag n-flag i-reg))
                  (bv-oprd-b i-reg)
                  reg-file
                  (bv (bv-alu-cv a-reg b-reg c-flag
                                 (bv-alu-op-code i-reg))))))
```

```
                    addr-out
                    (alu-c-flag i-reg a-reg b-reg c-flag)
                    (alu-v-flag i-reg a-reg b-reg c-flag v-flag)
                    (alu-z-flag i-reg a-reg b-reg c-flag z-flag)
                    (alu-n-flag i-reg a-reg b-reg c-flag n-flag)
                    a-reg b-reg i-reg


                    (trunc (default-visual-mem-value) 16)
                    (update-v-nth (and (not (b-direct-reg-b i-reg))
                                       (b-store-alu-result
                                          c-flag v-flag z-flag n-flag i-reg))
                                  addr-out real-mem
                                  (bv (bv-alu-cv a-reg b-reg c-flag
                                                   (bv-alu-op-code i-reg))))
                    (watch-dog
                     f
                     (mem-store-flag i-reg c-flag v-flag z-flag n-flag)
                     (mem-store-flag i-reg c-flag v-flag z-flag n-flag)
                     (bv (bv-alu-cv a-reg b-reg c-flag
                                      (bv-alu-op-code i-reg)))
                     addr-out))))
       ((disable ramp
                 b-direct-reg-b bv-alu-op-code
                 mar read write no-store-with-ifs
                 data-out-with-ifs addr-out c-flag-with-ifs
                 v-flag-with-ifs z-flag-with-ifs n-flag-with-ifs a-reg b-reg
                 i-reg-with-ifs visual-mem real-mem bv-adder-output
                 bv-subtracter-output b-store-alu-result
                 b-store-alu-result-with-ifs
                 append open-big-machine-on-listp big-machine-append
                 update-nth nth v-nth v-nat-inc v-nat-dec nat-to-bv bv-to-nat)
        (hands-off bv-alu-cv)
        (enable state-10-to-12-reg
                state-10-to-12-mem-no-store
                state-10-to-12-mem-store)))

(disable state-10-to-12)

(disable mem-store-flag)
```

```
;;;;;;;;;;;;;;;;;;;;;;;;;;;;;;;;;;;;;;;;;;;;;;;;;;;;;;;;;;;;;;;;;;;;;;;;;;;;;;;;
;;                                                                          ;;
;;                   Post-Increment Operations                             ;;
;;                                                                          ;;
;;;;;;;;;;;;;;;;;;;;;;;;;;;;;;;;;;;;;;;;;;;;;;;;;;;;;;;;;;;;;;;;;;;;;;;;;;;;;;;;

(prove-lemma state-12-to-13 nil
  (implies (and (ramp reg-file (machine-size) 8)
                (or (truep mem-store-flag)
                    (falsep mem-store-flag))
                (equal mar12 (nat-to-bv 12 (nxsz))))
           (equal (big-machine mar12 f
                               mem-store-flag
                               mem-store-flag
                               f
                               no-store data-out
                               reg-file addr-out
                               c-flag v-flag z-flag n-flag
                               a-reg b-reg i-reg
                               visual-mem real-mem
                               (watch-dog f mem-store-flag mem-store-flag
                                          data-out addr-out)
                               (list (list mem-store-flag f)))
                  (list (nat-to-bv 13 (nxsz))
                        f f mem-store-flag f no-store data-out
                        (update-v-nth (b-indirect-reg-a-inc i-reg)
                                      (bv-oprd-a i-reg)
                                      reg-file
                                      (v-nat-inc (v-nth (bv-oprd-a i-reg)
                                                        reg-file)))
                        addr-out
                        c-flag v-flag z-flag n-flag
                        a-reg b-reg i-reg
                        (trunc (default-visual-mem-value) 16) real-mem
                        (watch-dog f mem-store-flag mem-store-flag
                                   data-out addr-out))))
  ((disable bv-adder-output bv-subtracter-output b-store-alu-result
            v-nat-dec v-nat-inc fix-bool bv-oprd-a)
   (hands-off bv-alu-cv)
   (enable bv-decrementer-truncates-to-machine-size
           bv-incrementer-truncates-to-machine-size)))

(prove-lemma state-13-to-1 nil
  (implies (and (ramp reg-file (machine-size) 8)
                (equal mar13 (nat-to-bv 13 (nxsz))))
           (equal (big-machine mar13 f f dtack f
                               no-store data-out
                               reg-file addr-out
```

```
                              c-flag v-flag z-flag n-flag
                              a-reg b-reg i-reg
                              visual-mem real-mem
                              watch-dog-history
                              (list (list f f)))
                 (list (nat-to-bv 1 (nxsz))
                       f f f f no-store data-out
                       (update-v-nth (b-indirect-reg-b-inc i-reg)
                                     (bv-oprd-b i-reg)
                                     reg-file
                                     (v-nat-inc (v-nth (bv-oprd-b i-reg)
                                                       reg-file)))
                       addr-out
                       c-flag v-flag z-flag n-flag
                       a-reg b-reg i-reg
                       (trunc (default-visual-mem-value) 16) real-mem
                       (watch-dog f f f data-out addr-out))))
  ((disable bv-adder-output bv-subtracter-output b-store-alu-result
            v-nat-dec v-nat-inc fix-bool bv-oprd-b)
   (hands-off bv-alu-cv)
   (enable bv-decrementer-truncates-to-machine-size
           bv-incrementer-truncates-to-machine-size)))

(defn reg-file-post-inc (i-reg reg-file)
  (update-v-nth
   (b-indirect-reg-b-inc i-reg)
   (bv-oprd-b i-reg)
   (update-v-nth (b-indirect-reg-a-inc i-reg)
                 (bv-oprd-a i-reg)
                 reg-file
                 (v-nat-inc (v-nth (bv-oprd-a i-reg)
                                   reg-file)))
   (v-nat-inc (v-nth (bv-oprd-b i-reg)
                     (update-v-nth (b-indirect-reg-a-inc i-reg)
                                   (bv-oprd-a i-reg)
                                   reg-file
                                   (v-nat-inc (v-nth (bv-oprd-a i-reg)
                                                     reg-file)))))))

(prove-lemma state-12-to-1 (rewrite)
  (implies (and (ramp reg-file (machine-size) 8)
                (or (truep mem-store-flag)
                    (falsep mem-store-flag))
                (equal mar12 (nat-to-bv 12 (nxsz))))
           (equal (big-machine mar12 f
                               mem-store-flag
                               mem-store-flag
                               f
                               no-store data-out
```

```
                          reg-file addr-out
                          c-flag v-flag z-flag n-flag
                          a-reg b-reg i-reg
                          visual-mem real-mem
                          (watch-dog f mem-store-flag mem-store-flag
                                     data-out addr-out)
                          (list (list mem-store-flag f) (list f f)))
               (list (nat-to-bv 1 (nxsz))
                     f f f f no-store data-out
                     (reg-file-post-inc i-reg reg-file)
                     addr-out
                     c-flag v-flag z-flag n-flag
                     a-reg b-reg i-reg
                     (trunc (default-visual-mem-value) 16) real-mem
                     (watch-dog f f f data-out addr-out))))
  ((disable bv-adder-output bv-subtracter-output b-store-alu-result
            v-nat-dec v-nat-inc fix-bool bv-oprd-a
            bv-oprd-b b-oprd-mem-ref-with-ifs)
   (hands-off bv-alu-cv)
   (enable bv-decrementer-truncates-to-machine-size
           bv-incrementer-truncates-to-machine-size)))

(disable state-12-to-1)
```

```
;;;;;;;;;;;;;;;;;;;;;;;;;;;;;;;;;;;;;;;;;;;;;;;;;;;;;;;;;;;;;;;;;;;;;;;;;;;
;;                                                                       ;;
;;                  Pasting Together the Steps                           ;;
;;                                                                       ;;
;;;;;;;;;;;;;;;;;;;;;;;;;;;;;;;;;;;;;;;;;;;;;;;;;;;;;;;;;;;;;;;;;;;;;;;;;;;

; In state-4-to-7 we rewrite to something of the form (list ... (if a b
; c) ...).  When applying big-machine-append the variable M is bound to
; the rewritten version of this form.  But the rewriter moves the if's
; out, producing (if a (list ... b ...) (list ... c ...)).  We then, in
; simplifying the rhs of big-machine-append, rewrite (cadr M) to get the
; new read.  We want it to rewrite to f but in fact it rewrites to (cadr
; (if a (list mar7 f ...) (list mar7 f ...))).  Then, state-7-to-10
; doesn't unify.  So we prove the following two facts.  Because of these
; facts we don't really care whether our state steppers return lists with
; if's inside or outside.

(prove-lemma car-if (rewrite)
  (equal (car (if a b c)) (if a (car b) (car c))))

(prove-lemma cdr-if (rewrite)
  (equal (cdr (if a b c)) (if a (cdr b) (cdr c))))

(defn reg-file-after-a-b (reg-file real-mem)
  (fetch-oprd-b-reg-file
    (v-nth (nth 0 reg-file) real-mem)
    (fetch-oprd-a-reg-file (v-nth (nth 0 reg-file) real-mem)
                           (update-nth t 0 reg-file
                                         (v-nat-inc (nth 0 reg-file))))))

(defn addr-out-after-a-b (reg-file real-mem)
  (fetch-oprd-b-addr-out
    (v-nth (nth 0 reg-file) real-mem)
    (fetch-oprd-a-reg-file (v-nth (nth 0 reg-file) real-mem)
                           (update-nth t 0 reg-file
                                         (v-nat-inc (nth 0 reg-file))))))

(defn a-reg-after-a-b (reg-file real-mem)
  (if (b-direct-reg-a (v-nth (nth 0 reg-file) real-mem))
      (v-nth (bv-oprd-a (v-nth (nth 0 reg-file) real-mem))
             (fetch-oprd-a-reg-file
               (v-nth (nth 0 reg-file) real-mem)
               (update-nth t 0 reg-file (v-nat-inc (nth 0 reg-file)))))
      (v-nth (fetch-oprd-a-addr-out
               (v-nth (nth 0 reg-file) real-mem)
               (update-nth t 0 reg-file (v-nat-inc (nth 0 reg-file))))
             real-mem)))

(defn b-reg-after-a-b (reg-file real-mem)
```

```
  (if (b-direct-reg-b (v-nth (nth 0 reg-file) real-mem))
      (v-nth (bv-oprd-b (v-nth (nth 0 reg-file) real-mem))
             (fetch-oprd-b-reg-file
               (v-nth (nth 0 reg-file) real-mem)
               (fetch-oprd-a-reg-file
                (v-nth (nth 0 reg-file) real-mem)
                (update-nth t 0 reg-file
                               (v-nat-inc (nth 0 reg-file)))))))
      (v-nth (fetch-oprd-b-addr-out
               (v-nth (nth 0 reg-file) real-mem)
               (fetch-oprd-a-reg-file
                (v-nth (nth 0 reg-file) real-mem)
                (update-nth t 0 reg-file
                               (v-nat-inc (nth 0 reg-file)))))
             real-mem)))

(defn visual-mem-after-a-b (reg-file real-mem)
  (if (b-direct-reg-b (v-nth (nth 0 reg-file) real-mem))
      (trunc (default-visual-mem-value) 16)
      (v-nth (fetch-oprd-b-addr-out
               (v-nth (nth 0 reg-file) real-mem)
               (fetch-oprd-a-reg-file
                (v-nth (nth 0 reg-file) real-mem)
                (update-nth t 0 reg-file
                               (v-nat-inc (nth 0 reg-file)))))
             real-mem)))

(defn dtack-after-a-b (reg-file real-mem)
  (not (b-direct-reg-b (v-nth (nth 0 reg-file) real-mem))))

(defn a-b-oracle (reg-file real-mem i n m)
  (append (fetch-ir-oracle i)
          (append (fetch-oprd-a-oracle
                    (v-nth (nth 0 reg-file) real-mem) n)
                  (fetch-oprd-b-oracle
                    (v-nth (nth 0 reg-file) real-mem) m))))

(prove-lemma state-1-to-10 (rewrite)
  (implies
    (and (ramp reg-file (machine-size) 8)
         (sizep addr-out (machine-size))
         (ramp real-mem (machine-size) (exp 2 (machine-size)))
         (equal mar1 (nat-to-bv 1 (nxsz))))
    (equal (big-machine mar1 f f f f
                         no-store data-out
                         reg-file addr-out
                         c-flag v-flag z-flag n-flag
                         a-reg b-reg i-reg
                         visual-mem real-mem
```

```
                        watch-dog
                        (a-b-oracle reg-file real-mem i n m))
              (list (nat-to-bv 10 (nxsz))
                    f f
                    (dtack-after-a-b reg-file real-mem)
                    f
                    no-store data-out
                    (reg-file-after-a-b reg-file real-mem)
                    (addr-out-after-a-b reg-file real-mem)
                    c-flag v-flag z-flag n-flag
                    (a-reg-after-a-b reg-file real-mem)
                    (b-reg-after-a-b reg-file real-mem)
                    (v-nth (nth 0 reg-file) real-mem)
                    (visual-mem-after-a-b reg-file real-mem)
                    real-mem
                    (watch-dog (dtack-after-a-b reg-file real-mem)
                               f
                               (dtack-after-a-b reg-file real-mem)
                               data-out
                               (addr-out-after-a-b reg-file real-mem)))))
    ((disable fetch-oprd-a-reg-file fetch-oprd-a-addr-out
              fetch-oprd-b-reg-file fetch-oprd-b-addr-out
              fetch-ir-oracle fetch-oprd-a-oracle fetch-oprd-b-oracle
              b-direct-reg-a b-direct-reg-b
              mar read write no-store-with-ifs
              data-out-with-ifs addr-out c-flag-with-ifs
              v-flag-with-ifs z-flag-with-ifs n-flag-with-ifs a-reg b-reg
              i-reg-with-ifs visual-mem real-mem bv-adder-output
              bv-subtracter-output b-store-alu-result
              append open-big-machine-on-listp
              update-nth nth v-nat-inc v-nat-dec nat-to-bv bv-to-nat)
     (hands-off bv-alu-cv)
     (enable state-1-to-4 state-4-to-7 state-7-to-10)))

(defn reg-file-alu
  (i-reg c-flag v-flag z-flag n-flag reg-file a-reg b-reg)
  (update-v-nth (and (b-direct-reg-b i-reg)
                     (b-store-alu-result
                       c-flag v-flag z-flag n-flag i-reg))
                (bv-oprd-b i-reg)
                reg-file
                (bv (bv-alu-cv a-reg b-reg c-flag
                              (bv-alu-op-code i-reg)))))

(defn reg-file-from-alu-thru-post-inc (i-reg c-flag v-flag z-flag n-flag
                                             reg-file a-reg b-reg)
  (update-v-nth
    (b-indirect-reg-b-inc i-reg)
    (bv-oprd-b i-reg)
```

```
    (update-v-nth
      (b-indirect-reg-a-inc i-reg)
      (bv-oprd-a i-reg)
      (reg-file-alu i-reg c-flag v-flag z-flag n-flag
                    reg-file a-reg b-reg)
      (v-nat-inc (v-nth (bv-oprd-a i-reg)
                        (reg-file-alu i-reg c-flag v-flag z-flag n-flag
                                      reg-file a-reg b-reg))))
    (v-nat-inc
      (v-nth (bv-oprd-b i-reg)
             (update-v-nth
               (b-indirect-reg-a-inc i-reg)
               (bv-oprd-a i-reg)
               (reg-file-alu i-reg c-flag v-flag z-flag n-flag
                             reg-file a-reg b-reg)
               (v-nat-inc
                 (v-nth (bv-oprd-a i-reg)
                        (reg-file-alu i-reg c-flag v-flag z-flag n-flag
                                      reg-file a-reg b-reg))))))))

(defn real-mem-thru-post-inc (i-reg c-flag v-flag z-flag n-flag
                                    addr-out real-mem a-reg b-reg)
 (update-v-nth (and (not (b-direct-reg-b i-reg))
                    (b-store-alu-result
                      c-flag v-flag z-flag n-flag i-reg))
               addr-out real-mem
               (bv (bv-alu-cv a-reg b-reg c-flag
                              (bv-alu-op-code i-reg)))))

(defn alu-post-inc-oracle (i-reg c-flag v-flag z-flag n-flag n)
  (append (alu-oracle i-reg c-flag v-flag z-flag n-flag n)
          (list (list (mem-store-flag i-reg c-flag v-flag z-flag n-flag)
                      f)
                (list f f))))

(prove-lemma ramp-if (rewrite)
  (equal (ramp (if c a b) i j) (if c (ramp a i j) (ramp b i j))))

(prove-lemma ramp-update-nth (rewrite)
  (implies (and (ramp reg-file width number)
                (sizep value width)
                (boolp boolean)
                (not (lessp number place)))
           (ramp (update-nth boolean place reg-file value)
                 width
                 number)))

(prove-lemma state-10-to-1 (rewrite)
  (implies
```

```
(and (boolp no-store)
     (boolp c-flag)
     (boolp v-flag)
     (boolp n-flag)
     (boolp z-flag)
     (sizep data-out (machine-size))
     (sizep a-reg (machine-size))
     (sizep addr-out (machine-size))
     (ramp reg-file (machine-size) 8)
     (equal mar10 (nat-to-bv 10 (nxsz))))
(equal (big-machine mar10 f f dtack f
                    no-store data-out
                    reg-file addr-out
                    c-flag v-flag z-flag n-flag
                    a-reg b-reg i-reg
                    visual-mem real-mem
                    watch-dog-history
                    (alu-post-inc-oracle i-reg c-flag
                                         v-flag z-flag n-flag n))
       (list (nat-to-bv 1 (nxsz))
             f f f f
             (not (b-store-alu-result c-flag v-flag z-flag
                                      n-flag i-reg))
             (bv (bv-alu-cv a-reg b-reg c-flag
                            (bv-alu-op-code i-reg)))
             (reg-file-from-alu-thru-post-inc i-reg c-flag
                                              v-flag z-flag
                                              n-flag reg-file
                                              a-reg b-reg)
             addr-out
             (alu-c-flag i-reg a-reg b-reg c-flag)
             (alu-v-flag i-reg a-reg b-reg c-flag v-flag)
             (alu-z-flag i-reg a-reg b-reg c-flag z-flag)
             (alu-n-flag i-reg a-reg b-reg c-flag n-flag)
             a-reg b-reg i-reg
             (trunc (default-visual-mem-value) 16)
             (real-mem-thru-post-inc i-reg c-flag v-flag z-flag n-flag
                                     addr-out real-mem a-reg b-reg)
             (watch-dog f f f
                        (bv (bv-alu-cv a-reg b-reg c-flag
                                       (bv-alu-op-code i-reg)))
                        addr-out))))
((disable alu-oracle alu-c-flag alu-v-flag alu-z-flag alu-n-flag ramp
          b-direct-reg-b bv-alu-op-code bv-alu-op-code-with-ifs
          mar read write no-store-with-ifs
          data-out-with-ifs addr-out c-flag-with-ifs
          v-flag-with-ifs z-flag-with-ifs n-flag-with-ifs a-reg b-reg
          i-reg-with-ifs visual-mem real-mem bv-adder-output
```

```
            bv-subtracter-output
            b-store-alu-result b-store-alu-result-with-ifs
            append open-big-machine-on-listp bv-oprd-a bv-oprd-b
            update-nth nth v-nth v-nat-inc v-nat-dec nat-to-bv bv-to-nat)
    (hands-off bv-alu-cv)
    (enable state-10-to-12 state-12-to-1)))

(disable state-10-to-1)
```

```
;;;;;;;;;;;;;;;;;;;;;;;;;;;;;;;;;;;;;;;;;;;;;;;;;;;;;;;;;;;;;;;;;;;;;;;;;;
;;                                                                      ;;
;;   The lemmas that follow culminate in lemma STATE-1-to-1             ;;
;;   which is a statement of what FM8501 does upon executing            ;;
;;   an instruction.  FM8501 executes one memory-based instruction      ;;
;;   by starting in a state where the MAR is "1", executing some        ;;
;;   of micro-states eventually taking it back to a place where         ;;
;;   MAR is equal to "1".                                               ;;
;;                                                                      ;;
;;;;;;;;;;;;;;;;;;;;;;;;;;;;;;;;;;;;;;;;;;;;;;;;;;;;;;;;;;;;;;;;;;;;;;;;;;

(prove-lemma sizep-a-reg-after-a-b (rewrite)
  (implies (and (ramp reg-file (machine-size) 8)
                (ramp real-mem (machine-size) (exp 2 (machine-size))))
           (equal (size (a-reg-after-a-b reg-file real-mem))
                  (machine-size)))
  ((disable b-direct-reg-a bv-oprd-a
            fetch-oprd-a-addr-out update-nth nth)))

(prove-lemma sizep-addr-out-after-a-b (rewrite)
  (implies (ramp reg-file (machine-size) 8)
           (equal (size (addr-out-after-a-b reg-file real-mem))
                  (machine-size)))
  ((disable fetch-oprd-a-reg-file b-indirect-reg-a-dec v-nth bv-oprd-b
            b-indirect-reg-b-dec fetch-oprd-b-addr-out v-nat-dec)))

(prove-lemma ramp-reg-file-after-a-b (rewrite)
  (implies (and (equal m (machine-size))
                (ramp reg-file (machine-size) 8))
           (ramp (reg-file-after-a-b reg-file real-mem) m 8))
  ((disable fetch-oprd-a-reg-file b-indirect-reg-a-dec v-nth bv-oprd-b
            update-nth b-indirect-reg-b-dec
            fetch-oprd-b-addr-out v-nat-dec)))

(defn state-1-to-1-oracle (reg-file real-mem c-flag v-flag z-flag n-flag
                           ir-wait a-wait b-wait store-wait)
  (append (a-b-oracle reg-file real-mem ir-wait a-wait b-wait)
          (alu-post-inc-oracle (v-nth (nth 0 reg-file) real-mem)
                               c-flag v-flag
                               z-flag n-flag
                               store-wait)))

(prove-lemma state-1-to-1 (rewrite)
  (implies
   (and (boolp no-store)
        (boolp c-flag)
        (boolp v-flag)
        (boolp n-flag)
        (boolp z-flag)
```

```
      (ramp reg-file (machine-size) 8)
      (sizep data-out (machine-size))
      (sizep addr-out (machine-size))
      (ramp real-mem (machine-size) (exp 2 (machine-size)))
      (equal mar1 (nat-to-bv 1 (nxsz))))
 (equal (big-machine mar1 f f f f
                        no-store data-out
                        reg-file addr-out
                        c-flag v-flag z-flag n-flag
                        a-reg b-reg i-reg
                        visual-mem real-mem
                        watch-dog
                        (state-1-to-1-oracle
                         reg-file real-mem
                         c-flag v-flag z-flag n-flag
                         ir-wait a-wait b-wait store-wait))
        (list (nat-to-bv 1 (nxsz))
              f f f f
              (not (b-store-alu-result
                    c-flag v-flag z-flag n-flag
                    (v-nth (nth 0 reg-file) real-mem)))
              (bv (bv-alu-cv (a-reg-after-a-b reg-file real-mem)
                             (b-reg-after-a-b reg-file real-mem)
                             c-flag
                             (bv-alu-op-code
                              (v-nth (nth 0 reg-file) real-mem))))
              (reg-file-from-alu-thru-post-inc
               (v-nth (nth 0 reg-file) real-mem)
               c-flag v-flag z-flag
               n-flag
               (reg-file-after-a-b reg-file real-mem)
               (a-reg-after-a-b reg-file real-mem)
               (b-reg-after-a-b reg-file real-mem))
              (addr-out-after-a-b reg-file real-mem)
              (alu-c-flag (v-nth (nth 0 reg-file) real-mem)
                          (a-reg-after-a-b reg-file real-mem)
                          (b-reg-after-a-b reg-file real-mem)
                          c-flag)

              (alu-v-flag (v-nth (nth 0 reg-file) real-mem)
                          (a-reg-after-a-b reg-file real-mem)
                          (b-reg-after-a-b reg-file real-mem)
                          c-flag v-flag)
              (alu-z-flag (v-nth (nth 0 reg-file) real-mem)
                          (a-reg-after-a-b reg-file real-mem)
                          (b-reg-after-a-b reg-file real-mem)
                          c-flag z-flag)
```

```
                    (alu-n-flag (v-nth (nth 0 reg-file) real-mem)
                                (a-reg-after-a-b reg-file real-mem)
                                (b-reg-after-a-b reg-file real-mem)
                                c-flag n-flag)
                    (a-reg-after-a-b reg-file real-mem)
                    (b-reg-after-a-b reg-file real-mem)
                    (v-nth (nth 0 reg-file) real-mem)
                    (trunc (default-visual-mem-value) 16)
                    (real-mem-thru-post-inc
                     (v-nth (nth 0 reg-file) real-mem)
                     c-flag v-flag z-flag n-flag
                     (addr-out-after-a-b reg-file real-mem)
                     real-mem
                     (a-reg-after-a-b reg-file real-mem)
                     (b-reg-after-a-b reg-file real-mem))
                    (watch-dog f f f
                               (bv (bv-alu-cv
                                    (a-reg-after-a-b reg-file real-mem)
                                    (b-reg-after-a-b reg-file real-mem)
                                    c-flag
                                    (bv-alu-op-code
                                     (v-nth (nth 0 reg-file) real-mem))))
                               (addr-out-after-a-b reg-file real-mem)))))
    ((disable reg-file-from-alu-thru-post-inc real-mem-thru-post-inc
              reg-file-after-a-b addr-out-after-a-b
              a-reg-after-a-b b-reg-after-a-b
              a-b-oracle alu-post-inc-oracle
              alu-c-flag alu-v-flag alu-z-flag alu-n-flag ramp
              bv-alu-op-code bv-alu-op-code-with-ifs
              b-store-alu-result-with-ifs bv-oprd-a bv-oprd-b v-nth
              fetch-oprd-a-reg-file fetch-oprd-a-addr-out
              fetch-oprd-b-reg-file fetch-oprd-b-addr-out
              fetch-ir-oracle fetch-oprd-a-oracle fetch-oprd-b-oracle
              b-direct-reg-a b-direct-reg-b
              mar read write no-store-with-ifs
              data-out-with-ifs addr-out c-flag-with-ifs
              v-flag-with-ifs z-flag-with-ifs n-flag-with-ifs a-reg b-reg
              i-reg-with-ifs visual-mem real-mem bv-adder-output
              bv-subtracter-output b-store-alu-result
              append open-big-machine-on-listp
              update-nth nth v-nat-inc v-nat-dec nat-to-bv bv-to-nat)
     (hands-off bv-alu-cv)
     (enable state-1-to-10 state-10-to-1)))

(disable state-1-to-1)

(prove-lemma nth-update-nth (rewrite)            ; A helping lemma
  (equal (nth i (update-nth c j lst x))
         (if (and (truep c)
```

```
        (equal (fix i) (fix j))
        (lessp j (length lst)))
  x
  (nth i lst))))
```

```
;;;;;;;;;;;;;;;;;;;;;;;;;;;;;;;;;;;;;;;;;;;;;;;;;;;;;;;;;;;;;;;;;;;;;;;;;;;
;;                                                                     ;;
;;                Software Specification of FM8501                     ;;
;;                                                                     ;;
;;;;;;;;;;;;;;;;;;;;;;;;;;;;;;;;;;;;;;;;;;;;;;;;;;;;;;;;;;;;;;;;;;;;;;;;;;;


;;;;;;;;;;;;;;;;;;;;;;;;;;;;;;;;;;;;;;;;;;;;;;;;;;;;;;;;;;;;;;;;;;;;;;;;;;;
;;                                                                     ;;
;; Helping definitions for the specification of the software           ;;
;; machine.  Function SOFT is the actual definition defining           ;;
;; the operation of the FM8501.                                        ;;
;;                                                                     ;;
;; When programming the FM8501 the user sees eight general-purpose     ;;
;; registers (register file), four flag bits (carry, overflow,        ;;
;; negative, and zero), and the memory.  Instruction execution        ;;
;; is accomplished by reading the memory value pointed to by the      ;;
;; program counter (register 0), and interpreting this memory word    ;;
;; as an instruction to be executed.  The execution of an instruction ;;
;; may modify any visible registers.  The flag registers may be       ;;
;; updated only once per instruction.  The memory may be updated      ;;
;; only once per instruction.  The register file may be updated a     ;;
;; maximum of four times in six opportunities.  The first update to   ;;
;; the register file, which always occurs, is the incrementing of     ;;
;; the program counter.  Next comes the possible pre-decrement        ;;
;; operation for both operands.  The result of the ALU may be next    ;;
;; stored into the register file.  Lastly, there may be two           ;;
;; post-increment operations.  An operand cannot be both              ;;
;; pre-decremented and post-incremented.                              ;;
;;                                                                     ;;
;; The functions below generate the next state for the memory and     ;;
;; the register file given an instruction.  These are grouped         ;;
;; together into an interpreter called SOFT.  SOFT executed one       ;;
;; instruction per recursive call.                                    ;;
;;                                                                     ;;
;; The next state for the register file (REG-FILE) is created by      ;;
;; the composition of several functions.  Each function describes     ;;
;; the state of the register file at some point through the execution ;;
;; of an instruction.  Below are described the operation of the       ;;
;; functions that update the register file.  All of these functions   ;;
;; return a complete register file, which they may or may not have    ;;
;; updated.                                                           ;;
;;                                                                     ;;
;; REG-FILE-AFTER-PC-INCREMENT --                                      ;;
;;      increments the PC (register 0)                                ;;
;;                                                                     ;;
;; REG-FILE-AFTER-OPRD-A-PRE-DECREMENT --                             ;;
;;      performs a pre-decrement operation for operand A if required, ;;
;;      and included is the REG-FILE-AFTER-PC-INCREMENT operation     ;;
```

```
;;                                                              ;;
;;  REG-FILE-AFTER-OPRD-B-PRE-DECREMENT --                      ;;
;;      performs a pre-decrement operation for operand B if required, ;;
;;      and included is the REG-FILE-AFTER-OPRD-A-PRE-DECREMENT ;;
;;      operation                                               ;;
;;                                                              ;;
;;  REG-FILE-AFTER-ALU-WRITE --                                 ;;
;;      writes the output of the ALU to the reg-file if required, ;;
;;      and included is the REG-FILE-AFTER-OPRD-B-PRE-DECREMENT ;;
;;      operation                                               ;;
;;                                                              ;;
;;  REG-FILE-AFTER-OPRD-A-POST-INCREMENT --                     ;;
;;      performs a post-increment operation for operand A if required,;;
;;      and included is the REG-FILE-AFTER-ALU-WRITE operation  ;;
;;                                                              ;;
;;  REG-FILE-AFTER-OPRD-B-POST-INCREMENT --                     ;;
;;      performs a post-increment operation for operand B if required,;;
;;      and included is the REG-FILE-AFTER-OPRD-A-POST-INCREMENT ;;
;;      operation                                               ;;
;;                                                              ;;
;;  The ALU requires three operands so its result can be calculated.  ;;
;;  The C-FLAG is readily available, but the A and B value for the    ;;
;;  ALU must be generated under instruction control.  The A value is  ;;
;;  fetched either from the register file or the memory, but not until ;;
;;  both the PC has been incremented and the operand A pre-decrement  ;;
;;  performed.  The function A-VALUE-FOR-ALU-AFTER-OPRD-A-PRE-DECREMENT;;
;;  generates the appropriate value.  The B value for the ALU is      ;;
;;  fetched from either the register file or memory, but not until the ;;
;;  PC has been incremented and the possible operand A pre-decrement  ;;
;;  and operand B pre-decrement operations performed.  The function   ;;
;;  B-VALUE-FOR-ALU-AFTER-OPRD-B-PRE-DECREMENT generates the correct  ;;
;;  operand B value.                                            ;;
;;                                                              ;;
;;;;;;;;;;;;;;;;;;;;;;;;;;;;;;;;;;;;;;;;;;;;;;;;;;;;;;;;;;;;;;;;;;;;;;;;;;

;  This function increments the Program Counter (PC) by one.  The PC is
;  stored in register 0 in the register file.

(defn reg-file-after-pc-increment (reg-file)
  (update-nth t 0 reg-file (v-nat-inc (nth 0 reg-file))))

;  This function extracts the current instruction from memory.

(defn current-instruction (reg-file real-mem)
  (v-nth (nth 0 reg-file) real-mem))

;  The result of this function is the contents of the register file after
;  the possible pre-decrement for operand A and the increment of the PC.
```

```
(defn reg-file-after-oprd-a-pre-decrement (reg-file real-mem)
  (update-v-nth
   (b-indirect-reg-a-dec (current-instruction reg-file real-mem))
   (bv-oprd-a (current-instruction reg-file real-mem))
   (reg-file-after-pc-increment reg-file)
   (v-nat-dec (v-nth (bv-oprd-a (current-instruction reg-file real-mem))
                     (reg-file-after-pc-increment reg-file)))))
```

```
; The result of this function is the contents of the register file after
; the possible pre-decrement for operand B, the possible pre-decrement
; for operand A and the increment of the PC.
```

```
(defn reg-file-after-oprd-b-pre-decrement (reg-file real-mem)
  (update-v-nth
   (b-indirect-reg-b-dec (current-instruction reg-file real-mem))
   (bv-oprd-b (current-instruction reg-file real-mem))
   (reg-file-after-oprd-a-pre-decrement reg-file real-mem)
   (v-nat-dec
    (v-nth (bv-oprd-b (current-instruction reg-file real-mem))
           (reg-file-after-oprd-a-pre-decrement reg-file real-mem)))))
```

```
; This function returns operand A for use in the ALU after the PC has
; been incremented and the possible operand A pre-decrement has occured.
```

```
(defn a-value-for-alu-after-oprd-a-pre-decrement (reg-file real-mem)
  (if (b-direct-reg-a (current-instruction reg-file real-mem))
      (v-nth (bv-oprd-a (current-instruction reg-file real-mem))
             (reg-file-after-pc-increment reg-file))
      (if (b-indirect-reg-a-dec (current-instruction reg-file real-mem))
          (v-nth (v-nat-dec
                  (v-nth
                   (bv-oprd-a (current-instruction reg-file real-mem))
                   (reg-file-after-pc-increment reg-file)))
                 real-mem)
          (v-nth (v-nth
                  (bv-oprd-a (current-instruction reg-file real-mem))
                  (reg-file-after-pc-increment reg-file))
                 real-mem))))
```

```
; This function returns operand B for use in the ALU after the PC has
; been incremented, the possible operand A pre-decrement has occured,
; and the possible operand B pre-decrement has occured.
```

```
(defn b-value-for-alu-after-oprd-b-pre-decrement (reg-file real-mem)
  (if (b-direct-reg-b (current-instruction reg-file real-mem))
      (v-nth (bv-oprd-b (current-instruction reg-file real-mem))
             (reg-file-after-oprd-a-pre-decrement reg-file real-mem))
      (if (b-indirect-reg-b-dec (current-instruction reg-file real-mem))
          (v-nth
```

```
         (v-nat-dec
          (v-nth
           (bv-oprd-b
            (current-instruction reg-file real-mem))
           (reg-file-after-oprd-a-pre-decrement reg-file real-mem)))
          real-mem)
         (v-nth
          (v-nth
           (bv-oprd-b (current-instruction reg-file real-mem))
           (reg-file-after-oprd-a-pre-decrement reg-file real-mem))
          real-mem))))
```

```
;  This function returns the result of the ALU on operand A, operand B,
;  and the carry flag.

(defn bv-alu-cv-results (reg-file real-mem c-flag)
  (bv-alu-cv
   (a-value-for-alu-after-oprd-a-pre-decrement reg-file real-mem)
   (b-value-for-alu-after-oprd-b-pre-decrement reg-file real-mem)
   c-flag
   (bv-alu-op-code (current-instruction reg-file real-mem))))
```

```
;  This function returns the result of a possible storing of the ALU
;  result into the register file.  Note that this function takes into
;  account the possible changes that may have been inflicted on the
;  register file by some pre-decrement operations and the PC increment.

(defn reg-file-after-alu-write
  (reg-file real-mem c-flag v-flag z-flag n-flag)
  (update-v-nth
   (and (b-store-alu-result-with-ifs
         c-flag v-flag z-flag n-flag
         (current-instruction reg-file real-mem))
        (b-direct-reg-b (current-instruction reg-file real-mem)))
   (bv-oprd-b (current-instruction reg-file real-mem))
   (reg-file-after-oprd-b-pre-decrement reg-file real-mem)
   (bv (bv-alu-cv-results reg-file real-mem c-flag))))
```

```
;  This function returns the result of a possible storing of the ALU
;  result into the memory.

(defn real-mem-after-alu-write
  (reg-file real-mem c-flag v-flag z-flag n-flag)
  (update-v-nth
   (and (b-store-alu-result-with-ifs
         c-flag v-flag z-flag n-flag
         (current-instruction reg-file real-mem))
        (not (b-direct-reg-b (current-instruction reg-file real-mem))))
   (v-nth (bv-oprd-b (current-instruction reg-file real-mem))
```

```
          (reg-file-after-oprd-b-pre-decrement reg-file real-mem))
    real-mem
    (bv (bv-alu-cv-results reg-file real-mem c-flag))))
```

```
; This function returns the result of a possible post-increment of
; operand A after the possible storing of the ALU result, the
; pre-decrements of A and B, and the PC increment.
```

```
(defn reg-file-after-oprd-a-post-increment
      (reg-file real-mem c-flag v-flag z-flag n-flag)
  (update-v-nth
   (b-indirect-reg-a-inc (current-instruction reg-file real-mem))
   (bv-oprd-a (current-instruction reg-file real-mem))
   (reg-file-after-alu-write reg-file real-mem
                             c-flag v-flag z-flag n-flag)
   (v-nat-inc (v-nth (bv-oprd-a (current-instruction reg-file real-mem))
                     (reg-file-after-alu-write
                      reg-file real-mem
                      c-flag v-flag z-flag n-flag)))))
```

```
; This function returns the result of a possible post-increment of
; operand B after the possible post-increment of A, the storing of the
; ALU result, etc.
```

```
(defn reg-file-after-oprd-b-post-increment
      (reg-file real-mem c-flag v-flag z-flag n-flag)
  (update-v-nth
   (b-indirect-reg-b-inc (current-instruction reg-file real-mem))
   (bv-oprd-b (current-instruction reg-file real-mem))
   (reg-file-after-oprd-a-post-increment reg-file real-mem
                                         c-flag v-flag z-flag n-flag)
   (v-nat-inc
    (v-nth (bv-oprd-b (current-instruction reg-file real-mem))
           (reg-file-after-oprd-a-post-increment reg-file real-mem
                                                 c-flag v-flag
                                                 z-flag n-flag)))))
```

```
;;;;;;;;;;;;;;;;;;;;;;;;;;;;;;;;;;;;;;;;;;;;;;;;;;;;;;;;;;;;;;;;;;;;;;;;;;;;;
;;                                                                         ;;
;;    Function SOFT is the programmer's interpreter for FM8501.            ;;
;;    This function completely defines the effect of all instructions      ;;
;;    on the programmer visible state.                                     ;;
;;                                                                         ;;
;;;;;;;;;;;;;;;;;;;;;;;;;;;;;;;;;;;;;;;;;;;;;;;;;;;;;;;;;;;;;;;;;;;;;;;;;;;;;

;  This function returns the result of executing n instructions, where
;  n is the length of lst.

(defn soft (reg-file real-mem c-flag v-flag z-flag n-flag lst)
  (if (nlistp lst)
      (list reg-file real-mem c-flag v-flag z-flag n-flag)
      (soft
       (reg-file-after-oprd-b-post-increment reg-file real-mem
                                        c-flag v-flag z-flag n-flag)
       (real-mem-after-alu-write reg-file real-mem c-flag
                          v-flag z-flag n-flag)
       (update-v (b-cc-set (current-instruction reg-file real-mem))
                 c-flag
                 (c (bv-alu-cv-results reg-file real-mem c-flag)))
       (update-v (b-cc-set (current-instruction reg-file real-mem))
                 v-flag
                 (v (bv-alu-cv-results reg-file real-mem c-flag)))
       (update-v (b-cc-set (current-instruction reg-file real-mem))
                 z-flag
                 (zerop
                  (bv-to-nat
                   (bv (bv-alu-cv-results reg-file real-mem c-flag)))))
       (update-v (b-cc-set (current-instruction reg-file real-mem))
                 n-flag
                 (negativep
                  (bv-to-tc
                   (bv (bv-alu-cv-results reg-file real-mem c-flag)))))
       (cdr lst))))
```

```
;;;;;;;;;;;;;;;;;;;;;;;;;;;;;;;;;;;;;;;;;;;;;;;;;;;;;;;;;;;;;;;;;;;;;;;;;;;;;;
;;                                                                          ;;
;;    Function SOFT-RESET specifies what the programmer sees after          ;;
;;    reset has occured.  Note that SOFT-RESET calls the function           ;;
;;    SOFT.  After a reset, the software instruction interpreter is         ;;
;;    is the function SOFT.                                                 ;;
;;                                                                          ;;
;;;;;;;;;;;;;;;;;;;;;;;;;;;;;;;;;;;;;;;;;;;;;;;;;;;;;;;;;;;;;;;;;;;;;;;;;;;;;;

(defn soft-reset (reg-file real-mem c-flag v-flag z-flag n-flag
                            oracle)
  (if (nlistp oracle)
      (list reg-file real-mem c-flag v-flag z-flag n-flag)
      (soft (update-nth t 0 reg-file (nat-to-bv 0 (machine-size)))
            real-mem
            c-flag
            v-flag
            z-flag
            n-flag
            (cdr oracle))))
```

```
;;;;;;;;;;;;;;;;;;;;;;;;;;;;;;;;;;;;;;;;;;;;;;;;;;;;;;;;;;;;;;;;;;;;;;;;;;
;;                                                                    ;;
;;    The following contains the events leading up to and including   ;;
;;    the proof that an abstraction, containing the programmer        ;;
;;    visible registers, of BIG-MACHINE is equivalent to SOFT.        ;;
;;    This equivalence is the main result of this work; this result   ;;
;;    proves the correctness of a large piece of hardware with        ;;
;;    respect to a high-level description.                            ;;
;;                                                                    ;;
;;;;;;;;;;;;;;;;;;;;;;;;;;;;;;;;;;;;;;;;;;;;;;;;;;;;;;;;;;;;;;;;;;;;;;;;;;


;;;;;;;;;;;;;;;;;;;;;;;;;;;;;;;;;;;;;;;;;;;;;;;;;;;;;;;;;;;;;;;;;;;;;;;;;;
;;                                                                    ;;
;;    Help Lemmas for Proving the Correctness of "SOFT-MACHINE"        ;;
;;                                                                    ;;
;;;;;;;;;;;;;;;;;;;;;;;;;;;;;;;;;;;;;;;;;;;;;;;;;;;;;;;;;;;;;;;;;;;;;;;;;;

(prove-lemma
 a-reg-after-a-b-is-a-value-for-alu-after-oprd-a-pre-decrement
 (rewrite)
  (implies
   (and (ramp reg-file (machine-size) 8)
        (ramp real-mem (machine-size) (exp 2 (machine-size))))
   (equal (a-reg-after-a-b reg-file real-mem)
          (a-value-for-alu-after-oprd-a-pre-decrement
           reg-file real-mem)))
  ((disable nth bv-oprd-a update-nth v-nat-dec v-nat-inc)))

(prove-lemma
 b-reg-after-a-b-is-b-value-for-alu-after-oprd-b-pre-decrement
 (rewrite)
  (implies
   (and (ramp reg-file (machine-size) 8)
        (ramp real-mem (machine-size) (exp 2 (machine-size))))
   (equal (b-reg-after-a-b reg-file real-mem)
          (b-value-for-alu-after-oprd-b-pre-decrement
           reg-file real-mem)))
  ((disable nth bv-oprd-a bv-oprd-b update-nth v-nat-dec v-nat-inc)))

(prove-lemma hard-c-flag-is-soft-c-flag (rewrite)
  (implies
   (and (ramp reg-file (machine-size) 8)
        (ramp real-mem (machine-size) (exp 2 (machine-size)))
        (boolp c-flag))
   (equal (alu-c-flag (nth (bv-to-nat (nth 0 reg-file)) real-mem)
                      (a-value-for-alu-after-oprd-a-pre-decrement
                       reg-file real-mem)
                      (b-value-for-alu-after-oprd-b-pre-decrement
                       reg-file real-mem)
```

```
                              c-flag)
              (update-v (b-cc-set (current-instruction reg-file real-mem))
                        c-flag
                        (c (bv-alu-cv-results reg-file real-mem c-flag)))))
   ((enable alu-c-flag)
    (disable nth b-reg-after-a-b a-reg-after-a-b
             a-value-for-alu-after-oprd-a-pre-decrement
             b-value-for-alu-after-oprd-b-pre-decrement)
    (hands-off bv-alu-cv)))

(prove-lemma hard-v-flag-is-soft-v-flag (rewrite)
  (implies
    (and (ramp reg-file (machine-size) 8)
         (ramp real-mem (machine-size) (exp 2 (machine-size)))
         (boolp v-flag))
    (equal (alu-v-flag (nth (bv-to-nat (nth 0 reg-file)) real-mem)
                       (a-value-for-alu-after-oprd-a-pre-decrement
                        reg-file real-mem)
                       (b-value-for-alu-after-oprd-b-pre-decrement
                        reg-file real-mem)
                       c-flag v-flag)
           (update-v (b-cc-set (current-instruction reg-file real-mem))
                     v-flag
                     (v (bv-alu-cv-results reg-file real-mem c-flag)))))
   ((enable alu-v-flag)
    (disable nth b-reg-after-a-b a-reg-after-a-b
             a-value-for-alu-after-oprd-a-pre-decrement
             b-value-for-alu-after-oprd-b-pre-decrement)
    (hands-off bv-alu-cv)))

(prove-lemma hard-z-flag-is-soft-z-flag (rewrite)
  (implies
    (and (ramp reg-file (machine-size) 8)
         (ramp real-mem (machine-size) (exp 2 (machine-size)))
         (boolp z-flag))
    (equal (alu-z-flag (nth (bv-to-nat (nth 0 reg-file)) real-mem)
                       (a-value-for-alu-after-oprd-a-pre-decrement
                        reg-file real-mem)
                       (b-value-for-alu-after-oprd-b-pre-decrement
                        reg-file real-mem)
                       c-flag z-flag)
           (update-v
            (b-cc-set (current-instruction reg-file real-mem))
            z-flag
            (zerop
             (bv-to-nat
              (bv (bv-alu-cv-results reg-file real-mem c-flag)))))))))
   ((enable alu-z-flag v-zerop-equal-bv-to-nat-zero)
    (disable nth a-reg-after-a-b b-reg-after-a-b
```

```
                  a-value-for-alu-after-oprd-a-pre-decrement
                  b-value-for-alu-after-oprd-b-pre-decrement)
    (hands-off bv-alu-cv)))

(prove-lemma sizep-a-value-for-alu-after-oprd-a-pre-decrement (rewrite)
  (implies
    (and (ramp reg-file (machine-size) 8)
         (ramp real-mem (machine-size) (exp 2 (machine-size))))
    (equal (size (a-value-for-alu-after-oprd-a-pre-decrement
                   reg-file real-mem))
           (machine-size)))
  ((disable nth update-nth bv-oprd-a bv-oprd-b v-nat-dec v-nat-inc)))

(prove-lemma hard-n-flag-is-soft-n-flag (rewrite)
  (implies
    (and (ramp reg-file (machine-size) 8)
         (ramp real-mem (machine-size) (exp 2 (machine-size)))
         (boolp n-flag))
    (equal (alu-n-flag (nth (bv-to-nat (nth 0 reg-file)) real-mem)
                       (a-value-for-alu-after-oprd-a-pre-decrement
                        reg-file real-mem)
                       (b-value-for-alu-after-oprd-b-pre-decrement
                        reg-file real-mem)
                       c-flag n-flag)
           (update-v
            (b-cc-set (current-instruction reg-file real-mem))
            n-flag
            (negativep
             (bv-to-tc
              (bv (bv-alu-cv-results reg-file real-mem c-flag)))))))
  ((enable alu-n-flag n-flag-equals-negativep)
   (disable nth a-reg-after-a-b b-reg-after-a-b
            a-value-for-alu-after-oprd-a-pre-decrement
            b-value-for-alu-after-oprd-b-pre-decrement
            bv-to-nat-of-twos-compl bv-to-nat-of-incr all-onesp-of-compl
            bitn-on-implies-non-0 ramp)
   (hands-off bv-alu-cv)))

(prove-lemma
 addr-out-after-a-b-is-v-nth-of-reg-file-after-oprd-b-pre-decrement
 (rewrite)
  (implies
    (and (ramp reg-file (machine-size) 8)
         (ramp real-mem (machine-size) (exp 2 (machine-size))))
    (equal (addr-out-after-a-b reg-file real-mem)
           (v-nth (bv-oprd-b (current-instruction reg-file real-mem))
                  (reg-file-after-oprd-b-pre-decrement
                   reg-file real-mem))))
  ((disable nth update-nth b-indirect-reg-a-dec b-indirect-reg-b-dec
```

```
                      v-nat-inc v-nat-dec bv-to-nat)
       (hands-off bv-alu-cv)))

(prove-lemma hard-real-mem-is-soft-real-mem (rewrite)
  (implies
    (and (ramp reg-file (machine-size) 8)
         (ramp real-mem (machine-size) (exp 2 (machine-size))))
    (equal
     (real-mem-thru-post-inc
      (nth (bv-to-nat (nth 0 reg-file)) real-mem)
      c-flag v-flag z-flag n-flag
      (nth (bv-to-nat
             (bv-oprd-b
              (current-instruction reg-file
                                   real-mem)))
           (reg-file-after-oprd-b-pre-decrement reg-file real-mem))
      real-mem
      (a-value-for-alu-after-oprd-a-pre-decrement reg-file real-mem)
      (b-value-for-alu-after-oprd-b-pre-decrement reg-file real-mem))
     (real-mem-after-alu-write reg-file real-mem
                               c-flag v-flag z-flag n-flag)))
  ((disable a-reg-after-a-b b-reg-after-a-b
            a-value-for-alu-after-oprd-a-pre-decrement
            b-value-for-alu-after-oprd-b-pre-decrement
            nth update-nth b-store-alu-result b-store-alu-result-with-ifs
            addr-out-after-a-b reg-file-after-oprd-b-pre-decrement
            bv-oprd-a bv-oprd-b)
   (hands-off bv-alu-cv)))

(prove-lemma
 reg-file-after-a-b-is-reg-file-after-oprd-b-pre-decr
 (rewrite)
 (implies
   (and (ramp reg-file (machine-size) 8)
        (ramp real-mem (machine-size) (exp 2 (machine-size))))
   (equal (reg-file-after-a-b reg-file real-mem)
          (reg-file-after-oprd-b-pre-decrement reg-file real-mem)))
 ((disable a-reg-after-a-b b-reg-after-a-b
           a-value-for-alu-after-oprd-a-pre-decrement
           b-value-for-alu-after-oprd-b-pre-decrement
           nth update-nth b-store-alu-result b-store-alu-result-with-ifs
           addr-out-after-a-b bv-oprd-a bv-oprd-b
           v-nat-inc v-nat-dec nat-to-bv bv-to-nat
           b-indirect-reg-a-inc b-direct-reg-a b-indirect-reg-a-dec
           b-indirect-reg-a bf-indirect-reg-b-inc b-direct-reg-b
           b-indirect-reg-b-dec b-indirect-reg-b
           bv-alu-op-code)
  (hands-off bv-alu-cv)))
```

```
(prove-lemma hard-reg-file-is-soft-reg-file (rewrite)
  (implies
    (and (ramp reg-file (machine-size) 8)
         (ramp real-mem (machine-size) (exp 2 (machine-size))))
    (equal
     (reg-file-from-alu-thru-post-inc
      (nth (bv-to-nat (nth 0 reg-file)) real-mem)
      c-flag v-flag z-flag n-flag
      (reg-file-after-oprd-b-pre-decrement reg-file real-mem)
      (a-value-for-alu-after-oprd-a-pre-decrement reg-file real-mem)
      (b-value-for-alu-after-oprd-b-pre-decrement reg-file real-mem))
     (reg-file-after-oprd-b-post-increment
      reg-file real-mem c-flag v-flag z-flag n-flag)))
  ((disable reg-file-after-oprd-b-pre-decrement
            a-value-for-alu-after-oprd-a-pre-decrement
            b-value-for-alu-after-oprd-b-pre-decrement
            a-reg-after-a-b b-reg-after-a-b
            nth update-nth b-store-alu-result b-store-alu-result-with-ifs
            addr-out-after-a-b bv-oprd-a bv-oprd-b
            v-nat-inc v-nat-dec nat-to-bv bv-to-nat
            b-indirect-reg-a-inc b-direct-reg-a
            b-indirect-reg-a-dec b-indirect-reg-a
            b-indirect-reg-b-inc b-direct-reg-b
            b-indirect-reg-b-dec b-indirect-reg-b
            bv-alu-op-code reg-file-after-a-b
            reg-file-after-oprd-b-pre-decrement)
   (hands-off bv-alu-cv)))
```

```
;;;;;;;;;;;;;;;;;;;;;;;;;;;;;;;;;;;;;;;;;;;;;;;;;;;;;;;;;;;;;;;;;;;;;;;;;;;;
;;                                                                        ;;
;;  ORACLE generates an oracle for BIG-MACHINE given the oracle           ;;
;;  for SOFT.  The SOFT machine oracle is a list; each element of         ;;
;;  the list contains four arbitrary values.  These values are "fixed"    ;;
;;  into numbers and used to construct a BIG-MACHINE oracle.  These       ;;
;;  four-tuples describe the possible delay when BIG-MACHINE accesses     ;;
;;  memory.  The values are the number of waits to be inserted in         ;;
;;  memory accesses.  The four-tuples meaning is as follows:              ;;
;;                                                                        ;;
;;  (ir-wait fetch-oprd-a-wait fetch-oprd-b-wait store-oprd-b-wait)       ;;
;;                                                                        ;;
;;  ir-wait -- number of wait states for fetching an instruction          ;;
;;  fetch-oprd-a-wait -- number of wait states for fetching OPERAND-A     ;;
;;  fetch-oprd-b-wait -- number of wait states for fetching OPERAND-B     ;;
;;  store-oprd-b-wait -- number of wait states for storing OPERAND-B      ;;
;;                                                                        ;;
;;;;;;;;;;;;;;;;;;;;;;;;;;;;;;;;;;;;;;;;;;;;;;;;;;;;;;;;;;;;;;;;;;;;;;;;;;;;

(defn oracle (reg-file real-mem c-flag v-flag z-flag n-flag lst)
  (if (nlistp lst)
      nil
      (append
       (state-1-to-1-oracle reg-file real-mem
                            c-flag v-flag z-flag n-flag
                            (car (car lst)) (cadr (car lst))
                            (caddr (car lst)) (cadddr (car lst)))
       (oracle
        (reg-file-after-oprd-b-post-increment
         reg-file real-mem c-flag v-flag z-flag n-flag)
        (real-mem-after-alu-write reg-file real-mem c-flag v-flag
                                  z-flag n-flag)
        (update-v (b-cc-set (current-instruction reg-file real-mem))
                  c-flag
                  (c (bv-alu-cv-results reg-file real-mem c-flag)))
        (update-v (b-cc-set (current-instruction reg-file real-mem))
                  v-flag
                  (v (bv-alu-cv-results reg-file real-mem c-flag)))
        (update-v (b-cc-set (current-instruction reg-file real-mem))
                  z-flag
                  (zerop
                   (bv-to-nat
                    (bv (bv-alu-cv-results reg-file real-mem c-flag)))))
        (update-v (b-cc-set (current-instruction reg-file real-mem))
                  n-flag
                  (negativep
                   (bv-to-tc
                    (bv (bv-alu-cv-results reg-file real-mem c-flag)))))
```

```
      (cdr lst)))))

(defn big-machine-induction
      (no-store data-out reg-file addr-out c-flag v-flag z-flag n-flag
                a-reg b-reg i-reg visual-mem real-mem watch-dog lst)
  (if (nlistp lst)
      t
      (big-machine-induction
        (not (b-store-alu-result c-flag v-flag z-flag n-flag
                                 (v-nth (nth 0 reg-file) real-mem)))
        (bv (bv-alu-cv (a-reg-after-a-b reg-file real-mem)
                       (b-reg-after-a-b reg-file real-mem)
                       c-flag
                       (bv-alu-op-code
                         (v-nth (nth 0 reg-file) real-mem))))
        (reg-file-from-alu-thru-post-inc
          (v-nth (nth 0 reg-file) real-mem)
          c-flag v-flag z-flag
          n-flag
          (reg-file-after-a-b reg-file real-mem)
          (a-reg-after-a-b reg-file real-mem)
          (b-reg-after-a-b reg-file real-mem))
        (addr-out-after-a-b reg-file real-mem)
        (alu-c-flag (v-nth (nth 0 reg-file) real-mem)
                    (a-reg-after-a-b reg-file real-mem)
                    (b-reg-after-a-b reg-file real-mem)
                    c-flag)
        (alu-v-flag (v-nth (nth 0 reg-file) real-mem)
                    (a-reg-after-a-b reg-file real-mem)
                    (b-reg-after-a-b reg-file real-mem)
                    c-flag v-flag)
        (alu-z-flag (v-nth (nth 0 reg-file) real-mem)
                    (a-reg-after-a-b reg-file real-mem)
                    (b-reg-after-a-b reg-file real-mem)
                    c-flag z-flag)
        (alu-n-flag (v-nth (nth 0 reg-file) real-mem)
                    (a-reg-after-a-b reg-file real-mem)
                    (b-reg-after-a-b reg-file real-mem)
                    c-flag n-flag)
        (a-reg-after-a-b reg-file real-mem)
        (b-reg-after-a-b reg-file real-mem)
        (v-nth (nth 0 reg-file) real-mem)
        (trunc (default-visual-mem-value) 16)
        (real-mem-thru-post-inc
          (v-nth (nth 0 reg-file) real-mem)
          c-flag v-flag z-flag n-flag
          (addr-out-after-a-b reg-file real-mem)
          real-mem
```

```
                (a-reg-after-a-b reg-file real-mem)
                (b-reg-after-a-b reg-file real-mem))

        (watch-dog f f f
                 (bv (bv-alu-cv
                      (a-reg-after-a-b reg-file real-mem)
                      (b-reg-after-a-b reg-file real-mem)
                      c-flag
                      (bv-alu-op-code
                        (v-nth (nth 0 reg-file) real-mem))))
                 (addr-out-after-a-b reg-file real-mem))
        (cdr lst))))
```

```
;;;;;;;;;;;;;;;;;;;;;;;;;;;;;;;;;;;;;;;;;;;;;;;;;;;;;;;;;;;;;;;;;;;;;;;;;
;;                                                                   ;;
;;   Abstraction for looking at certain registers in BIG-MACHINE.    ;;
;;   Specifically, the definition below allows us to view the registers ;;
;;   REG-FILE, REAL-MEM, C-FLAG, V-FLAG, Z-FLAG, and N-FLAG, which    ;;
;;   are the registers used in SOFT machine.                         ;;
;;                                                                   ;;
;;;;;;;;;;;;;;;;;;;;;;;;;;;;;;;;;;;;;;;;;;;;;;;;;;;;;;;;;;;;;;;;;;;;;;;;;

(defn abstract (m)
  (list (caddddddddr m)               ; reg-file
        (cadddddddddddddddddddr m)    ; real-mem
        (caddddddddddr m)             ; c-flag
        (cadddddddddddr m)            ; v-flag
        (caddddddddddddr m)           ; z-flag
        (cadddddddddddddr m)))        ; n-flag

(prove-lemma abstract-list (rewrite)
  (equal (equal (abstract (list mar read write dtack reset
                               no-store data-out
                               reg-file addr-out
                               c-flag v-flag z-flag n-flag
                               a-reg b-reg i-reg
                               visual-mem real-mem
                               watch-dog))
               (list reg-file real-mem c-flag v-flag z-flag n-flag))
         t))
```

```
;;;;;;;;;;;;;;;;;;;;;;;;;;;;;;;;;;;;;;;;;;;;;;;;;;;;;;;;;;;;;;;;;;;;;;;;;;;;;;
;;                                                                          ;;
;;    The following lemmas ensure SOFT machine does not change the          ;;
;;    size of any registers.                                               ;;
;;                                                                          ;;
;;;;;;;;;;;;;;;;;;;;;;;;;;;;;;;;;;;;;;;;;;;;;;;;;;;;;;;;;;;;;;;;;;;;;;;;;;;;;;

(prove-lemma ramp-reg-file-after-oprd-a-pre-decrement (rewrite)
 (implies
  (and (equal m (machine-size))
       (ramp reg-file (machine-size) 8)
       (ramp real-mem (machine-size) (exp 2 (machine-size))))
  (and (every-member-sizep
         (reg-file-after-oprd-a-pre-decrement reg-file real-mem) m)
       (equal (length (reg-file-after-oprd-a-pre-decrement
                        reg-file real-mem))
              8)))
  ((disable bv-to-nat update-nth nth bv-oprd-a bv-oprd-b
            b-indirect-reg-b-inc current-instruction v-nat-inc v-nat-dec
            b-indirect-reg-a-inc b-store-alu-result-with-ifs
            b-direct-reg-b bv-alu-cv-results
            b-indirect-reg-b-dec b-indirect-reg-a-dec)))

(prove-lemma ramp-reg-file-after-oprd-b-pre-decrement (rewrite)
 (implies
  (and (equal m (machine-size))
       (ramp reg-file (machine-size) 8)
       (ramp real-mem (machine-size) (exp 2 (machine-size))))
  (and (every-member-sizep
         (reg-file-after-oprd-b-pre-decrement reg-file real-mem) m)
       (equal (length (reg-file-after-oprd-b-pre-decrement
                        reg-file real-mem))
              8)))
  ((disable bv-to-nat update-nth nth bv-oprd-a bv-oprd-b
            b-indirect-reg-b-inc current-instruction v-nat-inc v-nat-dec
            b-indirect-reg-a-inc b-store-alu-result-with-ifs
            b-direct-reg-b bv-alu-cv-results
            b-indirect-reg-b-dec b-indirect-reg-a-dec)))

(prove-lemma size-bv-alu-cv-results (rewrite)
  (equal (size (bv (bv-alu-cv-results reg-file real-mem c-flag)))
         (size (a-value-for-alu-after-oprd-a-pre-decrement
                 reg-file real-mem)))
  ((disable bv-alu-cv bv-alu-op-code
            a-value-for-alu-after-oprd-a-pre-decrement
            b-value-for-alu-after-oprd-b-pre-decrement)))

(prove-lemma ramp-reg-file-after-oprd-b-post-increment (rewrite)
  (implies (and (equal m (machine-size))
```

```
                    (ramp reg-file (machine-size) 8)
                    (ramp real-mem (machine-size) (exp 2 (machine-size)))))
             (ramp (reg-file-after-oprd-b-post-increment reg-file real-mem
                                             c-flag v-flag z-flag n-flag)
                    m 8))
  ((enable every-member-sizep-update-nth)
   (disable reg-file-after-oprd-b-pre-decrement
            bv-to-nat update-nth nth bv-oprd-a bv-oprd-b
            b-indirect-reg-b-inc current-instruction v-nat-inc v-nat-dec
            b-indirect-reg-a-inc b-store-alu-result-with-ifs
            b-direct-reg-b bv-alu-cv-results
            b-indirect-reg-b-dec b-indirect-reg-a-dec
            a-value-for-alu-after-oprd-a-pre-decrement)))

(prove-lemma sizep-b-value-for-alu-after-oprd-b-pre-decrement (rewrite)
  (implies (and (ramp reg-file (machine-size) 8)
                (ramp real-mem (machine-size) (exp 2 (machine-size))))
           (equal (size (b-value-for-alu-after-oprd-b-pre-decrement
                          reg-file real-mem))
                  (machine-size)))
  ((disable fetch-oprd-b-reg-file fetch-oprd-a-reg-file
            update-nth nth bv-oprd-b
            fetch-oprd-a-addr-out fetch-oprd-b-addr-out
            v-nat-dec v-nat-inc bv-to-nat
            reg-file-after-oprd-a-pre-decrement bv-oprd-a
            current-instruction)))

(prove-lemma ramp-real-mem-after-alu-write (rewrite)
  (implies (and (equal m (machine-size))
                (equal x (exp 2 (machine-size)))
                (ramp reg-file (machine-size) 8)
                (ramp real-mem (machine-size) (exp 2 (machine-size))))
           (ramp (real-mem-after-alu-write reg-file real-mem
                                             c-flag v-flag z-flag n-flag)
                  m x))
  ((disable a-reg-after-a-b b-reg-after-a-b
            a-value-for-alu-after-oprd-a-pre-decrement
            b-value-for-alu-after-oprd-b-pre-decrement
            nth update-nth b-store-alu-result b-store-alu-result-with-ifs
            addr-out-after-a-b reg-file-after-oprd-b-pre-decrement
            bv-oprd-a bv-oprd-b)
   (hands-off bv-alu-cv)))

(prove-lemma size-nth (rewrite)
  (implies (and (ramp lst 16 n)
                (lessp i n))
           (equal (size (nth i lst)) 16)))
```

```
;;;;;;;;;;;;;;;;;;;;;;;;;;;;;;;;;;;;;;;;;;;;;;;;;;;;;;;;;;;;;;;;;;;;;;;;;;;;;;;;;
;;                                                                           ;;
;;  The proof of equivalence between the hardware definition of              ;;
;;  FM8501 and the software definition of FM8501.  This lemma proves         ;;
;;  that BIG-MACHINE executes instructions in the same way as the           ;;
;;  interpreter SOFT.                                                       ;;
;;                                                                           ;;
;;;;;;;;;;;;;;;;;;;;;;;;;;;;;;;;;;;;;;;;;;;;;;;;;;;;;;;;;;;;;;;;;;;;;;;;;;;;;;;;;

(prove-lemma big-machine-is-soft-machine (rewrite)
  (implies
   (and (equal mar1 (nat-to-bv 1 (nxsz)))
        (standard-hyps mar1 f f f f
                       no-store data-out
                       reg-file addr-out
                       c-flag v-flag z-flag n-flag
                       a-reg b-reg i-reg
                       visual-mem real-mem))
   (equal (abstract
           (big-machine mar1 f f f f
                        no-store data-out
                        reg-file addr-out
                        c-flag v-flag z-flag n-flag
                        a-reg b-reg i-reg
                        visual-mem real-mem
                        watch-dog
                        (oracle reg-file real-mem
                                c-flag v-flag z-flag n-flag
                                lst)))
          (soft reg-file real-mem c-flag v-flag z-flag n-flag lst)))
  ((disable ramp boolp abstract
            nat-to-bv v-nat-inc v-nat-dec update-nth nth
            reg-file-after-oprd-a-pre-decrement
            reg-file-after-oprd-b-pre-decrement
            b-store-alu-result
            a-value-for-alu-after-oprd-a-pre-decrement
            b-value-for-alu-after-oprd-b-pre-decrement
            b-store-alu-result-ifs bv-oprd-a bv-oprd-b
            bv-alu-cv a-reg-after-a-b b-reg-after-a-b
            bv-alu-op-code nth reg-file-from-alu-thru-post-inc
            reg-file-after-a-b addr-out-after-a-b alu-c-flag alu-v-flag
            alu-z-flag alu-n-flag real-mem-thru-post-inc
            reg-file-after-oprd-b-post-increment real-mem-after-alu-write
            update-v b-cc-set current-instruction bv-alu-cv-results
            zerop bv-to-nat bv-to-tc
            append state-1-to-1-oracle
            open-big-machine-on-listp)
   (enable state-1-to-1)
```

```
(expand (oracle reg-file real-mem
                c-flag v-flag z-flag n-flag
                lst)
        (soft reg-file real-mem c-flag v-flag z-flag n-flag lst))
(induct (big-machine-induction
            no-store data-out reg-file addr-out
            c-flag v-flag z-flag n-flag
            a-reg b-reg i-reg visual-mem real-mem
            watch-dog lst))))
```

```
;;;;;;;;;;;;;;;;;;;;;;;;;;;;;;;;;;;;;;;;;;;;;;;;;;;;;;;;;;;;;;;;;;;;;;;;
;;                                                                  ;;
;;  The following events are concerned with the programmer's view    ;;
;;  of FM8501 during a reset operation.                              ;;
;;                                                                  ;;
;;;;;;;;;;;;;;;;;;;;;;;;;;;;;;;;;;;;;;;;;;;;;;;;;;;;;;;;;;;;;;;;;;;;;;;;

(defn oracle-reset (reg-file real-mem c-flag v-flag z-flag n-flag lst)
  (if (nlistp lst)
      nil
      (append (state-0-to-0-wait-to-1-oracle (car (car lst)))
              (oracle (update-nth t 0 reg-file
                                  (nat-to-bv 0 (machine-size)))
                  real-mem c-flag v-flag z-flag n-flag
                  (cdr lst)))))

(prove-lemma ramp-reg-file-after-reset (rewrite)
  (implies (and (ramp reg-file (machine-size) 8)
                (equal m (machine-size)))
           (ramp (update-nth t 0 reg-file (nat-to-bv 0 m)) m 8)))

(prove-lemma sizep-trunc-at-machine-size (rewrite)
  (implies (equal m (machine-size))
           (sizep (trunc x m) m)))

(prove-lemma soft-reset-works (rewrite)
  (implies
   (and (equal mar0 (nat-to-bv 0 (nxsz)))
        (standard-hyps mar0 f f dtack t
                       no-store data-out
                       reg-file addr-out
                       c-flag v-flag z-flag n-flag
                       a-reg b-reg i-reg
                       visual-mem real-mem))
   (equal (abstract
           (big-machine mar0 f f dtack t
                        no-store data-out
                        reg-file addr-out
                        c-flag v-flag z-flag n-flag
                        a-reg b-reg i-reg
                        visual-mem real-mem
                        memory-watch-dog-history
                        (oracle-reset reg-file real-mem
                                      c-flag v-flag z-flag n-flag
                                      lst)))
          (soft-reset reg-file real-mem c-flag v-flag z-flag n-flag
                      lst)))
  ((disable mar no-store-with-ifs data-out-with-ifs reg-file
            addr-out c-flag-with-ifs
```

```
            v-flag-with-ifs z-flag-with-ifs n-flag-with-ifs a-reg b-reg
            i-reg-with-ifs visual-mem real-mem
            bv-adder-output bv-subtracter-output
            b-store-alu-result append
            open-big-machine-on-listp update-nth
            update-v-nth nth v-nth v-nat-inc v-nat-dec nat-to-bv
            bv-to-nat nat-to-bv
            state-0-to-0-wait-to-1-oracle oracle soft
            ramp sizep boolp abstract)
  (hands-off bv-alu-cv)
  (enable state-0-to-0-wait-to-1)
  (expand (oracle-reset reg-file real-mem
                        c-flag v-flag z-flag n-flag
                        lst)
          (soft-reset reg-file real-mem
                      c-flag v-flag z-flag n-flag lst))))
```

```
;;;;;;;;;;;;;;;;;;;;;;;;;;;;;;;;;;;;;;;;;;;;;;;;;;;;;;;;;;;;;;;;;;;;;;;;;;;;
;;                                                                        ;;
;;                     Flag Interpretation Lemmas                        ;;
;;                                                                        ;;
;;;;;;;;;;;;;;;;;;;;;;;;;;;;;;;;;;;;;;;;;;;;;;;;;;;;;;;;;;;;;;;;;;;;;;;;;;;;

(disable bv-alu-cv-results)

(prove-lemma bit-vector-interpretation-of-z-flag (rewrite)
  (equal (zerop
           (bv-to-nat
             (bv (bv-alu-cv-results reg-file real-mem c-flag))))
         (v-zerop (bv (bv-alu-cv-results reg-file real-mem c-flag))))
  ((enable v-zerop-equal-bv-to-nat-zero)))

(prove-lemma integer-interpretation-of-z-flag (rewrite)
  (equal (zerop
           (bv-to-nat
             (bv (bv-alu-cv-results reg-file real-mem c-flag))))
         (equal 0 (bv-to-tc
                    (bv (bv-alu-cv-results reg-file real-mem c-flag)))))
  ((enable v-zerop-equal-bv-to-tc-zero)))

(prove-lemma bit-vector-interpretation-of-n-flag (rewrite)
  (equal (negativep
           (bv-to-tc
             (bv (bv-alu-cv-results reg-file real-mem c-flag))))
         (bitn (bv (bv-alu-cv-results reg-file real-mem c-flag))
               (size (bv (bv-alu-cv-results reg-file real-mem c-flag)))))
  ((disable size-bv-alu-cv-results)
   (enable n-flag-equals-negativep)))
```

Index

xor, 156

z-flag, 230
z-flag-ifs, 230
z-flag-with-ifs, 230
zero-not-less-than-anything, 199

References

[1] Backus, J., Can Programming Be Liberated from the von Neumann Style?, *Journal of the ACM* 21, 1978.

[2] Backus, J., The Algebra of Functional Programs: Function Level Reasoning, Linear Equations, and Extended Definitions, *Proceedings Symposium on Functional Languages and Computer Architecture*, June, 1981.

[3] Barrow, H.G., Proving the Correctness of Digital Hardware Designs, *VLSI Design*, July, 1984.

[4] Barrow, Harry G., VERIFY: A Program for Proving Correctness of Digital Hardware Designs, *Artificial Intelligence*, 24, 1984.

[5] Bell, C.G, Newell, A., The PMS and ISP Descriptive Systems for Computer Structures, *AFIPS Spring Joint Computer Conference*, 1970.

[6] Boyer, R.S., Moore, J S., *A Computational Logic*, Academic Press, Inc., ACM Monograph Series, 1979.

[7] Boyer, R.S., Moore, J S., *The Correctness Problem in Computer Science*, Academic Press, Inc., 1981.

[8] Boyer, R.S., Moore, J S., Proof Checking the RSA Public Key Encryption Algorithm, *American Mathematical Monthly*, 91:3, 181–189, 1984.

[9] Brock, B.C., Hunt, W.A., Young, W.D., Introduction to a Formally Defined Hardware Description Language, in *Theorem Provers in Circuit Design*, V. Stavridou, T. Melham, and R. Boute, eds., North-Holland, 3–35, 1992.

[10] Carter, W.C., Joyner, W.H., Brand, D., Microprogram Verification Considered Necessary, *Proceedings of the AFIPS National Computer Conference*, 1978.

[11] Darringer, J.A., Joyner, W.H., Berman, C.L., Trevillyan, L., Logic Synthesis Through Local Transformations, *IBM Journal of Research and Development*, 24:4, 1981.

[12] Digital Equipment Corporation, *Microcomputer and Memories*, Bedford, MA., 1981.

[13] Digital Equipment Corporation, *Micro/PDP-11 Handbook*, Bedford, MA., 1983

[14] Duley, J.R., Dietmeyer, D.L., Translation of a DDL Digital System Specification to Boolean Equations, *IEEE Transactions on Computers*, C-18: 4, April, 1969.

[15] German, S.M., Lieberherr, K.J., Zeus: A Language for Expressing Algorithms in Hardware, *IEEE Computer*, 18:2, February, 1985.

[16] German, S.M., Wang, Y., Formal Verification of Parameterized Hardware Designs, *International Conference on Computer Design*, 1985.

[17] Gordon, M.J., Milner, A.J., Wadsworth, C.P., *Edinburgh LCF*, Springer-Verlag, Lecture Notes in Computer Science 78, 1979.

[18] Gordon, M.J., LCF_LSM: A System for Specifying and Verifying Hardware, Technical Report 41, University of Cambridge, Computer Laboratory, 1981.

[19] Gordon, M.J., Proving a Computer Correct, Technical Report 42, University of Cambridge, Computer Laboratory, 1981.

[20] Gordon, M.J., Higher Order Logic, Description of the HOL Proof Generating System, Technical Report, University of Cambridge, Computer Laboratory, April, 1984.

[21] Gordon, M.J., How to Specify and Verify Hardware Using Higher Order Logic, Lecture Notes, University of Cambridge, Autumn, 1984.

[22] Hanes, L.H., *Logic Design Verification Using Static Analysis*, Ph.D. Thesis, University of Illinois at Champaign-Urbana, 1983.

[23] Hunt, W.A., *FM8501: A Verified Microprocessor*, Ph.D. Thesis, University of Texas at Austin, 1985.

[24] Hunt, W.A., FM8501: A Verified Microprocessor, Technical Report 47, Institute for Computing Science and Computer Applications, University of Texas at Austin, December, 1985.

[25] Hunt, W.A., and Brock, B.C., A Formal HDL and Its Use in the FM9001 Verification, in *Mechanized Reasoning and Hardware Design*, C. Hoare and M. Gordon, eds., Prentice Hall, 35–47, 1992. First published in *Philosophical Transactions of the Royal Society of London*, Series A, Vol. 339, 1992.

[26] Intel Corporation, *Intel Multibus Specification*, Santa Clara, CA., 1982.

[27] Jensen, R.W., Tonies, C.C., *Software Engineering*, Prentice-Hall, 1979.

[28] Johnson, S.D., Applicative Programming and Digital Design, *Proceedings of the 11th Annual ACM POPL Conference*, January, 1983.

[29] Johnson, S.D., *Synthesis of Digital Designs from Recursion Equations*, Ph.D. Thesis, Indiana University, 1984.

[30] Kernighan, B.W., Ritchie, D.M., *The C Programming Language*, Prentice-Hall, 1978.

[31] Kuck, D.J., *The Structure of Computers and Computations*, John Wiley & Sons, 1978.

[32] Kerrmann, H., Data Format and Bus Compatibility in Multiprocessors, *IEEE Micro*, 3:4, August, 1983.

[33] Moszkowski, B.C., Reasoning About Digital Circuits, Technical Report, Stanford University, Department of Computer Science, June, 1983.

[34] Motorola Corporation, Technical Information Center, *Eight-Bit Microprocessor and Peripheral Data Book*, 1983.

[35] Motorola Corporation, Technical Information Center, *M68000 16/32-bit Microprocessor Programmer's Reference Manual*, Prentice-Hall, 1984.

[36] Peano, Giuseppe, Arithmetices Principia, Nova Methodo Exposita, (1889), in *From Frege to Gödel*, Jean van Heijenoort, ed., Harvard University Press, 1967.

[37] Pitchumani V., *Methods of Verification of Digital Logic*, Ph.D. Thesis, Syracuse University, Electrical Engineering Department, 1981.

[38] Pitchumani, V., Stabler, E.P., An Inductive Assertion Method for Register Transfer Level Design Verification, *IEEE Transactions on Computers*, C-32:12, December, 1983.

[39] Premkumar, U. V., TRAC: Principles of Operation, Technical Report TRAC-3, University of Texas at Austin, Department of Electrical Engineering, 1979.

[40] Roth, J.P., *Computer Logic, Testing and Verification*, Computer Science Press, 1980.

[41] Shankar, N., A Mechanical Proof of the Church-Rosser Theorem, *Journal of the ACM*, 35:3, 475–522, 1988.

[42] Sheeran, M., μFP–An Algebraic VLSI Design Language, Technical Report PRG-39, Oxford University Computing Laboratory, September, 1984.

[43] Stoy, J.E., *Denotational Semantics: The Scott-Strachey Approach to Programming Language Theory*, MIT Press, 1977.

[44] Texas Instruments Semiconductor Group, *The TTL Data Book*, Texas Instruments, Inc., 1984.

[45] Waser, S., Flynn, M.J., *Introduction to Arithmetic for Digital Systems Designers*, Holt, Rinehart and Winston, 1982.

[46] Wagner, T.J., *Hardware Verification*, Ph.D. Thesis Stanford University, Department of Computer Science, August, 1977.

[47] Wagner, T.J., Verification of Hardware Designs Through Symbolic Manipulation, *Proceedings of the IEEE Symposium on Design Automation and Microprocessors*, February, 1977.

[48] Wilkes, M.V., The Best Way to Design an Automatic Calculating Machine, *Manchester University Computer Inaugural Conference*, Ferranti, Ltd., July, 1951.

[49] Wilkes, M.V., The Growth of Interest in Microprogramming: A Literature Survey, *ACM Computing Surveys*, 1, September, 1969.

[50] Wirth, N., Program Development by Stepwise Refinement, *Communications of the ACM*, 14:4, April, 1971.

[51] Zilog Corporation, *1983/84 Components Data Book*, Irvine, CA., 1983.

Springer-Verlag
and the Environment

We at Springer-Verlag firmly believe that an international science publisher has a special obligation to the environment, and our corporate policies consistently reflect this conviction.

We also expect our business partners – paper mills, printers, packaging manufacturers, etc. – to commit themselves to using environmentally friendly materials and production processes.

The paper in this book is made from low- or no-chlorine pulp and is acid free, in conformance with international standards for paper permanency.

Lecture Notes in Artificial Intelligence (LNAI)

Lecture Notes in Computer Science